An American Uprising in Second World War England: Mutiny in the Duchy

For Sylvia, my Mum, who encouraged me to write, always, and David, my Dad, who imbued me with my love of history and Cornwall.

An American Uprising in Second World War England: Mutiny in the Duchy

Kate Werran

PEN & SWORD
HISTORY

'... *the colored soldier over here is making good, and England will long remember the "Black Yanks"'*. Extracts from Letters from US Base Censor, March 1–15 1944

'... *the American race problem is being transplanted to British soil – sometimes with a venom unknown in the United States ... there are thousands of American Negro soldiers in England ... they are known affectionately as Black Yanks ...*' Roi Ottley's World War II

First published in Great Britain in 2020 by
Pen & Sword History
An imprint of
Pen & Sword Books Ltd
Yorkshire – Philadelphia

ISBN 978 1 52675 954 2

Printed and bound in the UK by TJ International Ltd,
Padstow, Cornwall.

Pen & Sword Books Limited incorporates the imprints of Atlas,
Archaeology, Aviation, Discovery, Family History, Fiction, History,
Maritime, Military, Military Classics, Politics, Select, Transport,
True Crime, Air World, Frontline Publishing, Leo Cooper, Remember
When, Seaforth Publishing, The Praetorian Press, Wharncliffe
Local History, Wharncliffe Transport, Wharncliffe True Crime
and White Owl.

For a complete list of Pen & Sword titles please contact

PEN & SWORD BOOKS LIMITED
47 Church Street, Barnsley, South Yorkshire, S70 2AS, England
E-mail: enquiries@pen-and-sword.co.uk
Website: www.pen-and-sword.co.uk

Or

PEN AND SWORD BOOKS
1950 Lawrence Rd, Havertown, PA 19083, USA
E-mail: Uspen-and-sword@casematepublishers.com
Website: www.penandswordbooks.com

Contents

List of Illustrations

Dramatis Personae

Court Martial President and Law Member
Lieutenant Colonel Raymond E. Zickel, 307th Quartermaster Battalion

Prosecutors
Trial Judge Advocate Major Frank P. Eresch, HQ Southern Base Section
Assistant Trial Judge Advocate Timothy J. Mulcahy, HQ Western District

Defence
Defense Counsel Captain John A. Philbin, General Depot G-50
Assistant Defense Counsel Alvin E. Ottum, 67th General Hospital

Alleged Ringleaders
Private First Class Clifford Barrett, 581st Ordnance Ammunition Company
Technical Sergeant Henry Austin, 581st Ordnance Ammunition Company
Sergeant Rupert Hughes, 581st Ordnance Ammunition Company

Accused Others
Private Freddy Blake, 581st Ordnance Ammunition Company
Private Tom Ewing, 581st Ordnance Ammunition Company
Private Charlie Geddies, 581st Ordnance Ammunition Company
Private Willis Gibbs, 581st Ordnance Ammunition Company
Private James H. Lindsey, 581st Ordnance Ammunition Company
Private James Manning, 581st Ordnance Ammunition Company
Private Arzie Martin, 581st Ordnance Ammunition Company
Private Henry McKnight, 581st Ordnance Ammunition Company
Private First Class Alexander Shaw, 581st Ordnance Ammunition Company
Private Carl Tennyson, 581st Ordnance Ammunition Company
Private Henry Tilly, 581st Ordnance Ammunition Company

Chief Prosecution Witnesses in order of appearance
Captain Richard Scott, Headquarters Company, 115th Infantry
Staff Sergeant Potocki, Headquarters Company, Second Battalion, 115th
  Infantry

Sergeant Ralph Simmons, E Company, 115th Infantry
Harry C. Poltraz, Criminal Investigator, Provost Marshal General's
    Detachment
Sergeant Marvin F. Richardson, Investigation Department, Provost
    Marshal General's Detachment
Corporal Alfred Joseph, 581st Ordnance Ammunition Company
Private First Class L.V. Edwards, 581st Ordnance Ammunition Company
Private Albert Smith, 581st Ordnance Ammunition Company
Staff Sergeant Kenneth Blanchett, 581st Ordnance Ammunition Company
Second Lieutenant Ariel W. Glenn, Camp Pennygillam, Launceston

Chief Defence Witnesses in order of appearance
Captain James E. Stevenson, Assistant Inspector General, HQ, Southern
    Base Section
Sergeant Rupert Hughes, 581st Ordnance Ammunition Company
Private Carl Tennyson, 581st Ordnance Ammunition Company
Sergeant Charles W. Bury, F Company, 115th Infantry, 29th Division
Private Henry Tilly, 581st Ordnance Ammunition Company
Private Willis Gibbs, 581st Ordnance Ammunition Company

Other Witnesses
Sergeant Alfred Faria, F Company, Second Battalion, 115th Infantry
Miss Joan Rendell, Werrington, Cornwall

Court Reporter
Miss Joyce Packe, US Army

Observers
George Orwell, English novelist, essayist and critic
Roi Ottley, American journalist and writer
Walter White, executive secretary of the National Association for the
    Advancement of Colored People (NAACP)

Associated
Learie Constantine, West Indian cricketer
First Lieutenant Robert Henne, Second Battalion, 115th Infantry

Maps

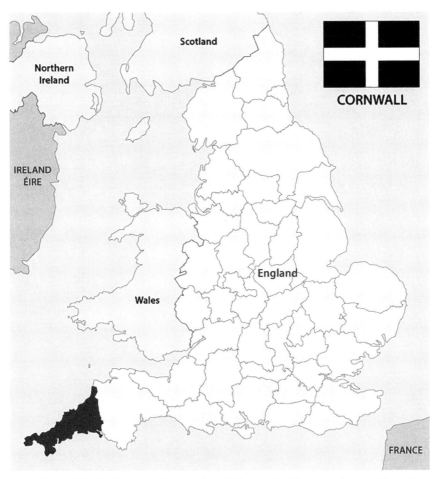

Map of the UK highlighting the position of Cornwall. (*Image used under license from Shutterstock.com*)

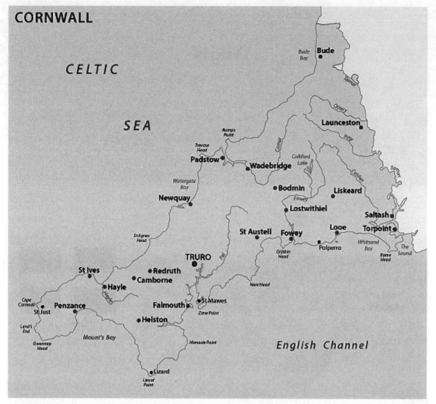

Map of Cornwall showing Launceston just over the county's border. (*Image used under license from Shutterstock.com*)

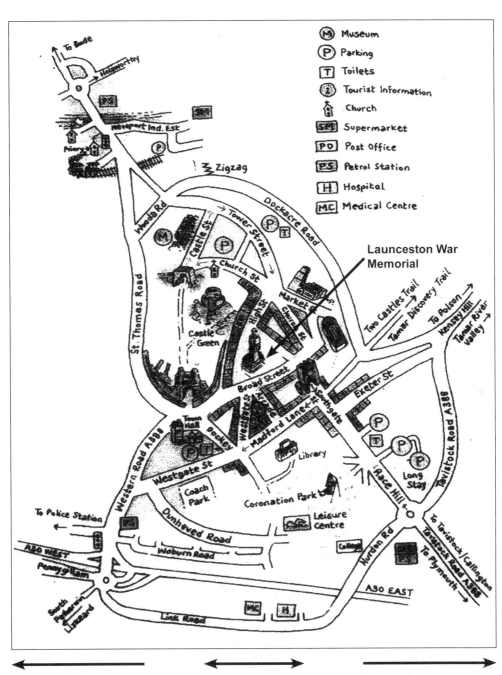

Street map of Launceston. (© *Jo Hunter*)

Prologue

6 June 1944: 10.00am

He could feel it turning. Despite the relentless pounding of giant guns that muffled mostly everything, he could sense a change in direction. They had been carving large, rough circles through unnaturally choppy waters for hours, but now the landing craft was straightening up. Finally, it had been commanded to break its holding pattern and head for the beach. Dry-mouthed and pale-faced, First Lieutenant Robert Henne stood in the left-hand side of the vehicle, gripping for dear life the line with which he had been entrusted. Comrades were counting on his 6ft 3in frame being enough to conquer the waves, so he could establish a safe line for them to cling to while landing. Their mission was to clear mines, allowing armoured vehicles to be grounded. He was a long way from home and this was a June day at the beach like no other.

Since before 6am heavy naval guns had pummelled the shoreline creating a colossal screen of black smoke. Wave after wave of bombers swept overhead, but still powerful enemy guns high in the French cliffs retaliated. As First Lieutenant Henne's craft now broke out of its arc, the stink of cordite mixed with wet woollen army-issue uniforms and vomit.

'I remember going past the US battleship Texas and it fired a broadside at the French coast, you could feel that wave and that big black smoke filled with fire,' he recalled more than seventy years later. 'I just wanted to get off the damn boat; when you're just a passenger your destiny is in someone else's hands.'

He and fellow soldiers from the 115th Infantry Regiment's Second Battalion knew the magnitude of the task ahead. Already the sea was bestrewn with the floating dead from previous assaults. Their sister company, the 116th Infantry Regiment, had earlier suffered catastrophic casualties, 'almost sixty per cent in the first two waves … young people think they're bullet-proof. I can remember being afraid of being maimed

– I thought about that a considerable amount – and that worried me, but not getting killed.'[1]

Beneath all the man-made smog and fumes that day, it was overcast. At around 10am, First Lieutenant Henne's battalion was fast approaching one of the most treacherous landing beaches in Fortress Europe. Ships of varying sizes filled every inch of the ocean as far as the eye could see. It was 6 June 1944 and they were part of the later invasion tides tasked with tackling Omaha Beach. At the last moment the beach master waved their ten landing crafts eastwards, away from the unit's original target, the deadly Dog Red stretch. One look at its watery scrapyard of burning vehicles, munitions and bodies, formed here by the first failed assaults, explained why. Now drivers had to navigate ferocious and bloody waters with extreme care. Commanders feared the sight of propellers chopping fallen comrades could shatter the collective nerve to land chest-deep in water and charge across slippery rocks under acute artillery fire.

Shunted 2,000 yards down the coastline, they prepared to jump out at neighbouring Fox Green instead, another of the four landing zones – no less daunting and singularly undeserving of its innocent-sounding name. Moments before the ramp lowered, Lieutenant Henne thought it had begun to rain, noting the flickering water ahead. But as the rhythmic patter reached his landing craft, it made the persistent rattle of metal on metal and he realised it was machine-gun fire. This was not what they were expecting; in briefings the previous week, Henne's battalion was told any opposition would be eliminated by the time they beached. Instead, at the last moment they realised they would have to land fighting. Now the ramp winched into action and Henne prepared to jump, weighed down by 70lbs of equipment on his back and clutching the landing line. This was that generation's moment and their brave, bold story has been told.

Meanwhile, somewhere in the United States another small band of soldiers, linked forever with this battalion of later-wave D-Day troops, was facing something entirely different. They had history with a handful of military policemen now battling their way onto Omaha Beach alongside First Lieutenant Robert Henne. The alternative for these stateside servicemen was equally life-changing – they too had been fighting for freedom. Two pathways, two army companies, 3,000 miles apart. They were bound together by one terrible clash which lasted five minutes in a small Cornish town and became an obscure historical footnote. Their two roads diverged after an extraordinary court martial the authorities tried to hush up. The trial injected unprecedented Hollywood-style drama to a war-weary Britain, captured world attention briefly before it flickered, moved on and was lost forever in an ever-escalating blitz of ultimate world conflict. This is the forgotten story of those forced down that less travelled road.

Their parallel journeys began in a pocket of Great Britain's south-west corner nine months earlier. When it dawned, 26 September 1943 was a quietish autumn Sunday of some national significance. That day marked the third anniversary of victory in the Battle of Britain but by 10pm, countrywide celebrations to commemorate it were long over. Since sunset, outdoor festivities had moved inside as dark curtains were pinned up across the country's windows. Small-town cinemas were closed, even ubiquitous fish and chip stands were shutting up shop. On this cool September evening, according to decades-old court martial records, a 'whole company' of American soldiers armed itself with rifles, tommy guns and ammunition. Their marching footsteps could be heard stomping downhill long before row upon row of them trooped into a quiet Cornish market square, three abreast. The night-time air was cool, pavements were wet from earlier rain and it was the pitchy-ink dark of blackout, wartime Europe.

Suddenly they appeared 'in a body', from out of the darkness, encircling a group of military policemen, fellow Americans, who were standing next to a jeep and chatting. A man seemed to be the spokesman for the group and he said, very quietly: 'Why don't you let us come into town, come to the pubs?' Flashlights snapped on. 'Hands up!' was shouted. The military police raised their arms and backed up. As they did, 'I heard bolts open on rifles,' said the jeep's driver. There was just time for the terrifying realisation that they were armed to sink in when: 'I heard a bolt crack and a shot landed at our feet. Someone hollered 'DUCK'. I jumped in behind the wheel of a jeep.' Next, a volley of fire. 'I felt a bullet whizz past me.' A flashlight revealed a soldier 'with a denim hat and overcoat firing a rifle from the hip and he was really pumping them out.'[2] A pause. Then chaos as British soldiers, Polish airmen, WAAFs and Land Army girls, as well as the Americans under fire, scrambled for cover amid ricocheting bullets.

Part I

The Prosecution – Day One 15 October 1943

Chapter 1

Court Opens

O ctober 1943 would go on to be the mildest of its kind in Britain for more than a decade – moderate, wet and mainly dull, according to The Met Office's monthly summary.[1] However, the forecast was anything but for a small town in the south-west, not 25 miles from Exeter. Day-to-day life momentarily suspended itself during the middle of that month as national and international pressmen descended daily on Paignton, Devon. For seventy-two hours they came, seeking the Victorian seaside resort's wood-panelled police court, to report a sensational trial that would lead front pages on both sides of the Atlantic. It was indisputable from day one that something extraordinary was playing out in this single room, a drama that stood out even in battle-hardened Britain.

When the trial started on Friday, 15 October 1943, Britain was 1,505 days into the Second World War. Since it began, losses to world freedom had been legendary. As the Nazi iron grip extended and tightened over Europe, Britain had been left alone, and increasingly beleaguered, to hold the line until January 1942, when Britain, USA and USSR formed the triumvirate of Allied powers. Four straight years of hostilities meant anything 'phony' was well and truly old news. Even the epic endeavours of Dunkirk and The Battle of Britain were receding three years hence. Since then, Britain's fortunes had plummeted to its nadir in 1942 when Singapore was lost to the Japanese in what Winston Churchill called 'the largest capitulation' in British military history. It was the nation's bleakest hour. When Generals Montgomery and Alexander's Eighth Army finally drove back Rommel in the Egyptian desert at El Alamein, church bells rang throughout the land proclaiming this watershed moment. The prime minister famously described it as 'not the end; it is not even the beginning of the end. But it is, perhaps, the end of the beginning.'[2]

By the time the Paignton court martial trial got underway, Churchill's thought was proving prescient as the tide was seeming to turn. The Germans had been defeated by the Russians at Stalingrad in February 1943 while British and American forces gained a foothold in Sicily after the ousting of its fascist dictator Mussolini later that summer. Meanwhile, closer to home, top-level preparations were in overdrive to run the Nazis out of mainland Europe with the biggest amphibious invasion ever conceived. Already the foot soldiers needed for this audacious assault were beginning to gather throughout Great Britain in their hundreds of thousands.

People waking up in Britain on 15 October 1943 would take heart from the morning headlines; the Fifth Army was giving '*The Hun*' 'what for' in Italy, the Red Army was storming Dnieper Dam City in the Ukraine while Bomber Command was hitting Germany hard at home with a massive strike against Bavarian ball bearing factories. On the home front, government ministers were dreaming up a better life with post-war plans to extend the new Pay As You Earn tax scheme to ten million people a year and serving troops were sketching out the kind of social housing they most desired, with up to 90 per cent of them fighting for detached or semi-detached houses close to cinemas, shops, pubs and schools.

Chairman of the Odeon cinema chain, J. Arthur Rank, was dreaming big too, declaring plans to expand in post-war Europe at his sixth annual meeting, in which he reported record profits. Entertainment in general was big business in this pre-invasion lull. The American Army's own ten-guineas-a-seat show was coming straight from Broadway to the West End under the artistic auspices of composer Irving Berlin who earned an unimaginable annual fortune of £100,000 – at a time when the average British soldier took home 2 shillings daily. American glitz and glamour were well and truly here thanks to the US Army Negro Chorus, which had first wowed the Royal Albert Hall's 10,000-strong audience and was now travelling northwards to extend its tour.

All this optimism and glamour, however, could not belie the dark underbelly of Britain at war. Clearly the price of nearly half a decade of conflict, rationing, blackouts, toiling the land and manning never-stopping factories – and the subsequent absentee parents who made much of it happen – was high, and rising fast. Readers that day saw stories and editorials tackling the new social problems of rushed marriages, collapsing home-life, newly labelled 'latch-key' kids and juvenile delinquency culminating in the controversial campaign against the birching of minors featured on the inside and back pages of local and national newspapers.

This mishmash of desperately sought victories, kaleidoscopic morals and shifting social dreams was as real and rich a national framework around what was about to commence as the more tangible colourful beach huts and golden sands belonging to Paignton, jewel of the English Riviera, where the stage was now set.

Here, at 9.30am on 15 October 1943, nearly three hours after blackout restrictions lifted, the Victorian courtroom in the upstairs of Paignton's Palace Avenue police station was full. Usually it was a police court, but for the time being it had been commandeered by the Americans. Their purpose? A court martial. American soldiers were about to be tried by an American court operating under American military law for crimes committed on Shakespeare's 'sceptred isle'. It was an extraordinary situation. A historical blip when a law other than English was to be freely practised in the home of justice vaunted and celebrated the world over. One of the biggest baits for newsmen that day was that this court martial offered a bird's-eye view of American military law in action. They had been given ringside seats at the enactment of one of the harshest legal codes, drawn up more than 150 years previously to guarantee strict discipline during America's revolutionary war. Never had it been allowed before, but suddenly these spectacles of New World trials were springing up in lawhouses and US camps throughout Britain.

In case anyone needed reminding that this show was American, Paignton police court's new temporary internal backdrop was an enormous stars and stripes flag. In fact, the entire court had been upended entirely.

'The furniture in the court was shifted until it resembled an American film court scene. There was no dock, no witness box, no Press seats,' reported Murray Edwards of the *Daily Herald*, precursor to the modern-day *Sun*.

The final touch was that every single member of the court, bar the defendants, were carrying guns at all times: 'All the judges, court officials and counsel – all white – were armed. Loaded Colt automatics stuck out of their belts.'

Despite the US Army's utmost efforts, however, they couldn't quite take the Devon seaside town out of the military court as 'witnesses sat on a deck chair [*sic*] with Paignton Urban District Council painted on the back.'³

Newly rearranged rows at the back of the court were filled with the frames of several US servicemen, who until the previous month had been stationed just 60 miles away in a small Cornish market town. Behind them sat two more rows bursting with newsmen representing an A to Z of British and American press spanning Chicago, Illinois to John O'Groats, Scotland. And right at the front of the court, facing the accused, sat Lieutenant Colonel Raymond E. Zickel, of the 307th Quartermaster Battalion, Law Member and President of this US Army Court Martial. He presided over a ten-strong panel of US Army majors and captains including Trial Judge Advocate Frank P. Eresch heading the prosecution and his counterpart, the Defense Counsel Captain John A. Philbin.

Immediately in front of and beneath the court president and panel sat a talented young English blonde. Miss Joyce Packe, a 21-year-old, from Torquay, had, even by the war's standards, an unusual job. She was one of just six women in the entire British Isles employed by the US Army as an official reporter for court martials. The geographical area she covered was the south-west. There was no looking back for Miss Packe a year after being drafted by the Minister of Labour from her previous role as secretary to the Principal of the National College of Domestic Sciences. This new job she described as 'loving' gave her a role and insight into the American Army legal system that was unique amongst Brits. Other than the president, she alone was entrusted to ask witnesses to repeat or clarify their statements as she made the official record of proceedings. Sporting the giveaway flash on her US Army-uniformed shoulder, as stenographer, Miss Packe was largely the only woman in court. In her spare time, Miss Packe, whose secretarial skills 'were among the best in Britain', was revising for an exam that Sunday, which would entitle her to an extra 3 shillings each week.⁴ She would get plenty of extra practice over the next eight hours as she proceeded to fill two notebooks with the words of twenty witnesses, eighteen statements and seven examinations and cross-examinations.

Before initial proceedings were over, and well ahead of the first witness even starting to stand, there were three red flags explaining why this court martial was attracting so much attention – from the free world's press to its highest echelons of power in London and Washington DC.

Right at the beginning came the first indication. As the accused American soldiers' names were read out it became clear that the case involved a shockingly large number of men. It was highly unusual for large gangs of defendants to stand together and when legal proceedings opened, it introduced no less than fourteen soldiers, including, significantly, two sergeants – Henry Austin and Rupert Hughes. The twelve privates were Charlie Geddies, James Lindsey, Alexander Shaw, Freddy Blake, James Manning, Henry McKnight, Henry Tilly, Private First Class Clifford Barrett, Tom Ewing, Arzie Martin, Carl Tennyson and Willis Gibbs. All fourteen were members of the 581st Ordnance Ammunition Company, stationed in the Norman town of Launceston, once Cornwall's ancient capital and known as the county gateway. Their sheer number made it truly significant and was also crucial in logistical terms. 'Paignton police court was borrowed from the British authorities. It was the only place big enough to hold all the people in the case', reported *The Herald*'s Murray Edwards.[5]

Each defendant stated they had no legal representative of their own, instead putting themselves at the mercy of the court-provided Defense Counsel and Assistant Defense Counsel, a role fulfilled by two army captains. After Miss Packe was formally sworn in as court reporter, the prosecution used a peremptory challenge to jettison a Major Dierdoff from the panel. The gallant major, from the 315th Station Hospital, retired promptly, even jauntily, according to observing journalists who saw he was smiling as if in relief that his role in proceedings was over in just a few minutes. The defence, however, waived its right to do the same thing.

Next, as a catalogue of charges was read out, came the second explanation for the court's heaving press benches. The allegations were not only many, but serious. Very serious. This was no ordinary criminal case, but mutiny with murderous intent. The soldiers were charged with attempted murder (violating the 93rd article of war); unlawfully taking up arms and discharging firearms in a reckless and unlawful manner while making inflammatory statements (breaking the 96th article); rioting and assembling in a violent and tumultuous manner specifically to disturb the peace (violating the 89th article of war) – and finally, actively mutinying to usurp, subvert and override military authority, to take up arms against and fire on military policemen. Their accuser was Captain James Bosson, of the Ordnance Department numbered 0-666, and the person in charge of the 581st Ordnance Ammunition Company stationed on land formerly used as a farm in Pennygillam, a mile south-west of Launceston.

Each man spoke only to plead 'not guilty'. For two-thirds of them, it would be the only time in the entire three-day court martial that their voices would be heard out loud. After a five-minute recess, granted at the request of the prosecution, the president got to the nub of the case – and why, most of all, this legal affair would grip groups around the world. It was the final and most significant signal that something extraordinary was about to unfold; that the crux of this case was different.

> 'Before continuing with the proceedings let it be understood that no report, publication or other communication may disclose the location of any unit, army postal office number, and any publication must clear through the Board of Censors prior to being released,' he started.

American military authorities were obviously trying to keep a tight lid on this stand-out case. Quickly, President Zickel moved to the heart of the matter – and to why this was a case with potential to cause controversy on a seismic scale.

Turning to the court, President Zickel made an exceptional demand: 'No reference will be made to race or colour of the accused or any parties who are witnesses of the proceedings.'

The president, confident he had thus quickly nipped any trouble in the bud, looked around to the waiting press non-expectantly, asking: 'Is [*sic*] there any questions in the mind of anyone as to that announcement?' But that cat was long out of the bag. Race was at the heart of this and too many people knew about it. The president had asked the impossible and the British press was not about to let him get away with it.

That instant, '… one of the press representatives stood, and said; 'Yes, sir. It has already been announced in the newspapers that the accused are coloured,' read the court transcript.

President: 'There will be no further announcement with regard thereto.'[6]

His concession was critical. For the first time, details of this case could be reported in the United States of America, home to the accused – who happened to be African American servicemen. Their race was at the heart of the controversy. And to be able to write about it was a breakthrough. For weeks, American newsmen had tried to file their copy to no avail. Banned from publishing details in the United States, this press challenge and victory in the courtroom meant news, long out in Britain, would get across the pond – albeit under the beady eye of the Board of Censors; and at a great personal and professional cost to those whose by-lines did make it into print. Effectively the British Press had forced the hand of President Zickel, setting the stage for a trial that would enthral the nation, publicly expose the climate of racial intolerance bred by US soldiers and a surprising British reaction to it. Ultimately, it was to shed light on two not-so-special relationships – both Anglo American and American/African American. Moments after the case was thrown open to the public, Trial Judge Advocate Frank P. Eresch stood up. The prosecutor was ready to start by calling his first witness. The game was on.

Chapter 2

Making the Case

C aptain Richard P. Scott would be one of the officers to battle his way onto Omaha beach during the Normandy landings. But now he was harnessing all the fight training he had for a different type of warfare altogether; a combat much closer-to-home than any far-flung enemy action. As the prosecution's first witness, Captain Scott, of the 115th Infantry's Second Battalion, was about to outline how so many of his fellow Americans had ended up facing such gravely serious charges. The nuts and bolts of his explanation would provide the prosecution case's framework.

What soon became clear, however, was that if ever the prosecution needed someone to downplay the root causes of riot in Cornwall, then Captain Scott was their man. On duty as Battalion Military Police Officer in Launceston on Sunday, 26 September 1943, he started by setting and painting the scene. It was a pretty town square, approximately 125 yards long by 75 yards wide, bordered on all sides by stores, shops and the White Hart Hotel, with a large war memorial in the centre and four separate streets leading in and out of the centre. Asked whether anything unusual happened there that night, he answered, with classic military understatement: 'At approximately 20 past ten, in the square of Launceston, in front of the White Hart Hotel, there was a group of men, armed, who fired at my military policemen.'

Elaborating on how things started, Captain Scott went on to describe his relentless night-time round of shuttling between closing pubs and Launceston town square to ensure all the soldiers had cleared out back to camp. He borrowed a torch around 10pm from one of his sergeants after breaking his own, and in the freshly acquired flashlight noticed a crowd gathering in the silent dark. The captain described them as giving no cause for concern, adding: 'There was just a group of men, milling round in the street, that was what was making the shuffling noise. The group did not seem to be causing any trouble or anything, so I went on about my business.'

There was little moonlight on 26 September, but enough to allow Scott to clock the thronging crowd on his return. He looked again and could see the group was larger than before but 'there was no noise, so I started to pass the group ...' But it was precisely at this point that the atmosphere darkened.

Captain Scott detected movement as he neared them and could see

> '[T]hey were in a sort of semi-circle with the monument and the military police on the open side of the semi-circle, and they started to spread out. I thought there must be some sort of a fight or something to cause the group of men to spread out like that, so I entered, to see what the trouble was.'

It was 10.20pm and gloomy, as Captain Scott pushed his way past three or four men into the gathering's core, leaving just one soldier between him and the centre. Suddenly a flashlight was shone from behind him onto the group. Just after noticing the dress uniform and leggings of what had to be his military police ahead, a shot fired out from behind him, on his right-hand side.

> 'I whirled around with my flashlight', he said, 'and there was, approximately 3 feet from me – a coloured soldier with a long coat, firing a rifle, or what appeared to be a rifle, from the hip,' he stated. 'I took my pistol out of my holster and yelled "what is the trouble?" or something like that, but there was too much noise then, several weapons being fired.'

Somewhat haplessly, the captain discovered his weapon was not loaded just as one of his own sergeants scuttled in front, 'so I had no chance to do anything to stop it'. This less than dazzling display would hardly have made the best of '*Boys' Own*'. Meantime, pandemonium prevailed in the noisy shadows as: 'there was several girls running in every direction in the Square ... commotion and confusion ... and someone was moaning and screaming. You could tell someone had been hit.'

With Captain Scott at that moment in Launceston town square were seven military policemen (two regular divisional military policemen from 29th Infantry Division and five sergeants from 115th Infantry Second Battalion), along with Captain Scott's driver and several RAF and Land Army girls who were waiting to pick up their transport.

'The group kept fanning out, the semi-circle getting larger, backing in the direction from which they had come. The girls were still running in every direction and screaming,' he continued.

Captain Scott said the shooters bolted immediately after ceasing fire, allowing him to check on the wounded military policeman who was 'hit pretty bad'. The officer forced his way into the square's White Hart Hotel to call for a doctor, but the telephone line to the camp was busy, according to a jobsworthy civilian operator who admitted he had 'heard the firing' even at the exchange. Scott demanded once more that the existing call be interrupted so he could be put through, but with typical British devotion to detail, 'he didn't do it, so I tried to call the camp at Pennygillam, the coloured camp to tell the officers what had happened. I judged the men were from there.'

By the time the captain returned to the square, the injured military policeman, Sergeant Charles Cox, who had lent him his flashlight just minutes before, had been moved to The Castle Inn, a hotel used at that time to billet British soldiers. Here he found another injured policeman, Sergeant Ralph Simmons, also laid out flat on a table. Luckily, Launceston's Medical Officer of Health, Dr D.H.A. Galbraith, was on hand to give the two men pain medication.

The prosecution gravitated quickly to the crux of the case, asking Scott directly: 'Did you recognise the race of the participants of that crowd?'

A: 'I did, Sir.'
Q: 'What was their race?'
A: 'Coloured, sir.'
Q: 'Did you see any members of that group with guns?'
A: 'I did, sir.'
Q: 'How many?'
A: 'I definitely saw two with weapons, distinctly two weapons. I saw a lot of flashes beside that, but I couldn't see the weapon in the dark.'[1]

In case there remained any doubt as to the perpetrators' ethnicity, he went on to say that most soldiers departed afterwards by the main and most direct route to Camp Pennygillam, that is, the 'coloured' camp. Asked as to the number of shots fired that night, Captain Scott said there were quite a few: a couple of single shots followed by a volley, a lull and then another volley. He reckoned there were at least thirty-five participants.

At this point the courtroom theatrics for which this court martial would become famous came in to play. In an original flash of not-so-amateur dramatics, the captain was rebuked by the prosecution and told to confine himself to what he 'actually' knew after he 'judged' the men to be from Camp Pennygillam. It was just the beginning of 'a truly novel and somewhat startling' approach, according to one British journalist witness, obviously used to gentler, more orderly court conduct. With a growing sense of amazement and alarm, the writer soon 'realised that counsel really do, in true film fashion, leap to their feet and yell 'I object', to which the president of the court replies 'objection sustained' or 'objection overruled'.[2]

But the fun was just beginning. Defense Counsel Captain John A. Philbin stepped up to face the prosecution's chief witness. The wooden walls of Paignton's central police court had never witnessed the like. Added to the gun-toting courtroom personnel and all the stars and stripes, was the frisson as 'every witness first saluted, although none of them wore caps. The president gravely saluted back.'[3] It was the closest Paignton would ever get to a certain type of legal television drama belonging to a distant future – and all the more noteworthy.

Captain Philbin's very first question set the tone. Curiously, Captain Scott was asked whether there were any British soldiers 'in that crowd of coloured men?' All prosecution witnesses would be asked this question. Captain Scott said 'no'. Nor could he identify any of the soldiers from that night among those in the dock, when asked. The Defense Counsel asked once more whether he had 'looked them over', but it was no use. The prosecution had established he could not identify even the hostile flashlight-holder that night.

After clarifying he had not, in fact, fired his weapon despite a previous statement to the contrary, Captain Scott, the officer in charge of patrolling his fellow countrymen that night, was asked about relations between the black and white American soldiers in Launceston. Specifically, he was asked: 'Had there been any trouble in town that night, or the previous night? Between the coloured and the white troops?'

Captain Scott replied: 'That night there was none, as far as I know, and I made a very thorough check that night.'

Somewhat implausibly, he said there had been no trouble between African American soldiers and their white counterparts either then, the night before or ever. What was the Defense Counsel getting at? Certainly Philbin persisted:

Q: 'You did not have the feeling that there would be any trouble or anything of that nature?'
A: 'Not anything of that nature, no sir.'
Q: 'It was just a quiet, regular night?'
A: 'It was a very quiet night.'
Q: 'You did not expect anything to happen?'
A: 'No, sir.'
Q: 'And there had been no previous trouble that night between the coloured and whites?'
A: 'There had not.'
Q: 'Had there the previous night?'

Finally, with Captain's Scott closing answer, came the rub:

'On the previous night I believe there was a slight incident.'[4]

As Captain Scott stood up to leave, the trial judge advocate announced the prosecution would wish to recall him later. Captain Scott, the most senior witness, in charge of policing United States' soldiers in Launceston on 26 September 1943, had not been able to identify either the soldier who had shone a flashlight in his face the night in question, or in fact any of the men in the dock that day. He had no explanation for the mutiny and nothing to say about race relations on his watch. And this was the prosecution's chief witness.

That day, the court would go on to hear from eleven more prosecution witnesses in succession. An unmistakeable, but sinister pattern was rapidly emerging in which not one of the large number of military police witnesses from either the 115th Infantry or 29th Infantry Division could identify any man sitting in the dock as actually being there on the night – some from as little as 10ft away.

Neither could the prosecution prove another key and, so far, inexplicable line of questioning, as to whether any British – soldiers or civilians – had involved themselves. Nor could they establish any trouble between black and white soldiers either that night, or any time before. They all, however, could identify the culprits as being African American. And each man's version of events added layers of tension and drama to the chaos of 26 September. Before lunch was called at 1.30pm, three men testified. Their names – Neilson, Potocki and Racey – were symbols of the United States' status as a world melting pot. Together their memories created a nightmare narrative of what had happened just nineteen days earlier.

First up was Sergeant Neilson, of G Company, 115th Infantry, a military policeman on duty that night, who described categorically how he knew there was trouble afoot.

'You could hear them before you could see them. There seemed to be a crowd, you could hear the marching feet,' he said. At that time the square was all but deserted save for a handful of Land Girls, sitting at the base of the monument, talking to a few military policemen standing between two parked jeeps. Estimating there to be between thirty and fifty soldiers, he added:

> 'They were marching in formation. When I first saw them it looked as though they were going to march on by, and then one after another they more or less peeled off and came over and surrounded us. I did not hear any comment 'Hands Up' but it appeared that the rest of the military policemen were backing up and raising their hands, so naturally I started too.'

In fact, words were spoken at that specific point and a voice was given to the mutineers, by the next witness for the prosecution, Staff Sergeant Potocki, of the 2nd Battalion, 115th Infantry. He said: 'He spoke very quietly too, and what he did say was "Why don't we let them come into town, come to the pubs and sort of have the freedom of the town?", and he seemed to step back just about then, and just as he stepped back on my right front that is where the firing started.'

Sergeant Potocki admitted skipping a beat before springing into action: 'I was sort of petrified for the moment, I didn't move. I knew I was a pretty good target standing there, and I had come to my senses and ran to the 'phone across the street, the New Market Inn, and called camp and asked for help.'

Ordered by the captain to drive off in search of an army ambulance, the following witness, Private Fred Racey, described how after, 'I started to pull away it felt like there was something under it.' On closer examination of the vehicle he saw how bullets had passed clean through one of the jeep's tyres as if it suffered 'from a puncture just like a bullet wound through it.'[5] It left more spent ammunition embedded in another. Subsequently it would take twenty men to carry off Private Racey's jeep, a vital piece of evidence, out of the square.

After hearing from the first four witnesses, time was called for a break. Even this part of routine procedure was elevated from the prosaic by its formalised informality, displaying a casualness that was alien to British journalists. Once again, they lapped it up. 'It was lunch time in the court. The president stretched his legs and stood up. 'Let's go,' he said. So they all filed out,' was how *The Herald's* front page splash opened the following day.[6]

After lunch, however, it was time for a gear change. British voices swelled in Paignton police court for the first time, adding extra dimensions of intrigue, colour and compassion too. The first Cornish civilian to testify was Tom Gossett, of the White Hart Hotel, Launceston. The sole reason compelling American authorities to hold this trial in public was the involvement of local witnesses such as Tom Gossett. He painted a graphic picture of military policemen under fire that night – but also conspicuously injected the one and only shot of empathy for the accused.

The publican, who had worked at the town square hotel for three months, described the sound of mutiny outside his workplace. It seemed, to him, like soldiers were firing in a circle: 'The sound of it seemed to start here and then go round.'

Q: 'You did not look out, did you?'
A: 'No, sir. I had more sense than that.'
Q: 'You mean the sound?'
A: 'The sound seemed to come and then go away, like, if you see what I mean.'

Talking about the armed soldiers he encountered that night, Mr Gossett did not portray a trio of crazed mutineers baying for blood. Instead, he described how easy it was for him to deal with them and his testimony makes transparent the kindness with which he treated them – an obvious new twist. He dealt briskly with the three armed soldiers who entered the hotel:

'One of them had a rifle, sir, and of some description, under his coat. I got them out and up the back passage, and this one with the knives I went up to him and just tapped him on the shoulder and said, "We haven't done you any hurt in here old man" and he said "no" and I said, "well come on out" and he followed me out.'

The five-minute rumpus could be heard nearly a mile away, said the following British witness, farmer George Robinson, a part-time member of Launceston Home Guard, who owned and still worked the land currently occupied by Camp Pennygillam. Testifying to the far-reaching explosion of sound that night, Farmer Robinson described hearing gunfire while next to the camp on the farm itself, three-quarters of a mile away up the hill. Nearly a week later he also found evidence, including a discarded rifle and a raincoat or groundsheet buried amid wheatsheaves on his land.

It was now that the courtroom audience would get its theatrical encore. Needing little introduction as he hobbled on crutches up several steps to take the courtroom stand, the next witness's role as one of the night's victims was beyond dispute. Sergeant Ralph Simmons, 29, formerly of Maryland and now belonging to E Company, 115th Infantry, was in obvious pain. He had taken cover behind one of the jeeps and been shot in both legs, which he proved to the court presently by rolling up his trouser legs to display dressings and scars in two places on the front lower third of the tibia. He offered to show them the instep on his left foot – which also received a bullet. Initially treated at the first aid station by a British officer, who gave him a shot in the arm, he was then transferred to his own unit's hospital. Staff Sergeant Simmons would recover to fight another day with fellow members of 115th Infantry's Second Battalion at Omaha Beach.

For now, however, his biggest concern was more mental than physical; specifically his imminent cross-examination. And he needed to keep his wits about him. Under close examination, Sergeant Simmons was challenged twice – firstly, given his role as shooting target that night, to double-check that he really could not identify any of those before him. Once again, and in common with every single witness before him, he could not put a face to any of the mutiny's perpetrators.

Secondly, he was pulled up for a mismatch between what he had just told the court under oath and his pre-trial sworn statement.

Q: 'You told the prosecution there was absolutely no disturbance that night?'
A: 'No, sir, I didn't see any at all.'
Q: 'But you have no idea of why these coloured fellows were a little bit peeved about things?'
A: 'I don't know – I don't know anything about it at all.'

On hearing this, the Defense Counsel begged to differ and showed a statement to the trial judge advocate, who clarified with the witness that it was indeed his.

Q: 'Will you read the last sentence please?'
A: 'It was because they were having trouble in some of the pubs,' he read, adding: 'Well, now, I don't know why the reason was they come up there, but I had heard that they had trouble in the pub, but I went down there and I didn't see nothing – everything was closing up then.'
Q: 'It was because they were having trouble in some of the pubs. You believed that that was the reason for the trouble?'

A: 'I imagined it would be, yes, but I didn't know anything about the trouble.'[7]

It seemed a small point, but for the first time a witness had been caught out. Admittedly it was just a detail, but it was one ranking high in the litany of mysteries surrounding the case. Why had there been trouble between black and white soldiers suddenly that night, out of the blue? Everyone so far had denied there being any friction at all. A very small fissure had appeared in the prosecution's case.

Chapter 3

Nailing the Ringleader

M iss Joyce Packe, US Army Court Reporter, was going to be extremely busy that afternoon. Not only did the official stenographer have to keep up with fast-talking, jargon-jiving American witnesses, but she had their New World spelling to contend with too. Miss Packe, however, was to be underestimated only at her beholders' peril. She swam in a busy stream of capable, unflappable British women underpinning the whole war effort – and was not to be trifled with under any circumstances. She had already proved her mettle at the age of 15 by becoming the first Torquay Girl Guide to pass a new test for rangers – and in so doing bagged for herself a prized viewpoint of King George VI's 1937 coronation. Six years on she was staying true to the guides' motto of doing her best and could well afford to enjoy the slight reprieve offered to the court in a ten-minute break.

It was one of many regular intermissions that day. From its start to finish three days later, each break in the court martial followed an exact pattern with predictable military precision: ten minutes of recess every hour. What made it extraordinary was its atmosphere. Described by those who saw it first-hand as strangely sociable, it felt like a pub, or, as Americans dubbed them, a 'poor man's club'. Each hour, 'without leaving the court everyone, including the prisoners, leaned back, lit cigarettes, and chatted animatedly,' noted the reporter from the *Western Morning News*.[1] Officers, witnesses and prisoners created a literal smokescreen at the back of the courtroom while, 'the defending officer strode across and laughed and chatted with the fourteen prisoners,' according to *The Daily Mirror's* man on the spot.[2] The absurdity of being able to kick back, laugh and joke while facing such grim charges underlines the naivety of these soldiers. Even while witnesses were being questioned and cross-examined under oath, they showed a frightening lack of awareness of just how serious their predicament was. 'They whispered freely among themselves. Some of them sat with their tunics unbuttoned,' remarked the *Daily Herald* reporter. For others, it was tantamount to disinterest: 'One of them unconcernedly read a Wild Western magazine throughout the day. No one stopped him.'[3] They literally didn't know what they were up against; that they were pitted against the full force of the US Army. Another British journalist there at the court martial later reflected how awkwardly this light-hearted reverie sat with the severity of charges prisoners faced that day. It was almost, he said, as if they didn't understand the sentences for their crime – which ultimately, if found guilty, was death by hanging.

The person aiming to prove their guilt was Trial Judge Advocate Frank P. Eresch, an ambitious 35-year-old lawyer from Kansas, already a major with both feet planted firmly on the army career ladder. Standing at 5ft 11in with blonde hair, blue eyes and just the hint of a scar on his upper right lip, Eresch was fresh from another court martial in Wiltshire just the previous week. Although appointed to the Judge Advocate General's department as one of only four new officers as recently as 3 August 1943, Eresch was already making a name for himself. In Marlborough, not ten days before, he had made waves defending a United States soldier accused of shooting dead one British woman and raping her friend. Eresch's swashbuckling court displays had not only made his name, but captured press attention too. Firstly, he had tried to bar graphic photographic evidence of the dead girl as unduly 'inflammatory' and then he advised another witness, not on trial, that by speaking up he could incriminate himself. That presiding judge told the young soldier witness here to disregard Eresch's advice adding: 'Be unafraid. Do you understand that you are not being tried here? I want you to speak up and be unafraid. Speak up without fear.'[4]

Coming back from the curiously convivial break, Eresch needed to bring his current case back on track in double-time. As prosecutor he now wanted to infuse some bolder colours into proceedings – and showed none of his previous coyness about illustrating violent injuries. In fact, he did the opposite by focusing on the severity of wounds suffered by the two military policemen. Three medics testified to treating both Simmons and his fellow sergeant, Charles Cox. Out of the two, the latter came off worse. Cox was originally thought to be in danger of losing his life and although now off the critical list, would need to stay in hospital for the next four to six months. The surgeon in charge of his care at the 115th Station Hospital, Captain M.C. Luthermond, said his leg injury was permanent resulting in 'an inch shortening of his left lower extremity.'[5]

After hearing testimony from ten witnesses, the vaulting prosecutor still had his work cut out because none of the targets that night could identify any one of the fourteen sitting in the dock. Strangely, given how busy the market square was that night, not one of the men so far had been able to accurately point the finger. It was time for the prosecution to speak to the only person who could, in fact, confirm the men in court as members of the 581st Ordnance Ammunition Company, based at Pennygillam. And that man was Captain James Bosson, who was the officer in charge of their 176-strong-unit. He alone could put faces to names read out by the court.

Originally the battalion adjutant, Captain Bosson had been part of the unit since its creation and in command since April that year. His testimony pointed to the interesting cultural mix within the company, with roughly half coming from the more enlightened northern and eastern parts of the United States and the others from the historic plantation-rich south where they volunteered for service in 1942 from the enlisted reserve corps. Even a rudimentary knowledge of the American Civil War would indicate these two groups would be light years apart in terms of their life experiences in twentieth-century United States and relationships with their fellow white citizens.

Captain Bosson confirmed his acquaintance with the men in the dock by acknowledging each of them as their names were read out and then feeding back their service record numbers. Eresch, secure in the knowledge that this was the only witness who actually knew those sitting in the well of the court, asked him somewhat unnecessarily to 'arise and look at the fourteen accused and tell the court whether or not they are members of your company. Take your time and make a complete inspection.'[6]

Captain Bosson correctly identified the men as being whom the prosecution said they were; that is, members of the 581st Ordnance Ammunition Company. This he could safely do. However, it was entirely different to confirming they were agitators in Launceston on 26 September. Captain Bosson himself was some 20 miles north of the town that night. It did not deter Eresch, who then asked for a ten-minute recess to arrange testimony for the next witnesses who 'will expedite the trial'. He was determined to get to the bottom of the second identity conundrum – to place the same fourteen soldiers in court at the scene of the crime. At 2.55pm, Captain Bosson was recalled, reminded he was still under oath, and then taken through each of the accused names individually to confirm they were present in the courtroom at that moment. And then he was gone.

Trial Judge Advocate Eresch now wheeled out his big guns to testify: army investigators tasked with extracting statements from those arrested in the hours immediately after the mutiny. Wartime conditions meant they had precious little time to gather evidence and now they too would be asked to confirm that the faces in front of them were in fact those they had interviewed in the riot's aftermath. The stakes were high and the scale and steeliness of the prosecution's intent were about to be laid bare as they attempted to prove once and for all who was actually to blame. High drama would return to the police court as names were named, because with this came serious qualifying questions: How sound were the statements containing these allegations? Who wrote them? Did the accused even knew what had been written? And more still. The fissure in the prosecution was about to come under pressure.

Harry C. Poltraz, Criminal Investigator for the Provost Marshal General's detachment, was stationed usually in London, but specifically seconded to Southern Base in Plymouth for the case. On 27 September, Poltraz had interviewed four soldiers in the military policemen's office at Camp Pennygillam and now needed to be able to identify each of them in turn so the prosecution could read those statements out loud to the court. Before each statement was read, several quick-fire questions established the interview was made voluntarily, without fear of threats or duress, promises or inducements and only after the accused was made aware of his rights. Poltraz was also asked to physically point to each man in turn.

First, Trial Judge Advocate Eresch battered down the defence team's objections to Poltraz's statements being read in full, regardless of who else was implicated. Eresch wanted to start by reading out the statement of 32-year-old Private Tom Ewing, an army veteran of just eight months. But Ewing's defence team resisted, saying that was fine as long as it solely referred 'to Private Tom Ewing, not to any other defendant.' Philbin feared the statement, if read in its entirety, would connect other parties to the crime. He asked 'if it would not be possible in reading the statement we eliminate the reading of those certain names and actions? Would it be possible to do that?'

His opponent, Trial Judge Advocate Eresch, was having none of it, arguing 'that would be approaching editing a statement … no harm can be done to any of the substantial rights of any of the accused by this court by the fact that it is read … the only purpose … is to expedite the trial.'

The president agreed, but Defense Counsel John Philbin stonewalled again, arguing that in 'some statements they deny what they have said in previous statements.'

The decision, however, was final. The statement, Exhibit C, was to be read in its entirety by the persistent prosecutor. And before long it was obvious why the defence team had objected. Ewing's statement named every man sitting at the back of the court and established a powerful precedent.

According to the statement, Ewing said that at 9.30pm a fellow soldier came into his tent saying 'they were having trouble in town' prompting him to get up, put on his overcoat and pick up a rifle he had, as well as a round of ammunition. Outside he saw Sergeant Austin passing around cartridges to fellow soldiers, identifying the remaining twelve in the court as among them. Marching into the square, he described hanging back at the corner. 'Most of the others went on up to the military policemen. All of a sudden, firing started,' he said. 'I heard a Tommy Gun being fired, which I think was handled by Barrett. After the shooting I ran away.'

After wandering around town for a couple of hours, he returned to camp where he was arrested and questioned. Completing his statement, he said: 'Barrett appeared to be the ringleader and instigator of the Trouble [sic].'

It was a turning point. The prosecution now had a witness statement that could positively say the men in court were the very same soldiers firing guns and rabble-rousing in Launceston on 26 September. The prosecution was making headway. But just how secure and sound was this or any subsequent statement?

Eresch quickly hammered home his advantage, keen to ensure from this point there was only one type of mutiny to be described in Paignton – and that was his. Riding roughshod over alternative accounts given by those who were actually there, such as Poltraz's next interviewee Sergeant Rupert Hughes, he objected strongly to any deviation being aired aloud. The defence team tried to object to Sergeant Hughes' evidence being read because he had changed his mind since speaking first, saying: 'I have a subsequent statement by this man Hughes, and he states that he–' But he was cut off before he could even finish his sentence let alone make his case by an objection from Eresch. This 22-year-old witness's subsequent and contradictory statement was ruled inadmissible and instead, the president allowed the defence a preliminary cross-examination.

Immediately, suspicions spiralled. For the defence, Philbin wanted to establish the exact manner in which this, and subsequent, statements were taken. Certainly, it was not taken under oath at the time it was made, as required. Investigator Poltraz tried to brush it off, saying it was sworn afterwards before Captain Bosson.

Sounding deeply unconvinced, Philbin asked: 'It was sworn before this captain, here?'

A: 'Yes.'
Defense Counsel: 'If that is true, no objection.'[7]

Even the press contingent was suspicious, as this questionable oath-taking and statement-swearing evolved into a dominant theme during the course of the afternoon, eventually surmising that 'Others said, that, having made statements, they were not sworn, as was customary under American procedure.'[8]

Regardless of its legitimacy, Sergeant Hughes, one of the two sergeants arrested, now had a statement, sworn under dubious circumstances, read on condition it could incriminate only himself. But how was that either possible or practical? It described trouble in the second pub visited on an unofficial visit into town. According to the statement 'Sergeant Austin had words with a white soldier, and later two white soldiers began fighting each other. Sergeant Austin and Barrett called us outside and Barrett asked us if we would all stick together against the whites.' Hughes described how the men, again naming every man in the dock, returned to camp, collected guns and that Barrett had issued the ammunition. Seeing the military policemen by the monument, he said, Barrett spoke to them asking why they didn't want them in town. 'The military policemen put their lights on us,' he said. 'Barrett then called to the military policemen again and told them to put up their hands. They put their hands up. Barrett had the only Tommy gun in our group. Firing started, and I knew the Tommy gun was fired, as I could tell by the sound.' Returning to camp and to bed Sergeant Hughes was arrested in the early hours of the morning.

One of the greatest gifts of jurors, judges and practising lawyers is their ability to disregard, to forget freely, what they have been told, when legally directed to do so during a court case. However, it must have been difficult to blot out names heard that day, especially when the same ones kept being repeated. Some of the people and actions included and read out under the pretext of not 'editing the statements' simply must have stuck. And it was in the prosecution's interest for it to do so – it needed to prove all fourteen were guilty as charged.

Sergeant Hughes, like Private Tom Ewing (the previous witness) had pointed to the same soldiers being led by the same man. Still more significant, was that Hughes (whose later statement was vetoed by the prosecutor's objection) concluded using the exact same words as the previous witness had in his statement. It echoed perfectly his fellow-accused: 'Barrett appeared to be the ringleader and instigator of the whole affair,' it read. Using the same text and even the same phrasing, this was surely a classic cut and paste job where simply the names of the accused were edited to elicit the story Poltraz wanted to tell.

In contrast with the white American officers, NCOs, privates and British civilians, who had taken the stand earlier, no black soldier had so far spoken in court. Instead they had to listen to statements read in their name. Eresch now asked to read the words of the man named ringleader and instigator: the 22-year-old Private First Class Clifford Barrett, a soldier for now nearly eighteen months, and son of a First World War veteran. It was by now beginning to appear that these statements gathered by Poltraz were more the product of literary fiction than original investigative nous. He had employed words and phrases not even known by the people meant to have uttered them. Again, the defence attempted to pour cold water, asking:

Q: 'Just how was this statement taken? What I mean is, did you ask the men: 'All right now, go ahead and tell me and I will put those things down?'
A: 'We first questioned him regarding the story of what happened in Launceston and we took it down.'
Q: 'And then who wrote – you?'
A: 'I wrote it.'
Q: 'You filled in certain words in certain places, and so on? For instance the word "instigator." Do you suppose that the last two–?'
A: 'No, I tried to explain what that was.'
Q: 'You put in some of your own?'
A: 'I explained to them.'
Q: 'You felt reasonable sure that the words … they used … were understood by them?'
A: 'Yes sir.'

Exhibit E was read to the court. It was the entire contribution to the case from the man meant to have masterminded the mutiny and centred on the word '*instigator*' – not even in his vocabulary. Clifford Barrett's statement said he was one of the only soldiers to have an official pass into Launceston on 26 September and that while in town, after having a beer, 'I heard some shots fired. I don't know how it happened or where. I started back to camp and went to bed. Sometime, the next morning, I was placed in custody. I don't know why, and that is all I know of the incident.'[9] It was the only time his words, let alone his voice, was heard in the court martial called to try the rioters he was meant to have rallied.

The sadness of a war veteran's son being championed as ringleader without so much as exercising his right of reply lingered – but not for long. There was no time for the moment's poignancy to resonate because some shocking admissions were coming that would cloud the tragedy of Clifford Barrett. The so-called mutineer's moment was about to be eclipsed.

Chapter 4

Turning the Tables

As the October darkness descended, court observers could not have known a truly mesmerising legal spectacle was heading their way. Shadowy army investigators' practices were about to be hauled under a brilliant spotlight to reveal sneaky shortcuts and a gaffe-littered investigation, topped off with some time-honoured perfidy. The rollercoaster first began picking up speed when the prosecution came to Exhibit F: the statement of 26-year-old Private Charlie Geddies, a sturdy soldier from Florida standing 5ft 5in, who reflected on his arrest and subsequent questioning by his colonel by acknowledging 'I did not tell him the full story.' After concocting Geddies' final statement, it seems Investigator Poltraz, responsible for its production, had also been selective with the truth. A terrible discovery was about to be revealed that might disrupt everything, leaving the prosecution's argument woefully weak.

'I am informed that this man Geddies cannot read', said the Defense Counsel Philbin. 'Did you read the statement to him in this particular case?'

Investigator Poltraz was on the cusp of an awful admission: that one of those who had put their names to a statement was physically unable to know what he was supposed to have said. The Defense Counsel continued:

Q: 'Then he did not read it?'
A: 'Well, I gave it to him to read.'
Q: 'Yes, but he couldn't read it if he couldn't read.'[1]

Shockingly, Geddies, facing the highest possible sentence for capital charges, did not even know what he was supposed to have told the investigator. Yawning gaps had opened in the prosecution's armoury.

So far it had been intimated that statements had not been recorded accurately. New and conflicting testimony had been shown to be barred; investigators admitted using unknown words and language to create the documents and right now there were firm fears about whether an illiterate soldier could even understand what was submitted as his own evidence. Watching journalists lapped up this tangible upping of the ante remarking how 'counsel … paced about the courtroom, sometimes spinning round on the witness with a particularly pertinent question' while those asked to identify any of the fourteen prisoners somewhat dramatically 'strolled across the court and peered at each of the accused in turn, hands in pockets and head quizzically on one side.'[2]

At 3.40pm, the president announced a recess of ten minutes which, bizarrely, like the switch of a light, extinguished the last hour's drama and tension, replacing it with something else. Resuming at 3.50pm, the prosecution had time for just two more witnesses before the close of business. So far, the bare bones of the story had been suggested – a leader, an accomplice or two, a few willing recruits, a handful of words, a shooting and injuries – albeit via the medium of increasingly questionable statements. Eresch hoped these next two men would flesh out the skeleton and indicate something of the story that caused an elderly Cornishman to tell the *Daily Mirror*: 'There hasn't been anything here like this since the days of the smugglers,' more than a century before.[3] But if he was expecting irrefutable evidence guaranteeing a classic open and shut case, Eresch and his assistant, Major Timothy Mulcahy, were in for a surprise. First up was the US Army's second investigator, Sergeant Marvin F. Richardson, also of the Provost Marshal General's detachment, responsible for writing five additional statements.

None of the explanations in his statements agreed on every detail. But they all started in the same way: with numerous men going into town, mostly without permission, and, after spending twenty minutes drinking a few beers in the first pub, moving to a second. Here, at this second tavern, a fight took place and the following confrontation certainly involved white soldiers. The million-dollar question was whether the group of illicit beer-drinkers were drawn in? It was difficult to see how merely witnessing two white soldiers scuffling among themselves could cause a mutiny of black soldiers – and this is what Private First Class

Alexander Shaw, from Tennessee, alleged as 'none of the coloured men were involved.' Another, more plausible version, that 'a white soldier pushed Clifford Barrett and told him to go on the other side or to go out,' came from 19-year-old Private Arzie W. Martin, adding: 'We all went to the other side but did not stay long.' Whatever happened during the tussle and whoever it involved, this pub punch-up was definitely the starting point for mutiny and riot. And this was according to all accounts collated by Sergeant Richardson – and most of those collected by his fellow investigator Poltraz too. Interestingly, it was the single point of information missing from the white military policemen's versions of events so far, but its chain effect was universally accepted.

Directly after, outside, 'someone said 'Do you all have ammunition' everyone said 'no' then whoever it was said "Will we all stick together?" everyone said "yes"', remembered Private Martin. More specific still was Private Shaw, 32, who said it was 'There [that] Barrett and Austin asked us if we would all stick together against the whites.'

Those two words – *'sticking together'* – were becoming common parlance in the trial, featuring in virtually every soldier's account of unfolding events that night. 'Sticking together' was singularly and indisputably the clarion call for action, the muster for mutiny. Promptly the men returned to camp picking up more arms and men as they got there. Twenty-year-old Private Freddy Blake, from Cook County, Illinois, and inducted barely six months earlier, told how he was 'in my tent when someone outside said there had been trouble down town. I got my bayonet and put it in my pocket and went out and joined the rest of them.' So too did Private James H. Lindsey, 22, who admitted collecting his rifle and six rounds of .30-calibre ammunition which had been in his possession since leaving Yeovil. Their mission was beyond doubt. 'We were looking for military policemen to pick a fight with,' said Private Martin. By the time they actually marched into Launceston town square, 'we had a great many more men with us,' said Private Shaw.

Various accounts of who actually addressed the military policemen found gathered and talking in the square were given – some said it was Corporal Joseph Alfred Joseph, others attributed it to Private Clifford Barrett. The gist of what was said, however, remained the same: 'Why don't you want us in town?' or 'Why can't we come down here and get along?' The refrain was muted. 'The military police replied something I could not hear,' said one.

Another that 'a scuffle started and I heard someone shout 'Don't anyone be a b–'. 'A shot was fired,' said Shaw. And that was the trigger for total mayhem and madness. With immediate effect.

Unquestionably the Saturday newspapers would have their fill alone on this powerful portrait of armed struggle – an intriguing case of blue on blue, Yankee-style. The universal editorial instinct to cover the case was justified one hundred times over. But what further compounded this lurid portrayal were the big, bold queries about how the admissions were made, which came again and again and again. Questions rained down on investigator Richardson as to how the statements were sworn and, once written, whether they were re-read properly to them. But it was over the question of who he had actually interviewed, that this particular investigator came unstuck and provided the press with the five-star field day it had been hoping for.

As was, by now, customary in the case, the investigator was asked to identify each man whose statement he had taken immediately after the shooting. The fifth and final soldier was 22-year-old Private James Lindsey, from Georgia, with a year's army service, four years of high school and yet more semi-skilled work warehousing in civilian life under his belt. Here came the moment reporters were waiting for and at this point the court martial manuscript reads like a drama script, complete with stage direction.

Defense Counsel:	'I just want to ask the Sergeant if he will identify Lindsey. Will you pick him out of that group?'
Witness:	'The third boy from the end of the back row.'
Defense Counsel:	'No that is not Lindsey. Lindsey stand up.' (Lindsey did so)
Q:	'How many times had you seen Lindsey?'
A:	'I had never seen him before.'
Q:	'You just saw him once?'
A:	'That is all, sir.'

It caused 'a sensation in the small court,' said one of the reporters, which would ripple far beyond Paignton police court. Only fast thinking by the prosecution stopped Sergeant Richardson repeating his error with the next witness, Private Martin. Asked to pick the soldier out, he replied:

A: 'I don't believe I could recognise him in court now.'

Quickly the trial judge advocate thought of a way round it, saying: 'The prosecution at this time would like to have Arzie Martin stand up for the purpose of determining whether Sergeant Richardson can identify him as being the same person.'

Even the president acknowledged this was a ridiculous way to conduct an identity parade, adding: 'For that purpose, how could Sergeant Richardson help to identify him, if I ask him to stand up, unless someone else stands up in his place?

Trial Judge Advocate: 'The prosecution withdraws that.'

This identity fiasco exacerbated existing concerns about the statements' reliability. Cumulatively, it could have threatened to undermine the prosecution's emerging narrative about the mutiny. But Eresch had an ace up his sleeve and there was never a better time for him to produce it.

By 4.30pm, the entire court was in position and waiting for the eighteenth and final witness of the day: the prosecution's star turn. In walked Corporal Alfred Joseph, a member of the 581st Ordnance Ammunition Company, who was taking the stand for the prosecution. Saluting the court president before sitting down, the courtroom was agog. What could have persuaded him to turn against his company? How had he been press-ganged into appearing? Before the prosecution commenced, Presiding Judge Zickel elaborately laid out the soldier's rights in this military court, boiling it down to the fact that 'no witness shall be compelled to incriminate himself or to answer any question ... when such answer might tend to degrade him.' In other words, Corporal Joseph was not, like fellow unit-members sitting at the back of the court, sticking together. He had turned US Army's evidence and there was little sign he was turning back again. Corporal Joseph may have been the first black witness to speak, but more importantly, he was appearing for the prosecution – and his impact was dynamite.

Corporal Joseph, who had belonged to the unit for eighteen months, gave an amusingly vague account of his movements before the mutiny, starting with 'three or four drinks with two British soldiers … and after we went to another pub to get some more whiskey and that one was about to close, so I didn't know my way back to the camp and these two soldiers went to take me back.' While returning they bumped into 'a gang of boys coming from my camp, so I stopped. I walked up behind them and I heard someone cry out "We will fix you" to some military policemen.'

Here, Corporal Joseph claimed to assume the role of peacemaker and asked the military policemen

'[W]hat was the trouble and he told me he didn't know, and when they said that, I knew it was fixing up a fight. I said "Can't we get along? What's the matter?" And then someone in the crowd hollered, "Put up your hands"'.

On doing so, according to his account, shooting started. Despite being in the company for more than eighteen months, acting as an eye-witness to the whole episode and reckoning between fifteen and twenty men to have been involved, Joseph was able to identify just four comrades: Private Clifford Barrett, Sergeant Kenneth Blanchett, Sergeant Rupert Hughes and Private First Class Alexander Shaw. And of those, one was not even standing trial.

Indulging his famous flair for showmanship, the trial judge advocate then produced Exhibit 2: a two-handed Tommy gun, which Corporal Joseph admitted was similar to that used by Private Barrett in Launceston. He also told Eresch that he did not see another gun fired after the fifteen or twenty rounds he guessed were shot by Private Barrett. Specifically, he said the bullets were low: 'He did not have it on his shoulder,' which surely suggested the attempted murder charge might have been wide of the mark. Asked whether he knew whether trouble was brewing, he said: 'No sir, I didn't even have no idea that anything was happening.'[4]

There was a pause as everyone absorbed this accidental bombshell. Seconds ticked by until the courtroom was jolted back into action by President Zickel adjourning court for the day. Now reality reasserted itself. Amid the cacophony of chatter, chair-scraping and flint-sparking as dozens of cigarettes were lit, various court-members left for the day – each preoccupied with their own thoughts. Trial Judge Advocate Eresch marched out, reflecting on his day's performance. To say it had not gone according to plan would be an understatement. Although disaster had been averted, it was only because of his eleventh-hour coup in those final few minutes. Surely, he could still be in a whole heap of trouble tomorrow?

It was true that evidence from his last witness, Corporal Joseph, had proved a powerful antidote to the mistakes and errors of US Army investigators laid shockingly bare before Paignton police court. This, plus the sheer doggedness with which Eresch had deflected questions about evidence-gathering and unreliable statements, had left him on ground much firmer than by all rights he should be. By using the testimony of a black soldier against his own company, the judge advocate had seemed to mask the fact that not one white soldier shot at that night recognised any of the supposed shooters sitting in the dock. Nor had anyone seemed to notice that the only person able to place anyone at the scene could barely put three of the fourteen there, just a fifth of the defendants on trial. Trial Judge Advocate Eresch had gone some way to creating a plausible narrative and identifying an instigator, all the while persuading the court to hear allegations incriminating every single one of the fourteen accused. But the harsh fact remained that eight hours after proceedings started, it was a little early to embark upon a victory lap. Even now, after court was dismissed for the day, Eresch's work was far from done.

Mostly there was no getting away from the serious questions raised that day including misidentified defendants and worrying allegations of shoddy evidence-gathering. Then there had been that very un-British playing to the gallery with courtroom theatrics more akin to a Hollywood B-movie than Paignton police court, which were bound to guarantee the kind of headlines so feared by President Zickel. The US Army would not be amused either. Publicising anything that might undermine the allies' relationship was not going to be welcomed, particularly before they attempted the world's largest seaborne invasion together. Worse still, the politically sticky subject of race was intrinsically involved here, providing further cause for aggravation. A bit of unseen back-corridor influence might just be needed to ensure the right outcome so that justice was seen to be done at this sensitive time. If Eresch was to be successful in getting the guilty verdict expected of him, much more was needed – and sharpish too because time was running out. With this in his mind he exited Paignton police court.

Eresch was followed closely by court reporter Miss Joyce Packe, who took her last note of the day, recording the time she did this as 5.05pm. She was exhausted, her hands ached after such diligent recording of court business, but she hastened out smartly like any other member of the US Army. It had been riveting. Secretly thrilled to be at the heart of such a famous trial, her head was nevertheless reeling because news had been made that day and Eresch's aggressive prosecution had posed as many questions as had been answered. Questions like precisely what role had British civilians or soldiers played in another free nation's fight? However much its army wished, this was not just about the United States. It had taken place on British soil, British civilians had spoken already and there had been plenty of talk about British soldiers milling around on the edge of events too. The Brits were part of this, but how? What was the mysterious line of questioning about British soldier and civilian involvement?

She dwelt on the president's clumsy attempt to censor reporting of the story in the UK as well as the United States. Reporters witnessed the official desire to put the kybosh on the most fascinating aspect of the story – race – but why? What was it about race relations in the American Army that drew its own platoon of pressmen on that first day? Crucially, why did African Americans need to stick together anyway? It is impossible to underestimate the shock value of American soldiers sticking together against each other. It was civil war in all but name –and they had already done that the previous century. How could things have come to this explosive point where sticking together was perceived as necessary and a reality too? Although being a signed-up member of the US Army, Miss Packe could see exactly why reporters were now fighting a war of their own to secure telephone lines to their editors.

These questions were beyond Miss Packe in October 1943. However, with the benefit of a fortuitous freedom of information request and access to newly opened archives, an attempt to explain her questions can be hazarded – but only by rewinding to the United States' entry to the war and, more specifically, the personal journey of the 581st Ordnance Ammunition Company.

Part II

The Road to Great Britain

Chapter 5

The Relationship Gets Special

Britain's solitary stance against Nazi Germany morphed into world conflict as the Axis enemy redrew the battle lines two years after invading Poland. First, on 22 June 1941, Hitler unleashed 3 million troops and thousands of tanks against his former Russian allies by attacking them on the eastern front in Operation Barbarossa. 'The war against Russia will be such that it cannot be conducted in a knightly fashion,' the Führer avowed. 'This struggle is one of ideologies and racial differences and will have to be conducted with unprecedented, unmerciful and unrelenting harshness.'[1] Next came an equally decisive blow. Writing in his diary on 7 December, MP Sir Henry 'Chips' Channon recalled how after turning on his wireless, 'I was flabbergasted to hear that Japan had declared war on the United States and Great Britain and that bombing of Honolulu had already begun. So this vast war spreads.'[2] Channon had happened to hear the destruction of the American fleet at Pearl Harbor in real time. Later that night, Churchill slept well. He was right to. Within four days President Roosevelt had declared war on Japan, Germany and Italy and effectively, by the start of 1942, a Grand Alliance of British, Soviet and American powers was in place to bring the fight back to Hitler in Europe. It was the first step leading men from northern and southern states of America to the 581st Ordnance Ammunition Company – then to the United Kingdom and ultimately Paignton police court.

What did this new alliance with the United States mean to Britain in practical terms? Before, there had been Lend Lease – a bill passed in March 1941 – which meant the Americans supplied food, oil and mothballed warships, planes and weapons to Free France, the UK and China (later Russia too) in return for ninety-nine-year leases on army and naval bases in Allied territory during the war. The slight sting in the tail was that anything left over when hostilities ceased had to be paid for – leaving Britain in hock to America to the tune of a crippling

$4.34 billion (more than $60 billion in today's money), a debt settled in full only sixty years later, under Gordon Brown's watch as Chancellor of the Exchequer in 2006. By March 1941, Lend Lease had watered-down America's totally splendid isolation from Hitler's machinations, but now the gloves were off – and so too was neutrality. It was all-out war and time to get battle-ready.

Within days, both Houses of Congress passed new orders extending the service period of recruits from two-and-a-half years to six months after the cessation of hostilities. President Roosevelt also sanctioned the deployment of United States forces anywhere in the world. Later in December, during a rapidly convened series of Anglo-American meetings in Washington, it was decided to send troops to the British Isles, Northern Ireland initially, and afterwards, a local command centre for 'American forces allocated to the European area' was plotted for Grosvenor Square, London. The European Theatre of Operations United States Army, soon to be better known as ETOUSA, was up and running. A plan was taking shape. Its code name was Operation Bolero, short-hand for the build-up of US troops in the UK just sanctioned by Washington. Here they would shortly begin to live, train and trial for the invasion and conquest of Nazi Europe. At its peak the operation would involve more than 1.5 million United States personnel being stationed simultaneously in the UK. The first 4,000 soldiers arrived in January 1942. Numbers steadily grew each month – as many as 74,000 came in August alone – and still they came, even after D-Day as troops in mainland Europe were reinforced by yet more GIs from America. Three million in total eventually passed through the UK to the European Theatre of Operations. Eventually, the United States troops occupied 100,000 buildings in more than 1,100 locations nationwide. But there was never to be any confusion over who was ultimately in charge of these troops, so far away from home. The little-remarked upon Visiting Forces Act was quietly passed in 1942 enshrining that these incoming soldiers would be subject to American military law, even for crimes committed on British soil or against British subjects. But back in the immediate aftermath of Pearl Harbor, before there could be any thought of soldiers moving across the Atlantic, they needed training. And in those salad days of war, America now plunged itself into a frenzy of combat preparations on a gigantic scale.

With the big decisions to move men to the UK and create a local command structure for them already taken, now the urgent requirement was for military machines and manpower – quick-sharp and in mind-numbing quantities. The task ahead of army planners in December 1941 was prodigious, but history would show the industrial drive for cutting-edge machinery in fact forged modern America. The war production effort into making uniforms, arms, military transport and weapons transformed the American economy, making unemployment (as high as 25 per cent pre-war) a thing of the past and catapulting its industrial output into the stratosphere. Its Gross National Product more than doubled to $212 billion (nearly $3 trillion today) in 1945 from $99.7 billion just five years earlier. The United States of America was never to look back. A new superpower had been born.

Meanwhile, the push to create a formidable fighting force would prove equally ground-breaking. Again, although more than 16 million Americans went on to serve in the Second World War, each spending on average sixteen months overseas, it seemed an impossible, quantum leap in the dark days of January 1942. Admittedly, the army had a small head-start thanks to the first peacetime military draft approved by Roosevelt and Congress in September 1940. America's military force at this moment was 2.2 million, which was something, but not enough. By late 1942, some 36 million men, aged between 18 and 64, were registered for the draft. From this vast pool, men were selected for examination by local boards, staffed by community members, who considered factors of occupation, health and family situation before deciding whether an individual was capable of being militarily fit. Ultimately, the draft alone would pull in 10 million or so volunteers. And somewhere in the mix were 2.5 million African Americans, of whom more than 130,000 would eventually serve in Britain.

Among them was Henry Tilly, who, as he joined up in August 1940, was the first of those 581st Ordnance Ammunition Company accused to enlist. He was followed by Freddy Blake in February 1942 and in March 1942, it was the turn of Virginia-born Henry Austin, who was later promoted to Technical Sergeant. The following month Charlie Geddies signed up. In May 1942, Clifford Barrett, dubbed by army prosecutors as 'instigator' of the Launceston mutiny, joined the army along with Henry

McKnight and Private Carl Tennyson. In September 1942 Privates James Lindsey and Alexander Shaw enlisted, followed by Rupert Hughes (later promoted to sergeant) in October. By February 1943, the remaining accused – Tom Ewing, Willis Gibbs, James Manning and Arzie W Martin – were all members of the US Army.

They ended up as part of an outfit that had started life in May 1942 as the 100th Ordnance Battalion in Camp Sutton, North Carolina. Originally, it had been formed by putting together two African American battalions led by white officers, one from each of the 301st and 302nd Ordnance Regiments. Coming exclusively from the National Automobile Dealers Association, the 100th Ordnance Battalion was made up of 1,000 or so mechanics, car salesmen, dealers and washers and was commanded by just twenty-five white officers. In the beginning, the battalion had four companies known as P, Q, R and S which became A, B, C and D. It was only on 8 August 1942 that A company was renamed 581st Ordnance Ammunition Company and that finally the company that was to take Launceston by storm was born.

After their selection, it was training. Here, 100th Ordnance Battalion bosses had their work cut out for them, right at the start, according to its official army history. Describing the battalion's early days as 'extremely complex', the account explained that 'few of the personnel had any military training prior to being assigned ... None of the personnel had any training in ammunition supply.'[3] Moreover, on top of acquiring the technical know-how, they had to get fighting-fit – and doing all of that in United States training camps was arguably a bigger battle for some than future hostilities with the official enemy. Especially when they were African American. For the 581st Ordnance Ammunition Company men, the next few months would prove a significant step on their march towards mutiny in Cornwall. All of those who were to fill up Paignton police court in October 1943 came together for the first time at the 100th Ordnance Battalion's new headquarters in Fort Sill, Oklahoma. If by any miracle they were unfamiliar with certain unsavoury customs practised in southern states and infamously known as *Jim Crow*, it was here that they quickly became acquainted with them.

Of America's 132 plus million population in 1940, nearly 10 per cent were of African origin and it was this ratio the army wanted to replicate.

Almost 80 per cent of African Americans were then in the south – half in rural communities; living proof of the slavery that for generations drove the antebellum economy. Most former slaves had stayed south of the Mason-Dixon Line in poverty as share-croppers after the watershed Civil War. Legalised racial segregation governed post-slavery society in these former Confederacy states. Dubbed *Jim Crow*, after a disrespectful show parodying an old black man dancing, it was supposed to enshrine 'separate but equal' treatment. Effectively it ensured African Americans lived totally separate lives from their former white masters with specially segregated public transport, schools, parks, cemeteries, theatres and restaurants. And when America entered the Second World War it was in their traditional homeland, these southern states, that the bulk of military training took place for draftees. However proud of its military tradition, the south was equally resolute in its racial segregation. Its cultural attitudes had been shaped by generations of blind-eyed ethnic violence, manifesting itself not just casually in total segregation but in thousands of terrifying lynchings and other Ku Klux Klan criminality.

To complicate things further, while Britain's newest ally's war machine cranked into action, its social fabric was also taking a radical new complexity and nowhere was this more apparent than in its military heartland of the southern states. Seismic change was on its way. One of the biggest and fastest mass movements of people in history, The Great Migration, began in 1940 and would result in 5 million African Americans leaving the southern countryside for the cities of the South, West and North. Sparked by the invention of revolutionary mechanical cotton-picking machinery, which obliterated wide-scale manual labour-requirements for plantations, it was bolstered by Roosevelt's Executive Order 8802 on 25 June 1941 which outlawed racial discrimination in the war production industry, ensuring there was factory work in the cities for African Americans to move to. It was already apparent on the army enlistment cards of 581st Ordnance Ammunition Company men, at least four of whom had moved from their birthplaces of Missouri, Virginia, Arkansas and Mississippi for Chicago and Ohio. For them, and others beginning to migrate north, it was as if they were leaving for another country.

This mounting insecurity of a transient community embarking on one of the biggest-ever migration surges exacerbated existing racial tension and unrest in the south. When the draft brought in 10 per cent of African Americans from every corner of the country here with the rest of the white intake, it was not a question of if the worlds of white and black recruits would collide, but when and how often. Men of the 581st Ordnance Ammunition Company were plunged into this obnoxious arena feet first.

They soon discovered their army roles and careers were on a different track to white counterparts and there was no doubt about which group was going slower. With rare exceptions such as the Tuskegee airmen and the 320th Barrage Balloon Battalion, most African Americans were denied the right to fight and instead given the hard, dirty and dangerous work of the Quartermaster Corps, The Corps of Engineers and the Transportation Corps. Grouped under the supply arm umbrella, they cooked, washed, cleaned, dug ditches, built bridges, drove trucks or as in the 581st's case, took responsibility for building ammunition dumps from their Cornish camp of Pennygillam. Although 581st men's individual accounts of training do not survive, a single, powerful overview of their shared experience is preserved in civil rights leader Walter White's account of his trip to the UK. It is a cautionary tale echoing thousands of other stories from various southern training camps, all of which follow the same sorry narrative.

After discovering they were not to be armed to fight in the Second World War, budding members of the 581st Ordnance Ammunition Company then found out that they, along with every other African American recruit, were rarely allowed to bring previous experience and talents to bear on their army careers – let alone bring advancement. In 1943, a Private Laurence W. Harris wrote to the *Pittsburgh Courier* to report the discrimination that he faced, which had all but stymied his hopes for advancement. By training as a small toolmaker, he dreamt of becoming an airplane mechanic, 'but the field doesn't seem open to Negro soldiers. I only hope and pray that I will get into some part of the service where I could use my trade.'[4]

His concern was typical. Instead of harnessing experience and trades to roles that might 'help win the war', according to another letter writer Jus Hill, with the 78th Aviation Squad in Texas, African Americans were used as 'servants and ditch diggers' mostly charged with 'washing dishes, working around the officers' houses and waiting on them.'[5]

It was plain from the outset that warriors came in just one colour – white. They 'were the only ones to be the heroes,' according to Benny Gordon, an American NCO who served with 498 Port Battalion, US Army in Great Britain and Normandy. Reflecting on his training, he said: 'there weren't to be any black heroes – they wanted to take it all. We shine their shoes but they gonna take the battle and that was very demeaning.'

Those sitting in Paignton police court dock in October 1943 had long known the universal truth that even a college education was no guarantee of better treatment in the US Army. Reports of some black soldiers being more intelligent, educated to a higher level and all round better-suited to lead than their own white officers are myriad. Interviewed after the war by the Imperial War Museum, Benny Gordon recalled: 'We had [white] officers that didn't even finish high school ... but "he was white" was enough to guarantee them more senior positions. Thereafter they were known as 'ninety-day wonders' by the black troops they commanded. Effectively the bright black NCOs were vital props in the chain because 'it was the black soldiers that made the white officers because the non-coms, like I was, we knew how and what; we ran these things for the officers. They got the credit but we were the person behind the scenes that made him,' he said.[6]

One rarity was the exclusively African American 92nd Division which came to be respectfully known as the Buffalo division in honour of their nineteenth-century namesakes: infantry and cavalrymen who courageously and famously patrolled America's Western Front. Perhaps a Buffalo officer was best placed to lament the egregious waste of talent during the twentieth century's most current war. Writing home while stationed in Arizona, one such Buffalo officer bemoaned that despite holding degrees from the nation's greatest universities, black officers, however brilliant, were consistently overlooked for promotion at the expense of lesser-qualified white candidates. Quite simply, he wrote, 'The poor colored officer who is his superior in service, tact and etc., is still a Second Lieutenant' consequently leaving 'colored officers fed up' because they knew 'that they [were] not being treated fairly, but there was nothing they could do.'[7]

Their gifts were ignored. Neither would they be given a proper outlet to object. Few official complaints from African American troops were recorded and little or no action was taken when they did. But the broad brushstrokes of discrimination, inequality and humiliation remain indelible in mountains of anecdotal evidence and contemporary letters written by outraged recruits and published by black newspapers.

Being second-class started in the army selection process itself (where segregation was a cornerstone) and accelerated the moment it hit the nation's capital Washington DC, where they were forced to board *Jim Crow* train carriages to their southern training camps and the segregation continued afresh.

Arriving at Fort Sill, men of the 581st Ordnance Ammunition Company were allocated bunks in one of twenty-three barracks earmarked exclusively for use by African American soldiers. There was enough space to host a garrison of 2,500 Negro soldiers but only six rooms available on the base for the use of their guests. Army planners had spent time working out the recreational facilities too and just to ensure segregation was complete, a new swimming pool had been built specifically for Negro soldiers at a cost of $17,000 in 1942. Supply Sergeant Marvin Wright, of the 3109 QM Company, said soldiers had to 'eat in separate facilities; live in separate facilities; sometimes there were no facilities at all and we had to sleep on the bus.'[8]

Sergeant Wright's suggestion was that African American amenities were not just separate, but notoriously worse. Everything in their world was second-rate, according to soldiers' accounts back home or to newspapers. Men like Benny Gordon said 'the white soldiers had the best of the best, the black soldiers were treated like dogs.'[9]

Writing to a Baltimore newspaper in 1943, another soldier reported how in his Florida camp, seeing the degradation was believing it:

'I wish I could snap a picture and send it because you wouldn't understand. Sir, we sleep on sand floors without no boards or anything to bed. We stand up and eat each meal in a mess kitchen. Sir we do not have running latrines. They have a group of colored soldiers who go around every morning and clean out the used bucket and put clean ones in.'[10]

In fact, even the enemy had it better when they were captured, according to leading civil rights activist Walter White, who was fed tales of German prisoners eating comfortably in Allied restaurants later in the war while African American soldiers were forced round the back to eat in kitchens.

But the one constant, relentlessly driving segregation, second-class facilities and skill-suppression in soldier training, was the everyday violence and endemic racism to which African American recruits were subjected.

One African American soldier from the 25th Infantry, stationed at Camp Bowie, Texas described how 'we have approximately 22,000 white soldiers, and from these white soldiers we're jeered both day and night, calling us various unpleasing names as "*niggers*", "snowball" and their Black African Army.'

If they were allowed the privilege of travelling on buses 'we're talked about like we're dogs and pushed and shoved around in the same manner.' In order to enjoy any of their precious leave it was better to hire special cabs, but however they journeyed to their free time, the rule was always the same: 'When we try to defend ourselves we're outnumbered ten to one.'

Unsurprisingly, when reported, abuse fell on deaf ears. Official advice given, was 'to not look at white soldiers, pay them no attention, just completely ignore them, if necessary walk a little faster.' It was also advised 'if the white soldier continues to hit you, get out of his way and do not hit them back.'[11]

It made a mockery of training, said one letter writer in 1943 describing the experiences of the 328th Aviation Squadron and the 908th Quartermaster Company in 1943. So far he and his colleagues had neither been drilled or even seen a gun 'except a 45 on the military policemen's side, ready to blow your brains out if you resent being treated like a dog and being called a *Nigger* or a Black Son of a B— much less call it Basic Training.'[12]

Such shameful, bullying training practised so widely could not go unchecked forever. What went on behind camp gates had already started to exact angry responses within the United States of America's army facilities throughout the nation. What's more, the conflict was spilling over outside into the wider community. But not from men of the 581st Ordnance Ammunition Company, just yet. They were still settling in.

Chapter 6

Heading South – the 581st Ordnance Ammunition Company Assembles

I f they were hoping for anything in Oklahoma other than the customary treatment thrown at African American servicemen elsewhere, 581st Ordnance Ammunition Company men were in for an abrupt awakening. Assembling in strength as part of a 1,000-men battalion offered scant protection from institutional racism in southern states like Oklahoma. Instead their time here marked a significant stage of an army career edging ever towards mainstream mutiny.

Fort Sill was a long-established camp, some 85 miles south-west of Oklahoma City and built originally as an outpost while the Indian Wars raged. With its history firmly rooted in America's pioneering conquest of the west, Fort Sill claimed to have played a significant role in every national armed conflict since. Its continuing importance was further cemented when it became home to the US Army's Field Artillery in 1930 and the Field Artillery Museum four years later. The 581st was directed immediately to the Field Artillery once they arrived at Fort Sill in August 1942. Quartered in the old civilian barracks, their new duties included supplying Fort Sill Artillery School with ammunition, keeping stock records and posting reports.

Just a few months into 1943, two factors in the countdown to Launceston's shooting slotted unremarkably into place. Firstly, in April a new commander was appointed to the 581st Ordnance Ammunition Company. One of the 100th Ordnance Battalion's founding twenty-five white officers, New Yorker First Lieutenant James Bosson, stepped up to the role and was still in charge when mutiny unravelled. He went on to play a leading role in Paignton's court martial.

Secondly, around this time an official inspection of the magazine area showed that not everything was adding up – and that more ammunition was stored there than permitted. A plan for what to do with excess supplies was drawn up directly, but it showed Fort Sill was awash with plenty of extra ammunition, which created ample opportunity for stray bullets to be bagged. Hidden stashes of illicit ammunition smuggled into Britain would become meaningful during the Launceston shooting itself – and in evidence during Paignton's court martial.

That spring, however, these two minor details slipped under the radar not least because to all intents and appearances, the company's star was actually rising. According to the company's official army history, the 100th Ordnance Battalion's eight months at Fort Sill were regarded as 'the most profitable from the standpoint of training received and results accomplished ever experienced by the battalion HQ until its arrival in Europe.'[1] During its time there, its troops trained five more ammunition companies and activated another three, all the while separating, stock-taking and restocking more than a million rounds of artillery ammunition.

Fort Sill was known by local tribes as 'the soldier house at medicine Bluffs' when it was built as part of a campaign to stop hostile raiders attacking border towns in Kansas and Texas in 1869. It is arguable what type of bastion, if any, it was to some of its own soldiers in the Second World War especially when, like every US Army camp, it expanded massively to keep up with demand. The 581st Ordnance Ammunition Company's whole experience at Fort Sill, at a time when it could house and train up to 26,000 soldiers, suffered many of the hallmarks of African American life in the US Army. At the outset, they had been allocated a barrack according to their race. In retrospect it was probably the most polite and discreet form of racism they were to experience in their soldiering service.

Life here would be a veritable baptism of fire for non-southerners among the 581st Ordnance Ammunition Company. Soldiers such as Chicagoans Freddy Blake, Tom Ewing and Willis Gibbs, now experienced *Jim Crow* close-up for the first time - with disastrous results. We know this from an impeccable source: a rare and eviscerating account that exists in the writings of no less than African America's most famous and vociferous leader, who went to the trouble of asking them about it when he visited Britain during the war.

Walter White, secretary for the National Association for the Advancement of Colored People (NAACP) was perhaps the greatest and most powerful civil rights advocate of his time – known for his charm, tenacity and steely determination. White's looks also distinguished him. *'I am a Negro. My skin is white, my eyes are blue, my hair is blond. The traits of my race are nowhere visible upon me,'* was how he began his autobiography *A Man Called White*.[2] The Aryan-looking, and appositely-named Walter White, from Atlanta, Georgia, wholly embraced his African American heritage. In fact, he originally used his looks to pass himself off as white so he could go undercover and investigate lynchings in the South (at great personal risk to himself) in the 1930s. This earned himself a senior role at the NAACP and by 1931 he became leader, a position he was to hold for nearly a quarter of a century, making him one of the founding architects of the American Civil Rights movement.

Walter White's secret weapon was undoubtedly his appearance which could prove deceptive for the uninformed – as demonstrated when he greeted certain fellow Americans during this UK wartime trip. When she saw him for the first time, Lady Astor, the Virginian-born, larger-than-life southern belle and since 1919, Member of Parliament, lived up to her reputation for straight talking. Now chatelaine of Cliveden, the infamous Berkshire house setting for political intrigue and scandal in the Profumo affair two decades later, the politician dispensed with any pretence at social niceties when she met her home country's most vocal and articulate apologist for racial equality. Walter White recalled: *'She shook hands, regarded me closely and exclaimed as her first words of greeting, 'You're an idiot!' Having heard of her frankness, I said nothing. 'You are an idiot,' she repeated, 'calling yourself a Negro when you're whiter than I am, with blue eyes and blond hair.'* She proved once again that you can take the girl out of Virginia, but not the Virginian out of the girl after lunch. Britain's first female Member of Parliament then told him: *'We never have any trouble with the good black boys. It's the near-white ones who cause the trouble. They're always talking about and insisting on 'rights.'"*[3]

With his nation at war and ten per cent of its army made up of African Americans, the NAACP leader was already fulfilling Lady Astor's observation and making *'trouble'* by investigating their fate overseas. Number one priority for the British leg of his trip was talking to 581st Ordnance Ammunition Company members and finding out first-hand from them about what army life in the south had been like. The result is an unblinking reflection of what it was for them to be based in a place where *Jim Crow* principles governed army life.

Men of the 581st Ordnance Ammunition Company described firstly how abysmal transport options perpetually left them 'forced to wait for buses into town until all the far greater number of white soldiers in the Southern camp had been accommodated.' On top of this 'frequently passes had expired before Negro soldiers could secure transportation'. The crux of it was that men of the 581st Ordnance Ammunition Company were denied access to recreation when not on duty. Prejudicial treatment did not end here, as they were also 'denied food or drink, called *nigger* and had discovered that the uniform of the US Army afforded no immunity from insult.' Interestingly, there were already signs that 581st men were not happy to take this discrimination lying down. Evidently there had been staged 'protests and a variety of incidents [that] caused them to be confined to camp for a number of weeks'.[4] Time spent in the south by the 581st Ordnance Ammunition Company therefore was a crucial staging post in their passage to 'mutiny'.

Every injustice they suffered on account of their race in Oklahoma was nothing compared to what came next for fellow battalion members in Kentucky, where the state motto *'Unbridled Spirit'* was about to take on a whole new meaning. Things took a dramatic turn for the worse on 22 June 1943, when the 100th Ordnance Battalion headquarters moved for a third time to Camp Breckinridge, 3 miles east of Monroe in Kentucky. Better-known now for bourbon, bluegrass and a certain type of cooked chicken, Kentucky had been officially neutral in the American Civil War, but one would be forgiven for not knowing it then – especially as its state star had taken central place on the Confederate battle flag.

It is unclear whether the 581st Ordnance Ammunition Company stayed in Oklahoma or moved with the headquarters of its umbrella battalion (the 100th Ordnance) at this stage. What is known is that the men they had lived and worked with at Fort Sill were to become party to a truly peculiar and troubling turn of events. What would unfurl was yet more evidence of generally dangerously high levels of racial tension within the ordnance sections of the army. It is pertinent to the story because it involved as a very minimum this same ordnance company's wider army family and possibly the 581st members directly themselves. It also serves to add more texture and depth to an understanding of what it was to be an African American soldier in June 1943. Ultimately, the insight it provides into how mutiny was becoming more likely for this ordnance company is razor-sharp.

A few curious pages contained within the unit's official history includes a detailed account of the 'disciplinary problems' arising after 581st Ordnance Ammunition Company's Battalion headquarters – the white-led 100th Ordnance Battalion – moved from Oklahoma to Kentucky, where existing companies were led by a mixture of black and white officers. The newcomers had been forewarned they were entering a troubled zone. But they can't have been expecting what subsequently happened.

According to the official version of events, it didn't take long for order to disintegrate once the ordnance battalion shipped in. Dozens of enlisted soldiers went AWOL. The fall-out was fantastic. But what was the cause? According to the official history there existed in the Kentucky ordnance companies 'a definite misunderstanding … between the officers, so much so that the company commanders had very little control over their organisations through their junior officers.'

It largely ascribed the worrying fact of 'uncontrollable' soldiers to disputes between black and white officers rooted in 'misunderstandings over duty assignments and certain details that the coloured officers were required to perform by their superior officers caused some of them to cry racial discrimination.' Briskly traducing African American complaints, it described the aggrieved officers' quest for revenge as fuelling rampant repercussions; that by telling their side of the story 'in a distorted manner' to their subordinates, in effect they were 'almost completely destroying effective control of the company commanders over their enlisted personnel.'

It wasn't long before things snowballed, the report continued. Such was the military breakdown that 'all duty assignments were carried out in a slovenly manner and signs of discipline were non-existent. One of the organisations had forty-five enlisted men AWOL at one time.'

Within just days, a clutch of investigators from the Office of the Inspector General were rushed in, quickly producing a 'detailed' report which they presented to the Battalion Commander during a two-hour conference. The commander used this time to outline a plan to 'restore the companies to usefulness', the gist of which was to get things back to basics. They would have to start as if from scratch with each 'staff section … [making] daily inspections of each of the companies and a very high standard of administration, discipline and general appearance was required.' Officers were expected to get up a full half an hour before the enlisted men so they could inspect their formations at reveille and retreat. All officers, 'both white and coloured' were required to perform 'unpleasant tasks' and anyone who failed to measure up to the newly-imposed 'army standards' were to be removed, again regardless of race.

Luckily, the investigators agreed the plan, warning with chilling foresight that 'drastic measures would have to be taken immediately, else a general mutiny was imminent.' Unfortunately for the Battalion Commander, Major W. Marshall Purvis, his scheme was then exposed to the elements, quite literally, as all his ordnance companies were drafted urgently to Missouri to complete flood control work. 'These orders came at an unfortunate time as the reorganisation had not had sufficient time to erase all the undesirable elements,' the army history narrated. When they returned thirty days later, much of the good work had been undone and 'it was immediately noted they had lapsed back into the same disagreeable, undisciplined organisations as before.'

According to this account, the Battalion Commander was now hell-bent on restoring the errant ammunition companies to their former glory, but on 28 August 1943, external factors thwarted his plans once more. Just two months after it had arrived, the 100th Ordnance Battalion HQ was ordered to move again, this time to the Tennessee Manoeuvre area. All reforming efforts were once again stopped in their tracks meaning the six ammunition companies had not achieved the 'perfection desired.' This part of the official army history ends on 28 August 1943 with the headquarters' move to Tennessee and an assessment 'that the period 26 June 43 to 28 August 43 produced a definite change for the better in the companies.'[5] Whether this was a case of wishful thinking or famous last words remains debatable.

It almost doesn't matter whether 581st men themselves were eye-witnesses or direct participants within the Camp Breckinridge debacle or not. A troubling breakdown of authority over racial inequality had taken place in front of their own battalion headquarters' eyes and it is inconceivable that they would not have at least known about it. Layered on top of the rich tapestry of what was being widely reported as happening in US army camps nationwide, it was in fact one more version of the increasingly common story in which race played a starring role. Dramatic racial tension was at the heart of this extreme chapter of the 581st's army career – whichever way one looks at it. They suffered in Fort Sill, Oklahoma, and may well have shared a taste of what their colleagues most definitely experienced in Kentucky. The end of their time in the American south, in the late summer of 1943, marked a pause in their journey. Freshly moulded by the deplorable training uniquely proscribed for African American soldiers in Oklahoma and possibly Kentucky, they waited for the next move. New orders for the entire 100th Ordnance Battalion came through on 28 August. While the battalion headquarters was moved south to Tennessee, the commanding officer of the 581st Ordnance Ammunition Company, First Lieutenant James Bosson, was given a different destination, even further away.

They didn't know it yet, but army life in America was nearly over for men of the 581st Ordnance Ammunition Company. Where would they go next? What lay ahead? Whatever the destination, they were travelling in the wake of thousands of white American soldiers. And what sort of act was this to follow?

Chapter 7

White Yanks in the UK: Anglo-American Relations

embers of the 581st Ordnance Ammunition Company were in fact one step closer to crossing the Atlantic – they just didn't know it yet. Word was that they were being transferred to the sweltering August heat of Camp Patrick Henry, a giant holding-pen for war zone-bound troops. A newly built facility cut out of more than 7 square kilometres of forest in the southern state of Virginia, Camp Patrick Henry had become one of the main staging posts for troop departures to Western Europe. However, at this stage nothing was certain.

Nobody in Fort Sill knew exactly where they were heading next, let alone their eventual destination. American servicemen had to endure interminable, tumultuous and nerve-wracking days at sea, running the gauntlet of both German U-boats and epic sea-sickness, only discovering their new location on stepping ashore. Restricted to camp, 581st Ordnance Ammunition Company men were not short of time and had ample opportunity to contemplate their forthcoming war-travels. Admittedly there were other theatres of war in which they could have ended up such as the Pacific, North Africa and now Italy, but Britain was the biggest. And it was towards Britain that the group's thoughts would have automatically turned.

What did the 581st Ordnance Ammunition Company really know about this nation, formerly America's colonial-master? More importantly, what impressions did Americans already experiencing wartime Britain hold? And what about the natives? In other words just how special was the relationship then that subsequent twentieth- and twenty-first-century British prime ministers have celebrated and harked back to ever since?

The omens were not good. Before Pearl Harbor changed everything, much American sentiment was anti-British both traditionally and more recently. In the twenty-odd years since the First World War, the two countries' economies had drifted apart while 'American foreign policy also sunk into a genuinely isolationist mentality'.[1] By 1935, a sequence of Neutrality Acts prohibited loans and trade with bellicose countries in wartime. And its famously patriarchal ambassador to the court of St James, Joseph Kennedy, was not necessarily the exception when it came to the isolationist views he espoused.

Two years into the Second World War, United States' opinion polls were expressing a wish to aid Britain, but the overriding desire was to keep clear of direct involvement – which may explain President Franklin D. Roosevelt's timid pre-Pearl Harbor political movements.

This lukewarm feeling was only reflected and entrenched further by ridiculous British stereotypes created, caricatured and circulating around the stage, screen and press in America. 'The typical Englishman is represented as a chinless ass with a title, a monocle and a habit of saying 'Haw, haw',' said George Orwell, writing in 1943 as literary editor of *Tribune*. 'We ought to face the fact that large numbers of Americans are brought up to dislike and despise us,' he continued.[2] Orwell had spotted what future actors Alan Rickman, Gary Oldman and Anthony Hopkins would come to discover in later twentieth-century blockbusting films – that British villains came straight from Hollywood's central casting.

Nor did things get off to a better start once the United States of America entered the war. Certainly, there was little evidence of hearts and minds being easily won in America, when British Home Secretary Herbert Morrison noted early in 1942 that: 'some people talk as though we were the Britain of 1776 and others as if we were the Britain of 1938 – and the second group is only slightly less out of date than the first.'[3] Soon after that, American-based British businessmen were warning the Foreign Office about the low 'stock' with which Britain was held across the Atlantic. In April 1943, *Daily Express* New York correspondent C.V.R. Thompson warned his British editor that 'If something drastic isn't done' about American regard for the British then 'we are going to have a much worse situation than after the last war before this war is finished.' Thompson worried that although the expected anti-British talk was rising it was 'worse than anyone expected. Now it sticks, even though I think a lot of Americans are trying hard to bury their instincts to bait the British.'[4] So penetrating was this insight regarded, that it was copied to the all-important Ministry of Information.

By July 1942, it was glaringly obvious the African American press had added its voice to the chorus of disapproval. That summer there was a great deal of comment on British policy in India, all of it very definitely anti-British. Columnist A.M. Wendell Malliet of the *New York Amsterdam Star News* wrote: 'While the British are remaining 'hard-boiled' against all appeals from their colored subjects, American leaders and statesmen are expressing words of hope and encouragement.'[5]

Most damning was an American opinion poll taken in December 1942 for the Bureau of Intelligence showing that one year into its participation in the Second World War, as many as one in four of its citizens were irrevocably anti-British, 'feeling that Britain is fighting the war primarily for motives with which they do not sympathise.'[6] This dire statistic was only equalled by a dismally low opinion of Britain's physical war effort. It didn't help that when Anglo-American forces went on to fight side by side in Sicily, the US press simply wrote Britain out of the story.

If naysayers' voices were strident in the United States both before the war and beyond, how did its servicemen feel once they had felt for themselves the brisk, bracing British weather on their faces? For many, their only preparation came from the unintentionally hilarious *Instructions for American Servicemen in Britain 1942* – a guidebook distributed to Blighty-bound soldiers to get them *'acquainted with the British, their country and their ways.'* Describing the United Kingdom as smaller than North Carolina or Iowa, the book explained how the 'reserved, not unfriendly' British spoke an 'English … you may not understand' using strange accents and words. Alerting Americans to the pitfalls ahead, it said: 'You will quickly discover differences that seem confusing and even wrong. Like driving on the left side of the road, and having money based on an 'impossible' accounting system and drinking warm beer.'

Everything in Britain, they were warned, was either miniature – such as 'dinky freight cars' on trains or the 'little and low powered' motor cars on roads – or just plain bad – like the coffee and weather: 'At first you will probably not like the almost continual rains and mists and the absence of snow and crisp cold.' Troops of Irish descent and other ancient enemies of Redcoats were reminded it was 'no time to fight old wars', but to reflect instead on the two nations' overarching similarities in ways of life, language, love of democracy, freedom of speech and worship.[7] The problem was, that a significant minority of Americans didn't see it that way once they arrived. And it skewed Anglo-American relations from the get-go, putting a new spin altogether on matters.

Contrary to the tsunami of wartime positivity about the 'special' Anglo-American relationship and a post-war profusion of rose-tinted GI and British home front memoirs – when the Yanks were famously and actually 'over paid, over sexed and over here', a good many of them didn't like it. And they weren't shy in making it known. We know this from the views of American servicemen interviewed or secretly recorded while stationed in the UK.

Speaking on conditions of strict anonymity, they let rip on what they really felt about Britain and its people, revealing an unpalatable reality about allied relations in 1943. And although it was by no means the majority feeling and the sample size was sometimes small, it was significant enough to be secretly reported, quantified and sweated over by both American and British authorities. Not only was the evidence sought and taken seriously, but determined efforts were consequently made to cover up the truth. And despite the best efforts of Anglo-American censorship, official propaganda machines and stories spun furiously then and now to depict a rock-solid friendship, the truth about it was never far below the surface.

While the 581st Ordnance Ammunition Company was training at Fort Sill, Oklahoma, there was already discernible disenchantment growing among Americans in Britain. On 11 March 1943, Foreign Office officials were horrified to receive a report entitled *What the American Soldier is thinking about in this Country.* Its subtitle might as easily have been 'Nothing Good.' Generated by the American division of Britain's Ministry of Information, the government department responsible for publicity and propaganda, it made for gritty reading, reeling off a long list of American pet-hates starting with the food and ending with English women. The very fact such a report was needed highlights how things were not quite cricket, but its findings were nothing short of a disastrous indictment of Anglo-American relations – at least on the American side. Covertly created 'without the knowledge of the American Army authorities', analysis of various interviews and eavesdropped conversations showed 'the excitement of coming to a new country has worn off.' Displaying a classic British restraint on the situation, the report went on 'This novelty did not last very long.'

Mostly it was the class system, rooted in Britain's unique history, that American servicemen rejected along with its royal trappings, the report found. Not only did Britain's history and traditions leave them numb, but they resented being perceived as brash by their British hosts. This inferiority complex was amplified by 'the Englishman's precision of speech, the clarity of his enunciation' which only served to 'embarrass the American soldier in England. The fact that even an English waitress seems to talk "better" than he does makes the American soldier in England feel uncouth.'

What remained, the report found, was the feeling that 'the country is inexcusably old-fashioned ... [and] ... the monetary system is an example of carrying a national joke a bit too far.' Unused to the privations of rationing and coming from a land of relative plenty, perhaps understandably, Americans found everything to do with British wartime cuisine diabolical. But their strongest and most sinister feelings were reserved largely for those who served it – the indigenous women. And ironically these were the people with whom, to all appearances, they were on best terms of all.

The report registered an antipathy bordering on misogyny towards 'English girls.' The sentiment was rooted in a sincere lack of respect for British women, a fervent belief they were inferior in every way to American women and manifested itself in a decidedly ungallant determination to use and abuse them. It concluded:

His attitude towards them is that they are all that is available and will have to do until he gets back to God's country. He considers them all fair game. He is convinced he can sleep with all of them and will, without much prompting, substantiate his statement with a variety of detailed and colourful examples out of his allegedly personal experiences.[8]

Things deteriorated rapidly the next month when research from Mass Observation, Britain's foremost social research engine, showed that less than one quarter of its interviews with American servicemen 'contained definite favour of the British.' Clearly, the Americans interviewed for '*Mutual Anglo-American Feelings*' had been drilled in the party line and rehearsed in how to answer such questions. What they reeled off smacked of insincerity and it didn't take much to perceive the underlying Brit-bashing. Reading between the lines, the astonishing statistic was revealed that less than 25 per cent of American soldiers based in Britain had anything good to say about its partner in war in April 1943. And that wasn't all.

Those old enough to remember the classic opener used by children to GIs 'Got any gum, chum?' would be mortified to think some soldiers saw this as evidence of Fagan-esque parenting. They hated 'the alleged habit of the British of sending their children out to beg candies from the Americans', and concluded its social service system left much to be desired. Brits they didn't see as beggars, they regarded as plain poor. Classic comments include: 'In America even the poorest people can afford a car' and 'is it on account of the war that you never have eggs? Did you used to have them?' And more general points such as: 'In the provinces they live almost like cavemen – but I suppose that's England.' Even elements not under British control were criticised with judgements such as: 'I can't understand why you British weren't the pioneers in central heating, the way your climate is.'[9]

The picture was bleak, but even harsher findings were to come in May 1943, when a new secret poll revealed just 5 per cent of Americans thought Britain was doing its utmost in the fight for liberty, ranking it fourth after Russia, America and even China in an international league table of endeavour. Equally stunning was the finding that more than 60 per cent of Americans blamed Great Britain rather than Hitler for starting the Second World War. These results contained in undercover research named *American Attitudes Towards the British* (conducted by the United States Office of War Information) revealed more than half the respondents mentioned their specific dislikes of the British and nearly 90 per cent thought the USA offered a better place to get ahead than Great Britain.[10]

So strained were relations that British-based VIII Bomber Command ordered its security officer to analyse 425 letters written by its officers and enlisted personnel, to learn, quite literally, what Americans were writing home about. By August 1943, it was clear that 'by far the most serious problem ... seems to be with the civilian population'. This top-secret analysis, which found its way to MI5 on the basis it would never be quoted, included yet more anti-British beefs such as the two prices shops and hotels had (one for British and one for Americans); the way British media referred to Allied rather than American efforts; and generally 'the British attitude regarding our entry into the war ... to grab all the glory.'[11] It reinforced a general theme detected by censors that summer and exemplified by a soldier writing home to his mother in July asking: 'Listen, do you think for one moment that our boys want to be here – do you think they like it here? Well, let me tell you they think it's the God-damnedest hole they've ever been in – antiquated – that's the word.'[12] And this wasn't mentioning the spiralling street battles breaking out between British and American servicemen.

Conversely, how did things feel for the hosts? What impressions had the Americans made on the British home-front? Even before the first arrivals, there was a healthy dose of British cynicism for the relationship. Mass Observation interviewees noted the Lend Lease ships given were out of date, but the naval bases they were exchanged for in return were extremely valuable. And abundant apocryphal tales abound – including George Orwell's notorious dubbing of Britain in 1943 as American 'occupied territory'. MP and diarist Harold Nicolson recorded a delightfully snooty account in January that year, in which perpetually gum-chewing 'doughboys' touring the Palace of Westminster were totally underwhelmed by the whole experience, even after bumping into the Lord Chancellor of England himself. Right at the end 'to my surprise and pleasure,' wrote Harold Nicolson, 'one of the doughboys suddenly ceased chewing, flung his wad of Wrigley into his cheek with a deft movement of his tongue, and said "Say, Sir, who was that guy?"'[13]

And when it came to the nylon-bearing GIs' popularity with women, myth turned to legend with notorious jokes about British war-issue underwear doing the rounds such as: 'Utility knickers – one Yank and they're off.' Minimal efforts were made to disguise the mutual attraction, to the disgust of one Falmouth Home Guard member who wrote, in a letter picked up by censors that 'if the Yanks can fight only half as well as they can chase our women, then I should think the issue is in the bag. As a Yank said to me the other day, "your liquor is dear but your women are cheap.""[14]

In fact, it was becoming increasingly obvious that for a significant minority, not only was the true sentiment enshrining Anglo-American relations unfriendly – but mutual too. Multiple sources of grass-roots public sentiment pointed to this inescapable conclusion, despite every weapon in the propaganda arsenal firing messages to the contrary. Although not universal, feelings ran highly enough to get every government department scrabbling for information. Secret reports produced by Mass Observation and two more top sources – the Ministry of Information and Home Intelligence, each accurate barometers of the national mood – ran to pages on every report detailing American transgressions. From the earliest impressions they were 'all talk' with their arrogant assertions that 'it's about time we came over to win the war for you,' reported in the Ministry of Information's weekly report on April 8 1942, there was little evidence that the 'special' bit in relationship meant 'good'.[15]

And the longer they stayed, the more people felt the same, according to Mass Observation which found only 27 per cent of people liked their 'friendliness' – a 10 per cent drop in January 1943 from the previous year. Interviewees punctuated their descriptions with adjectives such as 'bumptious'; 'full of baloney;' brimming with *'cockiness'* acting like they 'came over here to teach us everything' when describing their American so-called allies.[16]

And the fact these truthful feelings were rarely described in the censored newspapers may well have heightened things.

'Before the war there was no popular anti-American feeling in this country. It all dates from the arrival of the American troops, and it is made vastly worse by the tacit agreement never to discuss it in print,' said George Orwell in an article for *Tribune*. He concluded that the policy of not criticising Americans or responding to American criticism meant 'things have happened which are capable of causing the worst kind of trouble sooner or later.'[17]

By April 1943, nearly half of all Brits reported 'half and half' feelings about the Americans to Mass Observation – an increase of 16 per cent from two years before.

Whereas two years ago a fifth of the sample found nothing very much to say about the Americans, now only one person in fifty is without an opinion … more than one person in five had nothing good to say about the Americans … A third definitely liked Americans in 1943.

Which, followed to its logical conclusion, meant two-thirds of respondents did not.[18] Naomi Mitchison, mother-of-six, novelist and diary-keeper for Mass Observation, noted towards the end of 1943: 'One begins to feel no need to bother about anti-Semitism, as the Americans have completely taken the place of the Jews – stories about rape etc.. Nobody has a good word for them.'[19]

But what caused such vitriolic feelings against visiting GIs? From 1942 the Ministry of Information devoted a considerable chunk of its monthly reports to describing the nation's reaction to American servicemen. Each reads like a veritable catalogue of complaint. Four months before the 581st Ordnance Ammunition Company disembarked in the UK, came gripes 'of their alleged drunkenness, their lack of response to hospitality, their assumption that "money buys everything" and their bad behaviour – particularly with women and young girls.'[20]

By July 1943, the crescendo of criticism rose specifically against drunkenness, promiscuity, overly high pay, boastfulness, slovenliness, a preponderance of inexplicable army medals and a general lack of discipline. Further sources of resentment also included: 'The luxurious club facilities denied to some of our servicemen and the quantities and quality of food they have brought with them – "chicken twice a week and almost unlimited fruit.'[21]

Bomber Command's secret investigation into the 'strain' surmised:

The first (complaint) is the habit of Americans associating with the lowest class of women and the consequent habit of treating all women as though they were street walkers … underage girls … the British feel our troops drink too much … the British object to the American habit of bragging … the British feel we wear too many ribbons and decorations.[22]

This was but a tiny drop in the ocean of ill-will felt by British forces towards Americans in Britain. The most damaging blow to soldier morale in the Middle East was large numbers of US and Dominion troops at home 'wrecking the peace of mind of a very large proportion of the MEF,' according to a draft report about morale submitted to the Army Council Secretariat for May to July 1942. It recorded:

> The evidence, from home and abroad ... suggests that anxiety about infidelity of wives and 'girls' is in very many cases justified; in the words of a padre's letter from the M.E: 'The most efficient fifth column work done out here is carried out by the women of England.'

By October this anxiety was answered by the creation of a special organisation to assist men wishing to petition for divorce. Quickly it was swamped under a backlog of 2,000 cases while receiving 12 new applications each day.[23]

By July 1943, as the stateside 581st Ordnance Ammunition Company was awaiting movement orders, not only was the Ministry of Information reporting alarming skirmishes and street brawls between British and American soldiers all over the country, but the same Army Council Secretariat was told dryly that:

> They do not cease to create ill feeling among other ranks. They are not always, it seems, modest, sober, economical in their expenditure, or chivalrous and restrained in their bearing and behaviour towards women. It is evidently the street corner and public-house contact between the two Forces that leads to trouble.[24]

The urgent need for better relations between two armies needing to fight side-by-side in just a few months was recognised in the Morale Committee report minutes on 31 August 1943, when the chairman said that he understood that the prime minister had been invited to approach President Roosevelt on the question of joint action being taken by British and US authorities to improve the relationship of their respective forces.

By the time 581st Ordnance Ammunition Company men were receiving new travel orders, it is fair to say a sizeable number of Americans based in the UK mistrusted and disliked the Brits – and that this coolness was reciprocated. This relationship was special for all the wrong reasons and this equation only factored in the white population. What would happen when black Americans were thrown into the social mix and came within spitting distance of the beating heart of an empire ruling India and much of Africa? Who could forget Britain's role in the early slave trade? Surely relations were doomed to plummet into the abyss?

Chapter 8

Black Yanks in the UK – First Impressions

A s August drew to its sultry close, men of the 581st Ordnance Ammunition Company were about to take the last steps of their war journey on American soil. Rumours became orders and in answer to an advance request from European theatre commanders, their company prepared to ship out. Leaving the dry dust of Oklahoma's Fort Sill they headed, as expected, to Camp Patrick Henry in segregated railroad carriages. During the war, close to three-quarters of a million military personnel would pass through this camp before boarding troop ships at Hampton Port of Embarkation, the nation's third biggest military transport hub. The 581st was admittedly a tiny fraction of the 235,000 servicemen and women to pass through the camp in Warwick County, Virginia in 1943. But in those dying days of that famously long hot summer it wasn't just the temperature that soared.

On 13 August, the 581st Ordnance Ammunition Company arrived at Oyster Point railhead at Camp Patrick Henry to be met by a billeting officer who directed them to their assigned barracks. According to army PR, every company member should then have been subjected to a rigorous barrage of tests and examinations ranging from their physical health to soldiering skills and the state of their kit. They were encouraged to attend to personal admin – such as wills and taxes – and safety by learning how to scrabble down the side of a mock-up transport ship to prepare for their forthcoming sea journey. Hewn out of 1,700 acres of boggy pine forest, Camp Patrick Henry boasted barracks, mess halls, offices, theatres, clubs and warehouses enough to house and process 35,000 soldiers at a time before they departed. It even had its own hospital and post office, and was regarded as one of the best cogs in the system at getting troops combat-ready and away. It certainly prepared men of the 581st Ordnance Ammunition Company for action – it was just not the type army chiefs were expecting.

According to the port's historian Major William Reginald Wheeler: 'The camp's mission was to house, feed, process and entertain all those who were going overseas.'[1] Seemingly the final part of its mission was given no less consideration than the former, with stars of stage and screen appearing on celluloid and for real in the camp's ample assortment of cinemas, stages, concert halls, lectures, libraries and athletic facilities. For many young servicemen and women, their decisive send-off came in the appropriately named '*Last Chance*' nightclub.

'The staging area had an important role in keeping the soldiers' spirits up and holding disciplinary problems down,' according to Chief Historian Chester Wardlow.[2] Wartime Public Affairs Officer Captain Donald Higgins went further when he immortalised the camp's hundreds of temporary huts, systematically built around seven massive mess halls, as imbuing Camp Patrick Henry with 'certain aspects of a sylvan hotel managed by the Transportation Corps.'[3] Unfortunately, the 581st Ordnance Ammunition Company was unlikely to agree with either sentiment.

Its members would find it extremely difficult to find anything remotely spirit-lifting or hotel-like about a place more likely to serve up racism with breakfast than coffee. It was institutionalised here. So much so that several 581st men were driven to the drastic measure of securing arms for their own self-defence. Confidential US Army reports at the time revealed secret personal ammunition stashes showing up in routine spot checks all over the country's training camps – and it was no exception here. African American soldiers were stockpiling and hiding weapons throughout America – they were not going down without a fight.

The countless examples of common-or-garden prejudice reached its most famous zenith at Camp Patrick Henry in a full-scale riot between white paratroopers who clashed with the all-black 758th Tank Regiment the following year. Eye-witness Allen Thompson remembered:

> 'I saw it brewing. I could smell trouble, and I could see it too … the paratroopers on that base were antagonistic. They would gesture. They had shroud knives …They patted them and they made gestures with those knives … We were told when we got there we could go anyplace on the post … Well that wasn't the case.'

The mere sight of African Americans mixing with white girls at a dance triggered 50 paratroopers to come looking for trouble one night, and 200 more came the second, bragging they were looking for a kill. In the event the skirmish lasted a full 'hot minute' when paratroopers discovered their enemy was armed and lethal – and cleared out, leaving one of their own dead.[4]

It gives context to the kind of welcome received a few months earlier by men of the 581st Ordnance Ammunition Company. Admittedly, matters were slightly more in hand during their own three weeks at Camp Patrick Henry in August 1943. Certainly, they sensed danger keenly enough to arm themselves. But they never got to venture outside the camp as they were restricted once again – which could have been for their own protection, but was more likely than not a punishment. Although the potential for trouble was limited, the boredom was suffocating, and it was only a relief when the tension and uncertainty gave way. Finally, on 4 September they were given 24 hours' warning of their imminent departure. They were on their way.

Along with their embarkation notice, they were told to create an A and B bag: A for essential carry-on items while boarding such as helmets, backpacks, gas masks and weapons, and 'B' for less important stuff to be secured in the ships' holds. The following day dawned bright in Hampton, Virginia, as they returned on foot to the Oyster Point railhead. Here in bright, early autumn sunshine they were checked off on the passenger list and had individual boarding numbers chalked onto helmets. Eventually, they took a train for the short trip to the pier, alighting into long lines for various ships.

Here order reigned amid the noise and frantic movement of thousands of soldiers, military policemen, Women's Army Corp members and transportation officials at the pier. For five long hours, men of the 581st Ordnance Ammunition Company queued to the strains of *Boogie Woogie*, selected specially for African American soldiers to boost morale while keeping boarding lines moving efficiently. With each passing hour of port band jitterbug, they reflected on Fort Sill's brutal training regime, the inherent violence they had faced at Camp Patrick Henry – and contemplated their future overseas. Their wait was over. Britain beckoned at last. But were they simply out of the proverbial frying pan?

The first tantalising glimpse of what might lie ahead may have come as early as 5 September, departure day itself. No record remains of their specific troop-carrying vessel or its itinerary – all passenger lists, manifests, logs of ships and troop movement files of US Army Transports for the Second World War were destroyed in 1951 by army order according to the United States National Archives. However, the ship may well have been British and therefore staffed by a British crew.

Journalist Roi Ottley, commissioned as a lieutenant in the US Army to serve as a war correspondent in Europe, left a unique account of his own experience as an African American on such a ship. An entry from his lost wartime diary noted that: 'Negro troops get along excellently with English soldiers – boys from Wales, Scotland, England and Canada. They play a lot of stud poker together and exchange stories. There is not much fraternizing among the Negro and white troops. White Americans don't fraternise with the English soldiers.'[5] Having won literary plaudits for his book *New World A-Coming* in 1943 – a ground-breaking insight into life for black Americans – Roi Ottley was uniquely placed to comment on such social niceties. Had they been able to read this diary entry (unpublished and found well after the war's end), 581st Ordnance Ammunition Company men would have taken heart, but doubtless have been surprised. For this charming picture of comradely banter would surely upset the outside world's apple cart – and certainly those who believed they knew how many in British society's upper echelons thought.

Just how had the British first reacted to an African American presence? What was the reaction to their separation from white comrades, which was as much a part of the US Army to which they belonged as their star insignia? They were risking life and limb running the gauntlet of German-patrolled waters to reach Britain, but what was it all for? What were the parameters there for people of colour and what would the reaction be?

Although ruling 'an empire on which the sun never sets' incorporating a quarter of the world's population and land mass featuring jewels such as India and huge swathes of Africa too, there were surprisingly few people of colour in Britain itself when the Second World War started. The black British community was no bigger than about 15,000 and centred mainly in port-dominated cities such as Bristol, Cardiff and Liverpool.

Unsurprisingly, in such a mono-cultural nation, racism was bound to exist. Race riots exploded in 1919 around those same British port towns including Glasgow, London and mostly Liverpool leaving five dead, hundreds injured and 250 arrested. Learie Constantine, the famous West Indian cricketer who moved to the UK in 1923 described how 'personal slights' were 'an unpleasant part of life in Britain for anyone of my colour'.[6] Whatever ill feelings existed before the Second World War were bound to intensify when it came to the prospect of black Americans being imported to fight the good fight. With depressing predictability, prejudice proliferated further at the heart of the British Empire once American soldiers and with them, segregation, appeared. Even when just a tiny fraction of the subsequent 130,000 African American servicemen had trickled in, intolerance was inevitable.

It was implicit in a throwaway comment by Winston Churchill himself, who, after hearing that a black Colonial officer mistaken for an African American had been turned away from a West End restaurant, said: 'That's all right. If he takes a banjo with him they'll think he's one of the band.'[7] It extended to many of the prime minister's war cabinet including Foreign Secretary Anthony Eden, who, with a raft of excuses throughout the summer of 1942, tried to block black American servicemen from coming. Perhaps he was sensitive to army segregation backfiring in Britain. Nevertheless, in August, Eden argued, somewhat ludicrously, that African Americans should not come in ever-greater numbers because the climate was detrimental to their health. Even more preposterous was that the entire war cabinet agreed. Some of them were strongly supportive of US-style segregation and advocated falling in with demands to officially stop British soldiers from fraternising with African Americans. In October 1942, the cabinet eventually agreed the wording of a memo saying British troops should 'avoid intimate relations' with African American soldiers and warning that women mixing with them would cause 'controversy'. This guidance, quietly circulated among senior army officers, was to shape the way they advised soldiers –and was to be given strictly verbally only.[8]

Leading aristocrats with similar upbringings and experiences, including Churchill's cousin The Duke of Marlborough, shared the bigoted views of Lady Astor MP, the American daughter of a Virginian tobacco auctioneer. Attached to the American Forces as military liaison officer to the Regional Commander of the Southern Region, Marlborough shared with his cousin concerns specifically about the 'sexual behaviour' of black American soldiers and reported on a series of questions posed by the prime minister. He told Churchill 'there is a serious subversive element about them which I feel can do much to bring about a great deal of unpleasantness in the relationship between our two countries'.[9] Maurice Petherick, MP for Penryn and Falmouth, too breathed fire and brimstone about the 'sexual' dimension of black Americans coming to Cornwall. In letters to Foreign Secretary Anthony Eden, he listed a number of associated disasters starting with 'half-caste babies' and ending with suggested alternative destinations for troops, such as the Solomon Islands or Egypt.

Even God-fearing housewives in middle England were outraged by the prospective arrival of African Americans. In the autumn of 1942, a Somerset vicar's wife proved singularly not the Good Samaritan by creating an awful etiquette guide for female parishioners. Taking considerable time to think through every possible encounter they might have with African American soldiers, the vicar of Worle's wife came up with a six-point plan. Stipulations included serving 'coloured' soldiers who entered shops, but then telling them they must not return; moving away from any who happened to be sitting nearby in cinemas and walking out of any shop serving black soldiers. 'If she is walking on the pavement and a coloured soldier is coming toward her, she crosses to another pavement … White women, of course, must have no relationship with coloured troops. On no account must coloured troops be invited into the homes of white women.'[10]

Venomous views about soldiers of colour lurked in letters only to be picked up by censors who could read the zeitgeist. One, written in 1944, described a personal sympathy for America's *Jim Crow* attitudes and bemoaned the fact that it jarred with such a multitude of ignorant Brits:

'One of the slight awkwardnesses is the colour question and that is entirely the fault of the English – you see we are not used to having Negroes in the country and many stupid and soft-hearted people tend to treat them as if they were a sort of "super-white", they make more fuss of them than they do of the white men, merely to show in a pompous and short-sighted way that they are not afflicted with any "colour-baritis"'.[11]

It was not an isolated view.

Even more shrill were fears about the offspring of inter-racial relationships between American servicemen and British women, recorded by the Home Intelligence Unit, one of the nation's two agencies set up in 1940 to monitor public reaction. Weekly reports produced by the unit decried from 1943 onwards the 'wave of moral delinquency' or 'criticisms of their associations with white girls' and also 'the growing number of illegitimate babies, many of coloured men.'[12]

This prejudice, and some people's unquestioning acceptance of American-style segregation, reached its apogee in a striking tract written by the elderly, pompous and ultra-conservative Major Arthur Arnold Bullick Dowler, a career soldier, decorated in the First World War. Charged with administration in Southern Command, he put the unspeakable in writing when he produced *Notes on Relations with Coloured Troops* for his subordinate commanders in August 1942. Describing segregation as a Southern-States institution in which negroes 'have equal rights with white citizens and there is no discrimination between the two', he went on to completely contradict himself by outlining their separate churches, schools, living quarters, transport and entertainment. The reason was simple:

> 'While there are many coloured men of high mentality and cultural
> distinction the generality are of a simple mental outlook ... In short
> they have not the white man's ability to think and act a plan ... Too
> much freedom, too wide associations with white men tend to make
> them lose their heads.'[13]

Major Dowler recommended that in Britain neither white women should associate with them, nor soldiers take them as intimate friends. Major Dowler had articulated opinions and recommendations no-one wanted putting into words, yet alone circulated. Yet it snuck out to some soldiers and became the basis for a cabinet discussion in October 1942, when the Government had to decide to back or reject segregation in Britain.

Surely, the writing was on the wall for those travelling to Great Britain and destined to dock on 13 September 1943. Was segregated life as a subservient, sub-human part of the US Army to continue for men of the 581st Ordnance Ammunition Company once they reached dry land – home to officers like Major Dowler?

Chapter 9

The Real Special Relationship

Eugenics was a briefly respectable new science in the early 1900s geared at improving the human race's lot by breeding out 'undesirable' genetic elements. Up until Hitler hijacked the movement, it was quite fashionable. Around 1910, along with a great many others and 'probably under the influence of his reading of Darwin, Churchill was briefly a convinced eugenicist,' according to biographer Andrew Roberts.[1] Two or three decades later, a home-grown awareness of this morally dubious science still lurked in the shadows. More obviously, blatant racial prejudice existed in the United Kingdom before the Second World War. This patently found new channels for expression when African American soldiers arrived here from May 1942 onwards – and probably more frequently from the upper than lower echelons of British society. But a fresh look at evidence including top-secret Ministry of Information opinion polls, painstaking government data analysis of British reactions, censored letters, unpublished diaries as well as what we already know from newspapers and essayists shows overwhelmingly that Major Dowler's unreconstructed view was not the majority opinion. At all. And that changed everything.

At first, British judgement was befuddled by American segregation – that men coming to fight for freedom on the same side were being treated differently, let alone as inferiors. War Secretary James (PJ) Grigg reflected on this enduring catch-22 when he wrote to Churchill about the

'great difficulty in reconciling our policy of no discrimination or colour bar and the necessity for having to deal with what is manifestly the peculiar and special problem presented by the presence of thousands of coloured troops in this country who are by no means regarded as equals in their own country.'[2]

This was the root of the problem and it had taken Britain by surprise.

The host country 'is devoid of racial consciousness' reported Captain Harry Butcher, a United States naval aide to America's most senior General, Dwight Eisenhower. The English, he said, 'know nothing at all about the conventions and habits of polite society that have developed in the US in order to preserve a segregation in social activity without making the matter one of official or public notice.'[3] This fog of British ignorance was pierced for the first time by what the African American press labelled 'the race virus' which meant 'in essence there are those here who are still fighting the Civil War – this time on British soil,' observed Roi Ottley.[4]

Certain white GIs tried to make a case for segregation by poisoning the way for black comrades trailing behind. They assured naïve British countryside dwellers that African Americans were a different species. 'They'd tell all kinds of tales about the black soldiers, tell them [we] had tails like a monkey, and some of those English girls believed it. They went looking behind for tails,' recalled one private.[5] This mischief-making had a darker side because the lies always carried wicked character implications. NCO Benny Gordon, initially of the 498 Port Battalion, said that 'they would tell people we had tails, that we were murderers, that we were not to be trusted, that we would cut their throats, all this kind of thing to turn people against us.'[6]

As if bestrewing the African American path with obstacles was not enough at a grass-roots level, American top brass continued the pernicious publicity offensive. In July 1943, ETOUSA HQ sent out guidance to commanding officers of 'colored units and Officers assigned to or concerned with colored troops' that black servicemen were 'well-meaning but irresponsible children … they cannot be trusted to tell the truth … they are easily led.' It went on to isolate the difference between the UK and any other theatre of war:

> 'There exists in Great Britain the "colored soldier – white girl" complication which is a most potent factor and the one which will have the most lasting effect (even after the war). This in part is brought through the absence of a 'color-line' in England … This situation (except for recognised prostitutes) is unique.'[7]

However, evidence shows that although British racism from Churchill to un-Christian vicars' wives existed, it was not universally prevalent. In contrast there is a wealth of proof from a variety of sources indicating that the colour bar did not sit well with the British at all – from the moment it was imported. In July 1942, just a couple of months after the first arrivals, an enlightened Chief Constable, T.E. St Johnston, of Oxfordshire Police, wrote an impassioned letter to the Home Office arguing that segregation wouldn't work in the UK because civilians wanted to welcome all allies. People in Oxford were used to people of colour at any rate, he reasoned; that very year the Oxford University president was a West Indian. Therefore, 'the only persons who will take objection to the association of white people with the coloured troops will be the American white soldiers,' he wrote. Inspired probably by his scholarly beat, he channelled a classical argument, insisting that 'what is required is an intensive propaganda campaign against American white soldiers, particularly the officers that "when in Rome they must do as the Romans do."'[8]

Neither were all cabinet members accepting the colour bar lying down. Some felt the onus should be on the Americans to rethink. At 5.30pm on 10 August 1942, cabinet minutes recorded:

> 'There was also force in the argument that this country is not, in fact, the United States and we have our own way of looking at things here which many people would argue is a better way than the American. Moreover there is still a British Empire with a not inconsiderable number of coloured people in it.'[9]

Two days later, at the Bolero Committee, it was revealed that African American troops were making a very good impression on the British communities they encountered. The meeting heard that: 'local people were speaking in the highest terms of the courtesy and good behaviour of the coloured American troops and drawing distinctions between their behaviour and that of the white Americans, by no means to the credit of the latter.'[10]

In September 1942, the Minister of Information Brendan Bracken intervened in the argument with an essay published in the *Sunday*

Express entitled *The Colour Bar Must Go.* Warning that secretly-held racial prejudice 'should die a natural death as many prejudices have done in the past … If we have learned at least one thing from the two great wars in this century, it is to be less insular and to regard ourselves less as a nation apart.'[11] Letters appeared in newspapers up and down Britain decrying the unfair treatment of black American servicemen witnessed by members of the public. *The Times* reported a letter more suited for Paddington Bear than soldiers prepared to die for freedom, this time issued by a commanding officer to his black troops to give to restaurant owners telling them: 'it is necessary that he sometimes has a meal, which he has, on occasions found difficult to obtain. I would be grateful if you would look after him.'[12]

The British Government found the position it had been put in excruciating. Everyone at the highest level was painfully aware of just how fine the line was that needed treading. On one hand, after more than two long solitary years standing against the might of Nazi Germany, Britain now had a powerful ally with whom it had a fighting chance of winning. On the other, that ally's army was made up of two segregated races with tendencies to clash increasingly violently whenever they met. This was the army that came to Britain bringing with it malevolent clouds of prejudice, bigotry and hate. It was expected that Britain, as host nation, should suck it up, especially given its reliance on America's largesse – Lend Lease, aid and all. Britain was felt to be in no position to argue, let alone lecture America on its social policy, especially being an Imperial power itself.

So the delicately-named 'negro situation' rattled on, niggling away at cabinet discussion and arguments throughout the summer and early autumn of 1942. In August, war cabinet minutes show the dread of 'incalculable harm' being inflicted by large numbers of GIs seeing British women with African American soldiers. By October, the minutes eloquently captured the British dilemma that 'any difference of treatment between white and coloured troops may be regarded as racial discrimination which will give rise to bitter resentment.' It implored civilians to try and understand the risks associated with their acceptance of African Americans 'to prevent any tarnishing of our amicable relations with the US Army.' But there was recognition that positions were deadlocked and that navigating both standpoints – of America's state-sponsored segregation and the British distaste for it – was impossible. Consequently, the war office was 'on a razor's edge in trying to find balance.'[13] Arguably it never left that place.

The real nub of it was that white United States soldiers hated the welcoming British attitude towards black soldiers. And most of all they loathed the way British women opened their arms at a time when miscegenation legislation outlawed mixed marriages in thirty of America's forty-eight states. Censored letters sent from US soldiers were riddled with incandescence at the lack of a British colour bar. Southerners raised in segregated society vented their fury by writing home thoughts such as: 'Oh how I'm gonna love the South after this – where a *nigger* knows his place and the whites feel they are above sleeping and eating with the damned *niggers*! Grr I'm mad,' from an airforce corporal.[14] Another scribed 'One thing I noticed here and which I don't like is the fact that the English don't draw any color line … The English must be pretty ignorant. I can't see how a white girl could associate with a Negro' – this time from a lieutenant in the 566th Bomb Squadron's letter to home.[15] Another US soldier, based in Manchester, complained in his missive that

'So many girls dance with the colored troops the white ones are about ready for murder … But over here the British cannot understand our race prejudice … What makes me livid is that the darn Negro dare try it here when they know what would happen if they did it at home.'[16]

It didn't matter where in America they came from. African American soldiers' very existence was a headache for all white soldiers, it seemed, which drove an almost tangible behavioural wedge between the two allied nations. Curiously, it wasn't Southerners alone who were angered by the overall impact of black soldiers, according to the top-secret report *What the American Soldier is thinking about in this Country*. Foreign officials reading it for the first time on 11 March 1943 discovered that from a Southern viewpoint 'the American soldier in England is angry with the American authorities for putting the Negro into the army, with the Negro for daring to don the same uniform he wears, and with the English people for not sharing his views about the Negro.' If, however, he came from the North:

> 'he is angry with the Southern soldier for bringing his bigotry into a war and into a foreign country … with the American authorities for not having enough sense to work out some discreet system of segregation … and with the English people … for daring to take sides in a dispute about which they know nothing'

Acknowledging that Southern white soldiers had never seen straight on the Negro question, it compared their sufferings in war-time Britain to what 'Job might have experienced if, after all the sufferings he bore with so much patience, he found that someone had stolen his last razor blade. It is the last straw.'[17] For some, Anglo–American relations would never be special in a good way as long as 'the Negro question' existed.

That first summer of United States troops being in Britain, the government was constantly wrestling with the conundrum of how segregation sat in a nation not divided by race. Britain was riddled with archaic class division, but it was not split along race lines. Ultimately, and not without months of soul-searching, hand-wringing and deliberation, however, sense prevailed. In September 1942 the Home Office came to a bold and momentous decision.

The United States Army would do what it had to do, which ultimately was to segregate its men socially by designating certain pubs for white soldiers and others for African Americans, or whole towns to one or the other on different nights: Blacks Tuesday, Whites Wednesday and so on. But the British were not playing that game and it was decided at this turning point that they were not to be drawn into enforcing American segregation. Its 'bobbies' would sit back and watch, without interfering with or policing the mixing of two races. After all, how could a nation with hundreds of thousands of men and women of colour from all over the Commonwealth serving as equals in the British armed forces suddenly impose a colour bar?

What members of the 581st Ordnance Ammunition Company couldn't have known as their ship docked in September 1943 was that not only did a fair number of Britons hold a healthy disregard for American soldiers, but many felt stronger still about segregation. And the strength of this feeling would impact them directly shortly afterwards in Cornwall. Up and down the land British people were used to demonstrating their defiance of *Jim Crow* practises. Many, many months before even the watershed cabinet decision, the British writing was on the wall. It was proved by a raft of evidence including widespread testimony from African Americans themselves. And to generalise anything else does a huge injustice to the British public because their government's decision in September 1942 did not dictate policy towards African Americans so much as reflect what the general public was already thinking.

People witnessed prejudice being played out on the streets of Britain as black soldiers were pushed out of pubs, off buses and away from cinemas. 'I have personally seen the American troops literally kick, and I mean kick, the coloured soldiers off the pavement,' recalled a factory worker in Blackpool.[18] Not only that, US servicemen were indiscriminate in their discrimination, often picking on colonial troops of colour from the British Empire. In June 1943, Sergeant Arthur Waldron, an RAF pilot from Barbados, based in Suffolk, was beaten up by two American servicemen simply for asking a woman to dance. Incensed, he wrote an aggrieved letter of complaint, asking: 'is it fair, is it just, to ask me to risk my life nightly over enemy territory when behind me I have left something as treacherous to humanity as any [Nazi]ism?'[19] British authorities were able to quietly drop the matter when he died in a bombing raid over Germany the following week. Others did not forget his shabby treatment though and his words were published in the *Sunday Pictorial* in August that year, along with a plea for an apology from his friend Miss P.J. Palmer, from Wood Green. Neither did world-class champion status protect against racial prejudice, as boxer Joe Louis discovered in Salisbury, Wiltshire in 1944. After being directed to 'blacks only' seats by the cinema manager he recounted: 'I called my friend Lieutenant General John Lee and told them they had no business messing up another country's customs with American *Jim Crow*.'[20]

Weekly reports for the Ministry of Information by the Home Intelligence Division reported on British 'resentment at the attitude of white Americans to their black compatriots' or 'the attitude of white to coloured troops … is not liked – the less so because the coloured troops are usually popular and considered well behaved' and it 'was mentioned only to be condemned and used as evidence against the reality of American democracy.'[21]

Sometimes it was a bad attitude. Other times it was mindless murder. Dalton Slaughter, a member of the 116th Infantry's B Company, billeted in Ivybridge, some 35 miles down the road from the 581st Ordnance Ammunition Company's base in Launceston, recalled a fatality while drinking at the town's White Horse. A black serviceman inadvertently stepped into the 'white-only' pub when 'the ripple of silence reached the bar about the same time as a wooden chair rose up out of the crowd and came down on the man's head.'[22] Killed by that single blow, not one soldier witness could identify the culprit and the crime went unsolved despite the best efforts of American authorities.

This unwarranted and blatant bullying engendered a surprisingly adverse British reaction from a huge cross range of everyday people they met – from top journalists and opinion-formers to members of government and parliamentarians. In his first weekly article for *Tribune* as a new member of staff, George Orwell kicked off his debut column *As I Please* with a blistering conclusion about the new status quo: 'it is difficult to go anywhere in London without having the feeling that Britain is now Occupied Territory. The general consensus of opinion seems to be that the only American soldiers with decent manners are the Negroes.'[23] Foreign Secretary Anthony Eden's true feelings about 'the Negro question' are perhaps gleaned from a diary entry made by his private secretary Oliver Harvey in the summer of 1942 who noted:

'It is rather a scandal that the Americans should thus export their internal problem. We don't want to see lynching begin in England. I can't bear the typical Southern attitude towards the Negroes. It is a great ulcer on the American civilisation and makes nonsense of half their claims.'[24]

In September 1942 the Home Office had written to all chief constables and magistrates telling them it was illegal to discriminate and directed local police that 'if the American service authorities decide to put certain places out of bounds for their coloured troops ... the police should not make themselves in any way responsible for the enforcement of such orders.'[25] Later, on 29 September, Tom Driberg, the Independent (later Labour) MP for Maldon, Essex, waded into the debate during question time when he challenged Churchill's awareness of the fact that 'an unfortunate result of the presence here of American forces has been the introduction in some parts of Britain of discrimination against Negro troops.' After gaining the prime minister's attention, he asked 'whether he will make friendly representations to the American military authorities asking them to instruct their men that the colour bar is not a custom of this country and that its non-observance by British troops or civilians should be regarded with equanimity.'[26]

In November 1942, Foreign Secretary Anthony Eden attributed the many potential causes of ill-feeling between 'our visitors' and British soldiers and citizens to 'differences of tradition, custom and outlook on the one hand and special problems such as differences of rates of pay and rations and the Negro question on the other.'[27]

From the highest level downwards, that same feeling saturated the rest of society. It was there in the mythical witticism circulating widely that 'I don't mind the Yanks, but I can't say I care for those white chaps they've brought with them' to signs outside British pubs reading: 'This place is for the exclusive use of Englishmen and American Negro soldiers'. Everyday British people rejected racism. It went against an unwritten national code, reported the Home Intelligence Unit, in its 1943 report, *Anti-American Feeling in Britain*, and was deemed 'undemocratic' and 'as conflicting with the Englishmen's idea of fair play.'[28] Set up entirely to gauge public reaction, the Home Intelligence Unit's findings chimed precisely with what its social research equivalent, Mass Observation, was recording: That race was literally a black and white matter.

Mass Observation found 'feelings about the American troops in this country can be fairly sharply divided into feelings about white and coloured troops. As a general rule (although of course there are many exceptions) the latter have made themselves more liked in this country.'[29] In January 1943, the organisation found 'among those who had met Negro troops, opinions were very strongly favourable.'[30] The opinion was pretty much a national consensus. From Hull, where a canteen worker's censored letter revealed:

'We find the coloured troops are much nicer to deal with … they're always so courteous and have a very natural charm that most of the whites miss. Candidly, I'd far rather serve a regiment of the dusky lads than a couple of whites … All my friends … colour-conscious before – who serve in the canteens feel the same'

to Bristol where dockworkers praised their work ethic and politeness and Stoke-on-Trent where 'we all like the coloured ones better, they are a lot better behaved; they are what we call gentlemen, the manners nothing like it in England'.[31] The message was always the same. 'Bristol people who have come into contact with them have little but praise,' another Mass Observation report, *Feelings about America and the Americans*, found. In it, a port official was quoted as saying 'it's skilled work on the docks and not to be picked up in a day, but those negroes have done their best and been a great help' while 'Others are impressed by their politeness and their standard of education. On the interviews, there were several remarks, as: "they are not like we've seen on the films … not stupid and dull." '[32]

Ordinary people shied away from the overt discrimination suffered by African American servicemen and wrote letters to each other, newspapers and even the Foreign Office, beseeching British authorities to intervene. One father from Westcliff-on-Sea, Essex, wrote in disgust to the Foreign Office after witnessing a particularly ugly incident at a dance in Southend-on-Sea. He had taken his wife and two daughters to the Palace Hotel, where a group including one hundred plus United States sailors and officers and two 'coloured' soldiers were also attending the dance. According to the irate letter-writer, at 9pm a group of six white sailors attacked one of the black soldiers when he started dancing with a girl. The officers ejected the black soldier 'in spite of protests from several of the British people who were incensed at this absurd behaviour'. Things snowballed into a stand-off as the British women then refused to dance with white Americans whose 'feelings ran so high that the management stopped the dance'. Protesting at the part played by officers in the scene, the writer signed off: 'I am particularly disgusted that at this point of the war when so many men are dying in the fight for the rights of mankind, this sort of persecution should be allowed a free hand in our liberty loving Empire.'[33]

Chimes of ringing endorsements for African American servicemen were found in many censored army letters in comments such as 'it is always the white ones that start on the black as the people in Brixham like the black ones best as they are much better.'[34] A Hampshire resident wrote 'The Blacks are very quiet and well behaved and got along very well with the village.'[35] A 26-year-old soldier in the Royal Corps of Signals wrote in 1943 that 'what is certain is that the US coloured troops have behaved so excellently over here that everybody has good words for them. They were always cheerful and friendly and good mannered; never "fresh" like some American soldiers were.'[36]

Their appeal to women was universal – from those they met at church functions to town hall dances throughout the land – to the shock and disapproval of some letter writers who referred to them as 'little hussies' for chasing after them so. Even in red-light districts, British prostitutes preferred African American servicemen. According to the Mass Observation report *Feelings About America* while the white Americans made them feel like 'cheap little "chippies"' they received not only cash and gifts from the black GIs, but 'courteous and humble treatment; many of them are impressed to find that their black boyfriend holds a university degree, and yet treats her as if she was a lady.'[37] The female factor only entrenched mutual Anglo-American distrust as some GIs regarded something that was illegal back home as being positively flaunted in their faces.

This reaction filtered down and expanded through every strata of society combining to project a visceral support for the underdog as traditional in Britain as fish and chips. Ordinary British people wrote about their hatred of segregation in censored letters and their loathing was written about as they ostentatiously disregarded *Jim Crow* thinking in pubs, churches and dance halls across the country where they drank and socialised with black soldiers. They paraded their feelings. This increased with British exposure to progressively large waves of African Americans coming into the country, and then crystallised into something more tangible and prolific that came to haunt the authorities.

Violence began to break out all over the country that summer. In June, the Lancashire village of Bamber Bridge was home to a terrible shoot-out sparked by white Military Police officers attempting to arrest black soldiers from the 1511th Quartermaster Truck regiment in Ye Old Hob Inn. Things escalated when military police reinforcements arrived armed with machine guns, prompting the African American troops to raid the armoury for rifles themselves. One died and several military policemen and soldiers were wounded in the armed battle during the early hours of 25 June 1943. The ensuing court martial convicted thirty-two of mutiny among other charges.

Things came to a head on 6 September 1943, while the 581st Ordnance Ammunition Company was in transit and just days away from docking in Britain. Head of Southern Command, Sir Harry Haig, recorded the alarming number of American racial incidents in which British civilians and servicemen were involving themselves on the black soldiers' side. On the streets, Britons were not only accepting lifts from black Americans, but standing by their sides against white military policemen. Blood was being spilled and, like Bamber Bridge, even lives lost as soldiers and civilians took to the streets of Britain. In this memo, Sir Harry described another happening just reported to him from Corsham, Wiltshire, when at pub closing time a group of African American soldiers were gathered in the street slowing down traffic. A military police patrol moved in to order them on, but one soldier refused to budge.

> 'A large group of civilians gathered and were heard saying: "They don't like the blacks"; "Why don't they leave them alone?"; "They're as good as they are"; "That's democracy."
>
>   The situation eventually developed into one of mass insubordination by the coloured troops, and at one point a coloured sergeant who had been ordered to bring his Company Commander, replied: "We ain't no slaves, this is England."'

These worrying, and spiralling, incidents were not so easily explained away to the general public, according to Sir Harry. He wrote that however much 'education' the British received about how things were done in the American South, 'they will not acquiesce in what they regard as unfair and bullying treatment, and the incidents really arise out of this feeling.'[38] Secretary of State for War James Grigg went further when he wrote to the prime minister in October 1943 with further concrete examples of Brits muscling in on the side of African Americans. He described how near mutinies were being sparked when British witnesses saw over-zealous policing of minor uniform misdemeanours, prompting bystanders to cheer their support for the underdogs and occasionally 'laying hands' on the offending white officers.

Matters continued to deteriorate even after D-Day when a massive mutiny was sparked in Bristol by newly arrived American paratroopers rampaging against African Americans dating British women. The watching Bristol citizenry backed the African Americans for one simple reason, the British American Liaison Board minutes recorded:

> The people to whom we talked agreed that the British, seeing white American military policemen approach a Negro soldier, do not understand why the policeman always approaches with his truncheon in a position for attack. They say that the white military police never approach a white soldier in this way. Their natural deduction is that the white man discriminates against the Negro.[39]

In fact, for more than a year racial prejudice was the key reason for more criticism of US troops than anything else. In an analysis of censored letters and telegraphs from Britain to America written in July 1943, there were more 'adverse criticisms of Americans or incomprehension of their attitude towards coloured troops' (702 letters) than 'appreciations of Americans' (632). Analysing the letters' data revealed 'several compare them with the white troops, to the detriment of the latter.' A London letter-writer went to some length to compare and contrast the fact that African Americans were

> 'ten times as popular as the whites … Naturally they are the more popular with the youngsters, you'd expect that. But they are equally popular with grown-ups, police and such. They never find any trouble … They are clean and bright and cheerful, whereas the big-town white boys are a slovenly, hang-dog bunch …'

Admittedly the comments weren't unswervingly colour-blind; twenty-six writers were either 'scared' of them or despaired of the fights. Either imported racial bias had rubbed off or indigenous prejudice had risen to the surface. But the report said that overall: 'Incomprehension of American racial prejudice is the keynote of the remainder of these comments.' It included comments from a Leicester shopkeeper who registered sheer incredulity at how certain Americans expected the British to turn away customers on the basis of their colour: 'Our outlook is that anyone who comes over here to fight and help us should be treated decently and with courtesy … I've always thought England was the worst country in the world for snobbery and I should be pleased if I found it wasn't.' Another letter-writer saw bitter irony in the fact that an African American soldier might die 'to ensure the future of a white man,' reflecting on how 'Over here we don't shout out about our democracy and freedom and so on, [but] we do treat the black fellows a darned sight better than you appear to think necessary.'[40]

However, the most telling signal of how the British felt was recorded by African American servicemen themselves. Clearly the 'black yanks' reciprocated the positive British feeling – at every level. When America's first black general, Benjamin O.Davis Senior visited in October 1942 he was quick to praise the British 'good welcome to the Negro troops' despite the 'friction' it led from what he diplomatically described as 'individual white' GIs. It dominated much of the half-hour press conference and reporters noted his cool skill at 'parrying attacks from left and right about the colour bar' under such 'close-questioning'.[41]

Similarly, when the NAACP's executive secretary Walter White visited, he described how on one occasion 'without exception, the brightest note in the stories of all Negro soldiers I talked with … was the story of friendships they had formed with British people.' Knowing most were from America's rural South, he figured their synergy with the country people near whom most were posted connected them. Neither group knew the mod cons of twentieth-century life enjoyed by those from the industrial northern parts of America, and it was this shared experience – and possibly better manners – that stopped African Americans from insulting British living and offending their hosts. These were the foundations for respect and friendship so that consequently, 'For many of the Negroes it was their first experience of being treated as normal human beings and friends by white people.'[42] Roi Ottley also witnessed those living in the country warmly reach out to their black American visitors – sometimes over their fellow white servicemen. Pub-owners would often extend this to saving their whisky for African Americans alone, he wrote.

Summing up findings from censored letters sent by GIs in the European Theatre, Ulysses Lee, author of *The Employment of Negro Troops*, described 'the dominant tone of the letters was one of pleasant surprise on the part of Negro troops and an angry shock on the part of white troops'.[43] The contrast between what was reported by black and white troops could not have been starker. One of those pleasantly surprised was a corporal working in an ordnance ammunition company, who said: 'They are very friendly towards us and treat us like they do the white soldiers.'[44] Not only were they treated the same, but they felt positively preferred, wrote others. 'The conduct of the men has been splendid,' wrote one lieutenant from a Quartermaster Truck Company, 'the local people say that they are better behaved than the white troops who were here – which is a source of pride to us.'[45] One engineer summed up the feeling when he wrote home to tell how 'the colored soldier over here is making good and England will long remember the "Black Yanks."'[46] Spirits soared accordingly. 'The morale of the men is very high as they are well pleased with the hospitality accorded them by the Irish people,' wrote another first lieutenant. 'They knew nothing of race and we are treated royally. In fact they lean toward the American Colored Soldier with high respect.'[47]

This parity in treatment of black and white Americans meant much, much more, Roi Ottley recorded in his diary in August 1944: 'the Negro has social equality here in more ways than theory. To put it in the language of a Negro soldier, "I'm treated so, a man don't know he's colored till he looks in the mirror."'[48] Benny Gordon, a member of the 254 Tank Battalion said of his time in the UK: 'I found that the white people in England treated me better than the white people in America. It was a very good experience that I'll treasure as long as I live.'[49] Albert Grillette Wood of the 320th Barrage Balloon Battalion said he 'felt like a king' in South Wales. His comrade Arthur Guest said: 'It was a spark of a light. You can see a different way of living.'[50] Another private first class wrote home about the inspiration injected by this new-found equality:

'Dad ... Over here Negro soldiers are thinking about their chances
for employment after the war, their chances for a higher education
and a better way of life. They are ready to fight for it and die if
necessary. Some now speak of dying at home rather than over
here.'[51]

An anonymous staff sergeant in the medical section of an engineer's
battalion wrote that 'The lessons I have learned I shall never forget. The
impression the folk have of us as American citizens is quite contrary
to that of the American whites.'[52] Ollie Stewart, writer with the *Afro-
American* described that early British reaction as showing

'our lads every possible courtesy and some of them, accustomed to
ill will, harsh words and artificial barriers, seem slightly bewildered.
They never had a chance to leave their southern home before, and
therefore never realised there was a part of the world which was
willing to forget a man's color and welcome him as a brother.'[53]

It was a near universal experience.

When asked 'What sort of opinion do you have of the English people?'
in the first significant US Army survey of black soldiers in the European
Theatre of Operations in November 1943, 80 per cent answered
'favourable'.[54]

Such positive plaudits steered the African American press away from
its traditional criticism of Britain over Imperial India. According to a
Bureau of Intelligence memo on anti-British feeling by US citizens
in December 1942: 'Discussion of India was extremely rare after
September 1942, and where it did occur no anti-British feeling was
expressed.' It went on to explain that the British warmth had redirected
press attention:

The greatest amount of comment on Britain since September has
been in connection with the treatment of Negro troops in the British
Isles. In every instance the reports were pro-British. The issue was
treated as a matter of American prejudice being transplanted to
Britain and unsuccessfully urged upon the British.[55]

So it happened that while 581st Ordnance Ammunition Company men were powering through the Atlantic, it was impossible to keep stories about this extraordinary British situation from seeping out at home. The *Atlanta Daily World* was reporting race riots erupting all over the UK. With remarkable prescience it reported that:

> Riots are much more frequent than the press can publish. The troops break into the gun rooms and get their rifles and ammunition to protect themselves often. If something is not done by the US Army soon, I would not be surprised to see a major battle between Negro and white American soldiers.[56]

And it was to this strange paradox that men of the 581st Ordnance Ammunition Company docked in Britain one drizzly autumn morning in 1943. It was their first time out of the country. They were dazed by the eight-day sea voyage characterised by bad food, overcrowding and an intense seasickness – exacerbated by constant zigzagging to avoid enemy U-Boats. Having survived this and the terrifying training that had left them fearing for both sanity and safety, they were now in for the mother of all shocks. For against all expectation and to their eternal and abiding wonder, when they arrived in the UK on 13 September they were welcomed with open arms.

Through a peculiar accident of fate, two more incidents were about to explode in Britain that would throw their position into sharp relief, making mutiny in Cornwall virtually inevitable. They came to Britain as part of Allied plans for the most audacious amphibious assault ever attempted in history. 581st Ordnance Ammunition Company men had happened to arrive at a time and place perfect for the fight of their lives. It just wouldn't be against the Germans.

Part III

Britain at Last

Chapter 10

Coming to Cornwall

Americans swarming into Launceston during the Second World War did more than any single event since the Normans to restore it to its former glory as Cornwall's capital town. Launceston's geographical position on the main road between Devon and Cornwall and the spectacular eleventh-century castle dominating the skyline (built by no less than William the Conqueror's half-brother Robert of Mortain) ensured its place as county town for more than seven centuries from the 1100s. This crown was snatched by Bodmin in 1835 and although Launceston's Tuesday cattle and pig market maintained a weekly flurry of activity and the town's railway station gave direct access to Devon and Cornwall, it was still in gentle decline.

This all went into rapid reverse the moment war broke out, as wave upon wave of new blood surged into the ancient walled town, swelling by many times its 4,000-strong population. From 1940 it was the arrival of hundreds of Londoners, firstly, in June with nearly 500 evacuees including the teenaged Roger Moore, no doubt smooth, debonair and already eyebrow-arching. Fellow evacuee, 10-year-old Londoner Nick Appleyard remembered how the ancient town's newly-modern buzz allowed their fertile schoolboy imaginations to run wild. They fantasised about what the castle contained, he said: 'You can see the ruined tower from a distance, but there is a very thick stone wall round it, completely sealing it from trespassers. All kinds of rumours about what was kept inside were circulating in the war. High explosives, art treasures, secret papers, even, the Spy!'

Even greater mysteries and excitement lurked beneath the castle that crowned the hill-top town: an ancient parish church, a busy town square bustling with hairdressers and shops, a heaving cattle market and two cinemas ingraining children with memories of Roy Rogers and George Formby – some in colour – for life. Although Nick Appleyard and other evacuees at Launceston College, the town's grammar school, were attending lessons when Tuesday's cattle market took place from 11am, its smell left a lasting impression when school was out.[1]

Children escaping the capital's aerial bombardment were followed by more than a hundred mothers and babies in October. Coming hot on the civilians' heels were soldiers. In came British regiments including the 'Glorious Glosters' which incorporated other nationalities such as Free French and Polish individuals who had signed up after escaping Hitler. British troops came to inhabit Nissen huts and billets all around Launceston town centre and communities nestled in its surrounding hills of moss-green farmland, while late in 1943, prisoner of war camps were established for captured Italians and Germans. But the event that changed everything was when the Yanks came late in 1942 – bringing with them nylon stockings, candy and all that jazz. And of all American servicemen, it was the influx of 29-ers that was to have the most impact on Launceston – and ultimately on men of the 581st Ordnance Ammunition Company.

The 29th Infantry Division was in the UK longer than any other division. Based for nearly a year at Tidworth barracks near Salisbury, Wiltshire, it moved in May 1943 to the south-west to make way for increasing waves of newly arrived American servicemen coming into Great Britain. This Virginian infantry unit, formed in the First World War, was known affectionately as the Blue and Gray division, in homage to the fact it was made up of men from states who fought on opposing sides (Union blue and Confederate grey) in the American Civil War. Formed of three principal units, its men were now scattered throughout Devon and Cornwall as D-Day preparations ratcheted up. The 116th Infantry Regiment went to Ivybridge, Devon, and 175th Infantry Regiment was in Tavistock, Devon. Meanwhile, the 115th Infantry Regiment straddled both Devon and Cornwall county lines. It was the Second Battalion of the 115th Infantry Regiment that came to Launceston, Cornwall, and built a base for itself at a farm on the top of a hill nearly a mile from the town's market square. It was known as Scarne Camp and just half a mile away was Pennygillam, home exclusively to African American service soldiers. Meanwhile, the 115th Infantry Regiment's Third Battalion settled 20 miles away in Bodmin while the First Battalion moved slightly further afield to Fort Tregantle near Plymouth.

In the Second World War, Launceston, and indeed the whole of the south-west, was central to D-Day planning because of its role as a giant camp hosting the US Army. And to army chiefs, Launceston's main advantage as a military camp was its proximity to one of the best practice grounds for D-Day: Bodmin Moor. Bleak, bluff and boggy, its ubiquitous wind and mists made for ideal but tortuous training conditions. American GIs came to loathe it. Launceston's most famous son, Charles Causley, generally regarded as the greatest poet laureate Cornwall never had, christened his home county the 'granite kingdom' – but he could have been describing the moor. One wag, Captain Maurice Clift, a company CO in the 115th Regiment, created some poetry of his own by re-writing John Masefield's *Sea Fever*.

> '*I want to go out to the moors again,*
> *To the fog and the rocks and the rain.*
> *To the gorse and the marsh and the muddy pools,*
> *Wherein the boys have lain …*
> *Oh I'll go out to the moors again,*
> *But mind you and mark me well:*
> *I'll carry enough explosives,*
> *To blow the place to hell.*'[2]

Undoubtedly, Americans left a real impression just as forceful on communities bordering their detested training ground during the Second World War. It is difficult to exaggerate just how much swing and glamour forced its way through the cobbles and winding country roads of this market town edging Bodmin Moor. Clinging to the coat-tips of incoming US Army arrivals, it meant untold luxuries like Hershey's chocolate and oranges, Camel and Lucky Strike cigarettes and ice-cream all served up with voices straight from the movies. Legendary big band leaders like Artie Shaw swooped down on Launceston to entertain its men, world-heavyweight boxing champion Joe Louis showcased his talent here and military supremoes such as Generals Eisenhower and Bradley walked regularly among its townspeople. Cinemas worked overtime, star-spangled jeeps monopolised narrow old roads and careered around at crazy speeds while everything seemed to move at the speed of Lindy hop. It was life-changing. It created a heaving, throbbing cosmopolitan melting pot in an entire south-west region tapping to the same beat. First Lieutenant Robert Henne thought it 'difficult to imagine a better reception by the people of Cornwall (especially Launceston) than that accorded us.' It was towards this venerable Norman town, bulging with cutting-edge weaponry and a thoroughly modern mix of people, that men of the 581st Ordnance Ammunition Company were slowly shuttling.

Their mission was to create ammunition dumps. Part of a huge logistical supply chain network spun throughout Britain's roads, these ammunition dumps were to provide D-Day bound trucks with the firepower they needed for invasion day and ninety days beyond. One local, Joan Rendell, then a resident in her early twenties, remembers their overnight transformation of Launceston into one giant powder keg:

'We were amazed … They put up all these Nissen huts and they were ever so many yards apart. [They] came over night. Suddenly these Nissen huts were there and [they] were servicing them and they would throw these boxes about – they would throw them to one another and if they'd dropped one it would have blown up the whole of Launceston.'[3]

Their impact was equally explosive – but fortunately the shockwave was benign. Men of the 581st Army Ordnance Ammunition Company were treading in friendly footsteps when they arrived. African American soldiers already in Launceston had cut a dashing swathe with their generosity, kind manners and melodious contributions to church life. Arthur Wills, an 11-year-old schoolboy at the time said:

'They looked different, their uniforms were much smarter, they talked different, they used slang. They were very friendly, they gave us chewing gum and coins … I still have the coins they gave us. They gave us Christmas parties for the school children, it was good. We got jelly and ice cream which was absolutely amazing.'[4]

Joan Rendell remembered: 'They were so kind. They would always give you a bar of chocolate.'[5] Evacuee Nick Appleyard remembered waiting in the centre of town for his return bus ride home from school and seeing African American soldiers in expensive uniforms, big lace-up boots, oozing politeness and charm and always chewing gum.

> On one rainy occasion, sheltering in a shop doorway 'two huge black Yanks, dressed in dripping rubber capes, stepped into the doorway, crowding me backwards against the shop door.' Falling backwards into the shop, Nick was rescued when a 'proverbial giant black hand reached down from what seemed a tremendous height and picked me up. "Sorry, sir," I said. "Sorry."
> "That's perfectly alright son," said the black man, in American. "Have a piece of gum." I never really doubted that we would win the War, but this episode made me quite sure we would win it.'[6]

Joan Rendell recalled that people overcame any unfounded fears of African American soldiers to accept their generous transport offers, which were particularly valuable in an era of strict civilian petrol rationing. 'They would often lift little old ladies bodily into their large truck to provide (strictly speaking, illegal) lifts into town from the outlying districts when shortage and rationing of fuel meant car journeys could only be made for seriously essential purposes and bus services were almost non-existent.' And once acquainted, they were bowled over by the sheer glamour they brought with them. She remembered: 'Dixieland nights at the town hall – these were the finest shows we had ever seen in 'Lanson' [the local abbreviation for the town]. One of the men had been with Count Basie and a couple of the others were from well-known bands. And what dancers! The Dixieland shows were outrageous.'

Music was one thing – next came the moves, she remembered:

> 'They were wonderful dancers and all the farm boys would dance with you and jig you around and then [they] would sweep you off your feet and make you feel like Ginger Rogers. Especially Lucky Lee – everyone wanted to dance with him – he would make you feel like Ginger Rogers. They were so very glamorous. All their uniforms were such good quality compared with our boys – it was so different.'

What came with these American soldiers was a sense of the world coming to Launceston – and of giants walking with mere mortals. 'Joe Louis, the boxer, came to meet [them] and Glenn Miller played for the whites. Eisenhower, Bradley and Monty inspected troops down here – there was real Hollywood glamour. They were wonderful days. You were young and you just didn't worry about the dangers or the worries.'[7]

The most remarkable thing about living in a continual state of war, according to Arthur Wills, was that these quantum leaps were simply accepted as the new normal, particularly by young people:

> 'Joe Louis came to Launceston; we have a photo of him; I sat a couple of rows behind him in the cinema … I remember the war starting, how things changed, gas masks at school, the evacuees coming to school, troops around the town, US Army lorries at the station. Even bombs were dropped on Launceston – there was an unexploded bomb at St Stevens. We heard a horrible whistling sound then thud, thud, thud – it didn't explode. It was just normal life for us, we accepted it.'[8]

Launceston's solitary unexploded bomb was not the nearest the community got to witnessing German fire-power up close. Children remember gathering in the town's Coronation Park to watch the *'fireworks'* rain down on Plymouth's docks, 25 miles away, as it bore the brunt of Nazi bombers, night after night.

Part of that new order was the presence of African American soldiers in Launceston – and it was not just the young who approved of them. On a different level, the older generation in Launceston (more likely to be moved by church music than jitterbugging) was certainly not immune to their allure. Negro troops were spreading the good word by thrilling locals with their Baptist vocals. People still remember how African American singers took the church-going community by storm by performing at various local church events.

So the Cornish market town about to become home to men of the 581st Ordnance Ammunition Company was not only used to black soldiers, but fond of them too. This made for a good, special relationship and the newest arrivals were in for a warm welcome. In Launceston, as in every other base where African American soldiers were stationed alongside but segregated from white troops, the black/white divide was stark – and Cornishmen and women were picking their sides. A young Launceston woman at a 'mixed dance' in the town hall had partnered both a white and black soldier in June 1942. Writing in her diary she had no qualms in making her choice: 'The coloured boy was jolly and friendly … the white lad I thought was slovenly in his dress and I didn't like his swaggering walk.'[9]

Joan Rendell said:

'In 'Lanson' they used to frequent one pub and the whites used to frequent another so never the twain should meet. The whites used to go to the White Hart hotel and the blacks went to The Kings Arms (now the Bakers Arms) or the Ring o Bells. There was no love lost there. There was quite a lot of animosity. Some of the darkies were lovely looking lads – big, strong and the girls loved them. Lucky Lee was awfully good looking. He was a lovely dancer – everyone wanted to dance with Lucky Lee. And the whites didn't like that.'[10]

Another, an anonymous grammar-school boy at Launceston, was horrified that 'the coloured GIs seemed just the same as the white ones [yet] they were in their own camp down the road and obviously inferior. It seemed wrong to us.'[11] Arthur Wills, recalls his schoolboy confusion at segregation: 'We couldn't understand that people of the same country felt like that about each other. We didn't understand what had happened. There were different fish and chip shops; different pubs.'[12]

This was the frenetic, febrile and freaky atmosphere of Launceston in early autumn 1943. Adding to it at that exact moment was a new spirit travelling across from urban America. Back there, tension had built up throughout that long hot '*bloody*' summer with fights, riots and clashes erupting in five cities with ever-escalating violence. The Second World War had heightened inequality between black and white communities over housing, work and even over who got plaudits for fighting, and feuding broke out first in the streets of Los Angeles. It then flared ferociously in Detroit that June leaving thirty-four fatalities; twenty-five were black, of whom no less than seventeen were shot dead by police. It ended in New York in early August after a white policeman shot a black soldier who had involved himself in a couple's dispute. A young waiter who harboured acting ambitions, Sidney Poitier, was working in a downtown restaurant when he heard there was trouble in Harlem. He felt compelled to investigate:

> 'After work, I took a train uptown, came up out of the subway, and there was chaos everywhere – cops, guns, debris and broken glass all over the street. Many stores had been set on fire, and the commercial district on 125th Street looked as if it had been bombed.'[13]

The ripple effects were overwhelming. Reflecting on this summer of troubles, African American writer Lester B. Granger wrote in October 1943:

> 'It took race riots in five great cities to wake up white America to the dangers of racial conflict. It took a riot in Harlem to teach Negro America that all racial intolerance is not on one side of the fence and that a Negro riot in action is every bit as bestial and blindly destructive as a white mob.'[14]

Precedents had been set, lines drawn and then crossed with blood in America that summer. This new way of thinking came across the Atlantic with both communities as they poured across the ocean. It was inevitable that some of this should filter into their new British postings. By a quirky twist of fate, men of the 581st Ordnance Ammunition Company turned up in a Cornish market town at this very moment of rising racial tensions at home, now trickling abroad and playing out on British streets. It added to existing micro American tensions currently in the town and on a wider scale, reflected Anglo-American relations gone somewhat sour. The stars were aligning to make their arrival yet more ominous. By the time they pulled into Launceston in mid-September, shocking incidents directly involving British citizens were unravelling and thrusting race relations into an even more blinding spotlight. It came firstly with a racial slur involving the most quintessential bastion of British sport – cricket.

On 3 September 1943, a couple of days before the Launceston-bound soldiers set sail, news leaked that Learie Constantine, captain of the West Indies and a professional cricketer in Britain since the 1920s, had been thrown out with his family from a four-day stay at the Imperial Hotel in Bloomsbury, London. The reason? American servicemen guests there had complained about having to mix with their race. Newspapers had a field day as the story made headlines everywhere. The response was a national outcry.

The Home Intelligence Unit, set up specifically by the Ministry of Information to harness public opinion early in the war, reported little but indignation and bewilderment nationwide as the argument reverberated in newspapers and Parliament for weeks afterwards. 'If they are good enough to fight for us, they are good enough to live with us,' was a typical quote repeated in the weekly report on 9 September. 'In the Southern Region, people are said to feel that the matter cannot be left where it is, and in Scotland 'a number suggest that Mr Constantine should be invited to lunch with the Royal Family at Buckingham Palace.'[15] The following week's report proved indignation continued about 'this most abominable business' with one suggestion that the Imperial Hotel manager instead 'should have invited the complainant to leave if he did not wish to be in the same hotel as a distinguished coloured guest.' Another stated 'Talk about Hitlerism, it exists in this land of ours and must be rooted up.'[16]

By 30 September, blame was being laid squarely at the Americans' door.

Piling insult onto injury came the case of Amelia King, a young black British woman from Stepney, who was refused entry to the Women's Land Army because it was felt white farmers would reject her help on the sole basis of her ethnic heritage. Instead of taking her rejection lying down, she coolly raised it with her MP who voiced the outrageous situation in Parliament four days after the 581st arrived in Britain – and barely a week after the Constantine scandal erupted. It was the deciding blow.

What followed was an almighty row about the blindingly unfair treatment of Constantine and King. It rumbled on throughout September and October, culminating just four days before the Paignton Court Martial opened with a volcanic poll revealing 75 per cent of respondents felt 'definite disapproval' of the colour bar. It shone a light on how British feeling on race had crystallised since 'the American invasion'. Taken on the streets of London for Mass Observation (MO), the snap survey showed that the controversy surrounding both Learie Constantine and Amelia King had brought the 'colour bar' into sharp focus, because of the cricketer's fame and the fact both incidents happened within seven days of each other. The unconscionable ejection of Learie Constantine from a hotel and the snub of a would-be war volunteer prompted a vociferous reaction from everyday people, the MO fortnightly bulletin recorded in October 1943 'public opinion was very vigorously on the side of the two negroes.'

Expressions of resentment were often 'very strong indeed and many people were of the opinion that those responsible ought to be severely punished,' it surmised. 'Those people want wiping out,' said one interviewee. Another felt: 'People who encourage the colour bar would rather be friendly with enemy aliens and ought not to be allowed to hold these responsible positions.' Many felt people of colour were fighting for liberty and equality which should at least guarantee their own. 'It doesn't seem right to make a distinction. After all, they're God's children and many of them are willing to sacrifice their lives in the cause of freedom, just as our own children.' 'I hope they get a fairer deal,' said one. Someone else commented: 'if they came over here to give their lives for us, they ought not to be barred out of anywhere – they ought to be allowed in places. I don't think hotels and restaurants should refuse to have them – that just isn't fair.' Equal numbers highlighted the blatant hypocrisy of striving for freedom while not being allowed it themselves. 'It's very wrong, especially these days, when we're fighting against this so-called anti-racial intolerance (sic). It's to be regretted that we should want to imitate Hitler,' said one correspondent. 'Hypocrisy' was another favourite term,' concluded the bulletin. 'It was evidently very generally felt that the colour bar could hardly be reconciled to the claim to be fighting for democracy.'[17]

The dust seemed to settle once Amelia King's application to the Women's Land Army was processed successfully (later in October 1943) and when Constantine launched legal proceedings to sue the Imperial Hotel. But it had added the final ingredient for a perfect storm. A sturdy response to perceived injustice was now brewing in the most unlikely of places – the outer extremities of the United Kingdom. The countdown to mutiny had begun.

Chapter 11

26 September 1943

W hen the 581st Ordnance Ammunition Company's own D-Day came, it dawned as ordinarily as possible on this extraordinary British home front. It arrived at the end of a weekend of rare domestic highlights kicking off on Saturday, 25 September, when England footballers faced Wales in what was billed as the season's first international match. Quite how many internationals were physically possible during the Nazi-occupation of Europe was by the by; filling Wembley stadium once more with 80,000 fans was reason alone for British cheer. That £15,000 of Red Cross gate-money was raised in the process merely confirmed it as a truly beautiful game. It turned out to be a thrilling match in which England beat Wales 8–3 – the three final goals thumped home in five tantalising minutes making it the 'highest-scoring win ever recorded in an international at Wembley', according to *British Pathe's* newsreel.[1] And it wasn't just the goal glut that people loved. In the absence of a Welsh reserve player – and totally in keeping with the classic British wartime imperative to 'keep calm' and 'crack on' – England's Stan Mortensen was substituted for the opposition (after quickly changing out of his RAF uniform) when Welsh defender Ivor Powell was stretchered off with a broken collarbone.

Another cause for celebration came the next morning with Battle of Britain Day – to give thanks for the RAF's heroic success three years before. Hours before shooting began in Cornwall, the king and queen led an act of remembrance at St Paul's Cathedral, 200-odd miles away in London. Later that afternoon they took the salute outside Buckingham Palace, and the march-past of civil defence personnel, aircraft workers, members of AA Command, units of the RAF and dominion Air Forces was billed as 'one of the most representative processions ever to pass the palace.'[2] Churches and village halls up and down the country, including Launceston, hosted similar Battle of Britain commemorations – trying to blend in the annual harvest festival celebrations with which it coincided. This last festival was especially hard for Cornish farmers still counting the cost of thunderstorms and torrential rain that had swept the West Country two weeks earlier, leaving behind a trail of crop devastation.

There was just a hint of sparks threatening the now tinder-dry state of race relations. Prominent in that weekend's *Sunday Mirror* was a tail-flick over the Learie Constantine and Amelia King episode, courtesy of Tom Driberg MP. The independent member for Maldon had asked the Parliamentary Minister of Food whether 'he will consider withdrawing the catering licence of any hotel or other catering establishment, which tries to impose a colour bar on its customers?'[3] It was but a passing shadow that weekend. The silver screen, as ever, promised blissful escape and Launceston people were spoilt for choice with *Ship with Wings*; *Road Show; Not a Ladies' Man* and *Son of Monte Cristo* all showing. It was only as the weekend was drawing to a close and the football, festivals and films finished, that the tiny spark escaped.

Tension had been rising ever since 581st Ordnance Ammunition Company men awoke for their first day in Cornwall on 22 September 1943. Their commanders did not have the perfect clarity of hindsight to guide them. They might have been unaware of the strengthening British reaction to American racial segregation. Possibly, they had missed headlines expressing widespread British hostility to the second-rate treatment of Learie Constantine and Amelia King. Perhaps they overlooked the back-to-back confinement to camp already suffered by the 581st Ordnance Ammunition Company. Eyes could have been blind to persistent prejudice they had faced ever since joining the United States of America's army. Intentionally or not, however, 581st Ordnance Ammunition Company's commanders blanked out all this – as well as racial violence back home, echoing outbreaks in Britain and growing nervousness in their newly adopted Cornish town. Unaware of the volatility of all these factors, they made a dreadful decision. They decided to restrict the new arrivals to camp – again. It was an atrocious oversight. This meant men of the 581st Ordnance Ammunition Company were banned from venturing into town as access passes for them alone were blocked. It was the third successive camp in which they had been virtually incarcerated. For fourteen of them it would be the last.

American Civil Rights leader Walter White prioritised investigating this specific restriction when he arrived in the UK a few months later. Describing the 581st Ordnance Ammunition Company's plight, he said the moment they arrived in England they were restricted allegedly because they did not have the correct dress uniforms to wear into town but noted that 'white units nearby suffered no such restrictions.'[4] Journalist Roi Ottley was under no illusion about the role restrictions like these were meant to play. In his diary he described it as the quickest and most effective shortcut to establishing home-grown rules in an alien territory: 'an effective strong-armed instrument for establishing the *Jim Crow* pattern in public places. To reinforce these discriminations, Negroes are sharply restricted.'[5]

To men of the 581st Ordnance Ammunition Company, this most recent restriction to camp was a firm indication that *Jim Crow* rules used in Fort Sill and Camp Patrick Henry had been successfully transplanted into British territory. To make matters worse, even when a few finally secured passes, there was still no guarantee of a hassle-free furlough – especially when seen publicly socialising with Launceston people. Walter White described the frustration of discovering that white military policemen required them to produce not only their passes but dog tags too, requiring coats and shirts to be unbuttoned in the unforgiving damp that Cornish autumn. 'When this was made necessary by the military policemen every few yards, bitter resentment began to well up among the Negro soldiers,' he recorded after hearing the men's complaints.[6]

Explosive forces were now in play. Men of the 581st Ordnance Ammunition Company had suffered for their race multiple times at successive US Army camps. They had been restricted at least three times in a row. The pattern of humiliation and prejudice was repeating itself all over again, but in a brave new political climate altogether. Was anything other than trouble likely if they ever ventured out?

Around 10pm, the few Launceston residents still out and about with nothing but intermittent moonlight to guide them, began to sense that something unusual was up. More than anything, it was what they heard during that evening's blackout that gave the game away. John Pearce, a grammar school boy, returning to his town centre home late that night, told how he could not have missed the sound while 'walking down Western

Road when he came upon a whole load of GIs walking in formation – plod, plod, plod.'[7]

At that moment a young Joan Rendell, then 23, was unknowingly heading towards the crescendo of marching. In Launceston to meet her civil servant father as he came back from the Admiralty Department in Bath, she was keen to move quickly: 'It wasn't good for a young girl to be seen outside the town hall looking hopeful and I started to walk away from the hall towards the square and I was looking at my watch. It is all so vivid.'[8]

On spotting young John Pearce, African American soldiers called out to warn him, specifically saying he was 'not to go into the market square, but to seek refuge in Castle Green as there was going to be trouble. They were prepared for trouble. They had rifles under their great coats.'[9]

The unique confluence of explosive external factors thrown together at the very time when 581st Ordnance Ammunition Company men arrived in Launceston six days before was about to ignite.

Joan Rendell had nearly got to the old garage by now and was almost at the square when 'suddenly I heard this screaming and shouting. I do remember that woman's scream. I can hear it today. It was an unearthly scream – and then I heard these shots.'[10]

Something quite exceptional was now in motion. In the minutes after 10.15pm on 26 September 1943, the sparks had caught light.

Part IV

Day Two 16 October 1943

Chapter 12

The Body of Evidence

This sensational Cornish drama was evidently on the British public's radar before anyone so much as set foot in Paignton's hastily reconfigured courtroom. The nation's tabloid press had seen to that ten days previously. Coming when it did, the mutiny was a slam dunk of a lead story. It brought together all the volatility from previous weeks – America's 'bloody summer' of race riots; spiralling British indignation against the grossly unfair treatment of popular African American troops and righteous outrage over Learie Constantine and Amelia King's 'colour bar'. So when things did collide in a monumental way at a small market square in Cornwall, it struck a nerve. The story headlined everywhere to a totally captive audience. Splashed on front pages of the four biggest-selling nationals *The Herald*, *The Mail*, *The Mirror* and *The Express* – with combined sales alone pushing 12 million – tabloids jockeyed with each other for the most vibrant detail. With 85 per cent of Brits getting their daily news in black and white, the spectacle was inescapable.

Headlines such as 'US Men in "Wild West" Fight' in *The Mirror* screamed to Britons' inner cowboy and played on stereotypical action associated with American movies.

'With revolver shots echoing across the main square, shop windows shattered and civilians diving for cover, a quiet Cornish market town resembled a wild west settlement when fighting broke out between American soldiers,' was how it broke the news to its readers in early October. 'The town had heard little gunfire of any kind for the past century.'

One old man told the *Daily Mirror*: 'There hasn't been anything like this since the days of the smugglers.' It gave the violence some context too, by noting it was the third time in as many weeks that US servicemen were facing court martials for serious charges.[1]

Similar tales of derring-do spilled over from *The Mirror's* tabloid rivals:

'A party of men each with rifle and with 60 rounds of ammunition hidden under his jacket, came into the square,' was how *The Daily Herald*, forerunner of today's *Sun*, told it.

Using a pace redolent of its more recent incarnation, it described how 'from behind a monument and from across the street they ambushed troops leaving an hotel. As shots were fired British police pushed civilians into the cover of doorways or shepherded them from the danger zone. The battle lasted ten minutes.'[2]

Then a Labour-supporting tabloid boasting more than 2 million readers, *The Herald*, warned of imminent consequences such as a new, strong and immediate disciplinary code to be imposed and zealously enforced in American army camps throughout Britain.

The story was flying off printing presses up and down Britain, but of all Fleet Street's finest, it was the *Daily Mirror* that played a blinder. Its first front page scoop on 5 October revealed the inconvenient truth that those involved 'are said to have been coloured troops and white.'[3] The *Daily Mirror* was the only national to report this tiny detail, but it blew the case wide open. Without this single fact being published before the trial opened, the presiding judge might well have been able to censor the reporting of races involved. But when the trial opened it was impossible because too many people knew about it.

If the nation's taste buds for this sensational drama were well and truly teased before US Army legal action started on 15 October, by the time court resumed for day two they were hooked. There had been time enough for newspaper commentary from the previous day to sink in before court started at 9.30am. From that morning's headlines it was clear that prior tales of armed battle had morphed into mutiny, plus there were plenty of juicy snippets to spice things up further. Highlights included the prosecution's parading of a Tommy gun; images of the injured Military Policeman Sergeant Simmons limping on crutches to take the stand; reports of bizarrely sociable hourly 'smoke breaks' in the specially recreated court and the equally surreal but repeated intrusion into proceedings from 'an elephant from a local circus [that] trumpeted loudly somewhere outside.'[4] Court reporter Miss Joyce Packe was given

Paignton, Devon – The South Sands, Goodrington – The Pier and South Sands, The Bandstand and Pier, The Preston Promenade and The Cliff Gardens and Promenade. (*Mary Evans/Grenville Collins Postcard Collection*)

Palace Avenue Police Station, Paignton, scene of the USA Army Court Martial, 15–17 October 1943, photographed before demolition. (*Courtesy of Paignton Heritage Society*)

Schools, transport, housing and restaurants, as this 1938 photo shows, were separated for African Americans. (*Library of Congress, Prints & Photographs Division, FSA/OWI Collection* (*LC-USF3301-006392-M4*))

Even water fountains were segregated according to Jim Crow lines. (*Library of Congress, Prints & Photographs Division, FSA/OWI Collection* (*LC-USF34-9058-C*))

Race riots broke out in the five American cities of Detroit, Los Angeles, New York, Mobile and Beaumont, Texas in the summer of 1943. Here, a black man is seen being chased through the streets of Detroit by a white mob armed with sticks and beer bottles. (*Mary Evans/Sueddeutsche Zeitung Photo*)

Jitterbugging was one of the most famous American imports during the Second World War. Here a couple demonstrate the 'special relationship' in action at a hayride and picnic lunch for the US forces and their friends organised by the American Red Cross for Independence Day celebrations. (© *Mirrorpix*)

A Metropolitan police officer talking to two American servicemen. (© *Metropolitan Police Authority/Mary Evans*)

African American soldiers and local girls dance to swing music at Bouillabaisse on New Compton Street, London (© *Hulton-Deutsch Collection/CORBIS/Getty Images*)

The first African American troops the United States ever sent to England are pictured having a beer at a local pub. (© *Photo by David E. Scherman/The LIFE Picture Collection/Getty Images*)

Learie Constantine (right) and George Headley (left), of the West Indies head out to bat after tea at Lord's during the 1939 test. (© *Illustrated London News Ltd / Mary Evans*)

As executive secretary of the National Association for the Advancement of Colored People (NAACP), Walter White prioritised visiting Launceston when he travelled to the UK in 1944. (© *Mary Evans / Everett Collection*)

George Orwell wrote much about the American 'occupation' of Britain and was one of those who identified racial tension between United States' troops stationed here during the Second World War. (© *Mary Evans / Everett Collection*)

Journalist Roi Ottley's 'lost diary', written while he was war correspondent during the Second World War, contains much commentary on how Britain treated African American servicemen. (*Courtesy of the Photographs and Prints Division, Schomburg Center for Research in Black Culture, The New York Public Library*)

Joyce Packe, British star of the Paignton Court Martial, went on to set up the local Liberal Club and became an acclaimed local historian. She died at the age of 75 in 1991. (© *Herald Express, 22 Febuary, 1991*)

Historian, writer and prolific matchbox collector Joan Rendell was an eye-witness to the shooting in Launceston. This portrait, taken by John Lyne, was her favourite. (© *John Lyne*)

The Home Secretary, Herbert Morrison, seen here visiting a mobile kitchen in 1941, introduced The Visiting Forces Act, which would prove hugely significant for those accused of mutiny in Launceston. (© *London Fire Brigade / Mary Evans Picture Library*)

Winston Churchill holding a Tommy gun while visiting America. (© *Mary Evans Picture Library*)

African American soldiers receiving rifle instruction at Fort Sill, Oklahoma in 1943. (*Courtesy of US Army Artillery Museum, Fort Sill, Oklahoma*)

Soldiers performing rifle drill in front of their barracks at Fort Sill, Oklahoma in 1943. (*Courtesy of US Army Artillery Museum, Fort Sill, Oklahoma*)

Soldiers enjoying some downtime with Spotty at Fort Sill, Oklahoma in 1942. (*Courtesy of US Army Artillery Museum, Fort Sill, Oklahoma*)

Camp Patrick Henry was carved out of Virginian forest and provided a bucolic setting for servicemen making final preparations to go overseas. This is the entrance. (*Courtesy of the Mariners Museum and Park, Newport News, Virginia*)

African American troops arrive at Camp Patrick Henry as the last staging post before embarking overseas. (*Courtesy of the Mariners Museum and Park, Newport News, Virginia*)

Launceston Castle has crowned the town since Norman times; it was built soon after the conquest. This view of it, taken across Newport, was captured in 1985. (© *John Lyne*)

Surrounded by a patchwork of fields spread over undulating hills, Launceston was the top entertainment destination for many GIs based in and around the town. (© *John Lyne*)

Hollywood came to Cornwall during the Second World War as the American entertainment industry put top stars out on parade for its servicemen. Here Bob Hope is playing for laughs when he visited Bodmin Barracks in July 1943. (*E7296, George Ellis Collection, courtesy of Kresen Kernow*)

Actress Frances Langford was a regular singer on Bob Hope's *The Pepsodent Show* along with guitarist Tony Romano. Together they entertained thousands of troops across the world. Artie Shaw, Glenn Miller and Joe Louis were regular visitors to Cornwall too. (*E7297, George Ellis Collection, courtesy of Kresen Kernow*)

Boxing supremo Joe Louis, regarded as one of the world's best champions ever, proved himself as popular with white as black troops when he dropped in on Bodmin Barracks during the month before D-Day. (*E8685, George Ellis Collection, courtesy of Kresen Kernow*)

The United States Army's colour bar even filtered down to how its troops watched the host of celebrities who turned out to entertain them. Notice how troops watching World Heavyweight Champion Joe Louis in Bodmin 1944 are separated. (*E8681, George Ellis Collection, courtesy of Kresen Kernow*)

American GIs marching under the Stars and Stripes flag head towards the town square for this fundraising Wings for Victory Parade held in June 1943. The whole of Launceston turned out to see allied servicemen march through the town before assembling in the town square. (*E7046, George Ellis Collection, courtesy of Kresen Kernow*)

American servicemen assembling in happier times in Launceston town square – this is the Wings for Victory fundraiser on 12 June 1943. Ironically these troops are stationed immediately in front of the drapers Hicks and Son, which was to be shot up during the mutiny a few weeks later. (*E7047, George Ellis Collection, courtesy of Kresen Kernow*)

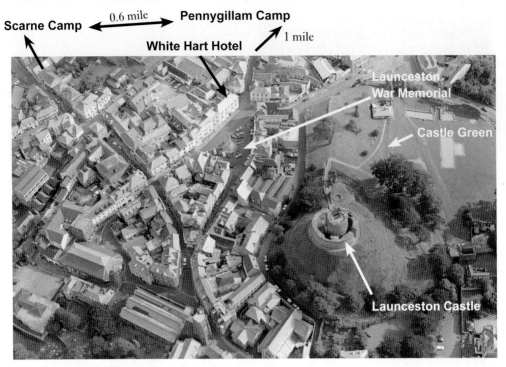

Scarne Camp ←——— 0.6 mile ———→ Pennygillam Camp

White Hart Hotel ↗ 1 mile

Launceston War Memorial

Castle Green

Launceston Castle

This aerial shot of Launceston, taken in 1995, shows the castle sitting high on its mound. The market square's war memorial and the various exits used to leave the scene of the shooting are clearly visible. (© *John Lyne*)

The White Hart was central to the action in 1943. It had changed little by the time this picture was taken in 1984. A couple of the men sought refuge here after the shooting and were calmly talked down by the kindly publican Tom Gossett. (© *John Lyne*)

The court martial of the fourteen coloured accused of mutiny, riot and intent to murder ended here tonight, after a three-days' hearing, including an all-day Sunday session; *Daily Herald*, 18 October 1943. (© *Mirrorpix*)

American assault troops mass behind the protective section of their landing craft as it approaches the beach head, Omaha Beach, on D-Day. The smoke visible in the background attests to the massive naval artillery assault, supporting the landing. (© Imperial War Museum / Robert Hunt Library / Mary Evans)

a starring role in most stories but was afforded the headline itself in *The Herald's* front page entitled 'A Briton at the Court of Yankees.'[5]

Key players were no doubt feeling the pressure of such intense media exposure. Despite all the prosecutor's wins from the previous day in court, there remained a subtle shadow in the papers that morning. For a start, Trial Judge Advocate Frank Eresch's charismatic showmanship, used to devastating effect by his unashamed playing to the audience, added much lineage to the morning coverage. Consequently, attention had been directed to a story army bosses wanted sweeping under the carpet. Worse, despite establishing a clear ringleader, narrative of events and accomplices, all backed up by testimony from a turncoat company soldier, real doubts persisted. Beneath all the shock and awe reportage of that first day, there was a definite sense that not all was cut and dried about the prosecution case – particularly the investigators' inability to harness watertight witness statements. When one failed to spot and identify witnesses he had interviewed, it caused simply 'a sensation' in Paignton police court, said watching journalists.[6]

It was this shred of doubt that kept needling the chief prosecutor, Trial Judge Advocate Frank Eresch, as he walked in from his Paignton billet that morning. Heading a couple of streets inland from Paignton seafront, past the once picturesque and ornamental Palace Avenue Gardens (now dug over for victory vegetables) and towards the police station, he wondered whether he had done enough thinking and fine-tuning of the case overnight. There had not been much time to fully secure the result his superiors wanted. Once there, he neatly side-stepped the front desk and took the stairs up to the first floor. Loitering before the US Army's borrowed courtroom, he took a moment. Inside was US Army court reporter, Miss Joyce Packe, ready and waiting. So too was the man he needed to beat, Defense Counsel Captain John A. Philbin. Despite lingering qualms, in that brief minute of repose Trial Judge Advocate Eresch reminded himself of his knock-out line up of witnesses, the strength of his case and the need to secure a conviction. Eresch was the man and this was his hour. By 9.30am sharp on Saturday, 16 October 1943, he was ready to launch his opening salvo.

Eresch prepared to weaponise the prosecution argument with an all-out bid to nail the mutiny's 'instigator'. After the laborious swearing in

of all court personnel and fourteen accused, in walked Private First Class
L.V. Edwards, member of the 581st Ordnance Ammunition Company for
a year and now the unit's second to change sides by appearing as witness
for the prosecution.

He described the chain of events as starting at '*chow time*', around
7.00pm that fateful Sunday, when word circulated that 25 per cent of
the company was to be allowed into town. Sergeant Hughes led them,
dressed up in smart overcoats, to the first sergeant who wrote out 'little
slips of paper to take to the Lieutenant Songy,' – but their hopes were
then dashed as the lieutenant refused flatly to sign them because 'we did
not have no blouses.' In outright defiance they decided to venture into
town anyway, said Private Edwards, and at the first pub met 'these two
British soldiers [who] … takes us down to another one on round from
there.' It was at this second pub where Private Edwards spotted 'Clifford
Barrett … on the other side … standing up on some bench. What he was
saying I don't know. He was talking to some white soldiers and when he
come back on to the side where we was, he called us all outside.'

Private Edwards was one of nine to return to camp after first agreeing
to Barrett's request for them to 'stick together.' Pressed by the trial judge
advocate, he described the logistics involved in what happened next:

> 'Barrett said to get the carbines out of the tents and told them to
> assemble back there near the little road that goes through where you
> come in … and Sergeant Austin when he comes back to the road,
> that's when he brought the ammunition out there and passed it out.'

Having acted first as group quartermaster, Private Barrett then
transformed himself into a sergeant major, directing the men's drill.
According to the witness, 'he told us to all move out in threes, let three
go on like here, and then after they got so far three more, and three more,
and three more, like that, that's the way he had them moving.'

To make things crystal clear here, Trial Judge Advocate Eresch
intervened:

> Q: 'Do I understand you mean to say more or less of a formation?'
> A: 'Yes, sir.'

Q: 'Was Barrett directing them?'

A: 'Yes, sir.'

Briefly, Trial Judge Advocate Eresch dwelt on Barrett's Tommy gun; pointedly reflecting on the significance of this choice as a weapon built for rapid fire and therefore able to inflict maximum damage. Next, Eresch moved onto the crime scene, reacting harshly when Private Edwards painted the encounter between 581st men and military policemen as accidental, almost spontaneous, rather than a pre-meditated and clinical attack on the said representatives and upholders of army law. 'They wasn't going back to get the military policemen,' he said. 'They left the camp to go back to this pub, not the military policemen. After they saw the military policemen standing there round the jeep that is where they stopped.'

Trial Judge Advocate Eresch was not going to let his own witness get away with deviating from the party line on motive and exploded at this hint that military police, known by locals as snowdrops because of their white helmets, were not the original target. Surely the mutiny charge would not stick if this were the case.

Q:	'Were you told that by anyone or was it just your thought?'
A:	'That was just my thought.'
Trial Judge Advocate:	'The prosecution desires that all parts of this witness' testimony which refers to just his thoughts be stricken from the record.'
Law Member:	'Let it be stricken.'

Eresch had successfully squashed the notion of this merely being retaliatory action for a pub slight. But he was itching to get to the heart of Edwards' real purpose for appearing that day: the character assassination of Private First Class Clifford Barrett. Eresch asked Private Edwards whether he had anything else he wanted to say.

'When we was coming from Fort Sill to [Camp] Patrick Henry I had Clifford Barrett's gas mask through a mistake. I didn't know I had it, I thought I had my own. I opened the gas mask and he had some carbine ammunition in there and I took it to him in this car, and he is in the back of the car, sir, where he is. When I told him about it he grabbed me by my collar, and pulled out one of those long Swiss made knives, and he said if I'd say anything about it he would cut my head off, and I was scared to say anything about it.'

Before court started that morning, Trial Judge Advocate Eresch needed more colour on the man held up as orchestrator of the military strike in Launceston town square – and now he had it. It had taken mere minutes to achieve. The prosecution had its textbook villain. Rather than indicating a dastardly intent, Clifford Barrett's secret stash of ammunition was in fact much more likely to be for his personal protection. Even more likely was that he actually needed to safeguard himself against the everyday violence he experienced first in Fort Sill and Camp Patrick Henry. African American servicemen up and down the United States were doing the same thing and secretly amassing ammunition for self-defence. But Eresch was not about to let the truth get in the way of a good story, and sadly, neither was Barrett's defence team.

Gaining momentum, Eresch ploughed on with his argument that Private Barrett had masterminded the mutiny, ably and freely supported by everyone else in the dock. He barely flinched when Defense Counsel Captain John A. Philbin tried a challenge, by suggesting to Private Edwards that Barrett had strong-armed fellow soldiers against their will:

Q: 'And were most of them afraid of Barrett, or afraid that if they did not go along something might happen to them? Were the others afraid?'
A: 'Was the others afraid?'
Q: 'Were there quite a number of them afraid? Were there quite a number afraid, were there others afraid, and—'

It was more than the trial judge advocate could bear. Once again, his witness was meandering away from the official position – and Eresch wanted to shut down his challenger's line of cross-examination.

Trial Judge Advocate:	'If the court pleases, the prosecution objects to that line of questioning, as to whether they were afraid. That is something which the individual alone can determine. If he wants to ask whether they told him—'
Law member:	'Will you amend your line of questioning?'

Stutteringly, Philbin tried to get his argument back together, but seemed thrown as the barrage of objections quickened.

Q: 'Did anyone say anything "Well now you had better come along" or anything of that nature?'
A: 'Well he – Clifford – told them that they'd better go.'
Q: 'What was it he said? He said "You all better go?"'
A: 'Yes sir. I don't know whether they was scared or not.'
Q: 'Well then, they were afraid to back out then, is that it?'
A: 'Yes sir.'

The attempt was less than feeble. Philbin had made no effort at all to explain why Private Barrett might be stashing illicit ammunition in the first place. He had also run out of steam in attempting to show Private Barrett had forced other men to do his bidding. It was a limp, under-cooked and half-hearted performance. Even more damning, however, was the pointed intervention of the court president himself at this juncture, who was trying to establish why exactly so many accompanied Clifford Barrett on his armed trip back to town, when according to this witness, they didn't know where or why they were going. President Zickel was about to shoot down any remaining tatters of Private Barrett's reputation.

Quite literally holding court, the president started:

Q: 'Why did you say "Yes" if you did not know where he was going or what he was going to do?'
A: 'Well, I was scared if I didn't say "yes" what he was going to do. He had threatened me once. I thought he might git me.'
Q: 'Then you knew if it was something serious that was going to happen. Is that right?'
A: 'Yes, sir.'

Soon after, President Zickel returned to this line of questioning by asking what made Private Edwards think it was such a serious situation:

> A: 'I saw him when he was in the pub, I saw him in there talking. It seemed like to me he was standing up on something talking to some white soldiers.'
> Q: 'What was there about his manner that convinced you that it was something serious?'
> A: 'By him talking. He looked to me like he was angry.'
> Q: 'He looked angry?'
> A: 'Yes sir.'

The court president's questioning merely served to tighten the noose and it was at this point that Eresch leapt into action once more. Anxious to capitalise quickly on the president's key findings – that Edwards went along with it all because he feared an 'angry' Barrett would 'git' him – he directed Edwards to do what only members of the 581st Ordnance Ammunition Company men could do: identify the defendants on the bench as being present that night.

Indulging his trademark penchant for stage direction, he asked the witness to stand up, look around and positively identify the fourteen accused as mutineers – which Private Edwards did.

There was only one problem. An obvious addition had been made to the people Private Edwards named in his original statement and the individuals he now reeled off. Private Willis Gibbs' name had been inserted after the first statement was taken by Harry C. Poltraz, criminal investigator. Unwittingly, the defence was about to expose the bogus statement-gathering techniques used on African American soldiers in the immediate aftermath of the shooting in Launceston town square. Philbin asked first:

> Q: 'Is there any certain reason why you mention this particular person. You did not mention him originally when this incident was fresh in your mind. Was Gibbs present?'
> A: 'Sir, when I made this statement he told me if there was any more when I was making the statement, I was making it, and he

went, he started reading names off, after I had told him some
of the names, and I read off some and he read so many names
and he did not put them names down, the man who I made the
statement to.'

Q: 'But you did see Gibbs?'

A: 'Yes sir.'

Investigator Poltraz had his own private list of alleged suspects before he
interviewed Private Edwards and clearly had not been interested in taking
note of those actually named during the process. With that, there were no
further questions and the witness was excused and withdrew. Amazingly,
Defense Counsel Captain John A. Philbin had let one of the biggest
admissions about the interview procedure go by without comment. It
was a terrible blunder. For his opponent, however, this shambling cross-
examination of a critical prosecution witness made for an excellent
start. Trial Judge Advocate Eresch was on a roll. He had proved Private
Edwards was at the heart of the action with a birds'-eye view of events –
in the marching formation's second row and just ten yards from Private
Clifford Barrett. Private Edwards' court appearance also notched up
another definite confirmation that Private Clifford Barrett was one of, if
not, the principal shooter that night.

Next up was Private Albert Smith, the third 581st Ordnance
Ammunition Company man to appear and the one Eresch hoped would
be able to prove that military policemen were the intended target that
night. And not just for Private Clifford Barrett, but for all of the strong-
minded servicemen setting out from Camp Pennygillam. It was critical to
proving the mutiny charge.

Private Smith told the court that before dark he had been at camp
talking to someone casually claiming to be a Russian prince when he
became aware that a group were after passes to go into town. Much later
he saw them return. The first he knew of it was when Sergeant Austin
asked whether he could enter his tent:

'I told him … "Yes because I don't own the tent" so Sergeant
Austin he went in the tent and when he come back out he had a
box of ammunition and he goes to give the ammunition out and so

all the boys they left and went out into the street, and some more
boys come out from round about, and from by the office and they
stopped round on the side and they went down the street, so in all
that time it looked like the whole company fell out.'

Having achieved the prosecutor's first objective, by graphically describing
the uprising as involving what looked like 'the whole company', Smith
then went through the identification parade. He said he had clearly seen
Private Barrett and Sergeant Austin as toting Tommy rifles and that
Privates Carl Tennyson, Willis Gibbs, Henry Tilly and Henry McKnight
were there too, but denied seeing Private Arzie Martin.

Philbin tried to defuse the impact of this testimony by attempting to
pin Private Smith down to precise numbers involved that night. In his
first cross-examination of Private Smith, he asked:

Q: 'I believe you said it looked like about the whole Company went
along back down town?'
A: 'Yes.'
Q: 'And how many men in the Company do you know?'
A: 'Well, sir, I don't know about how many men there were there.'
Q: 'One hundred men?'
A: 'Well, sir, it was a right smart lot.'
Q: 'A big crowd?'
A: 'Yes sir.'

Unable to find any wiggle room here, the defence next picked up on a
curious anomaly.

Q: 'Did you have a rifle that night or two rifles?'
A: 'No, sir, I didn't have a rifle.'
Q: 'Didn't you have a rifle? '
A: 'No sir.'

The defence weren't about to give up quite so easily this time and moved
to resolve the matter by getting something read from Private Smith's
original statement to Investigator Harry C. Poltraz at officers' quarters

in Manton House, Dunheved Road, Launceston. Even this, Trial Judge Advocate Frank Eresch managed to turn to his advantage by insisting the entire statement be read out – thereby using this witness to score his second goal: putting military policemen standing around Launceston town square firmly in the target range for retaliatory action.

Defense Counsel Philbin read to the court that 'Carl Tennyson of our unit came along from the direction of town, and spoke to me and said 'Come on, let's go to town, and we are going to get even with those mother fucking military police.'

Private Smith went on to describe how men rallied to the battle cry. Philbin read that in addition to Clifford Barrett: 'Willis Gibbs, Arzie Martin, Henry McKnight, had O3 and A3 rifles and fired them. I was carrying an O3 and A3 rifles also. I fired one shot out of my gun towards the military policemen.'

No one seemed to notice that this statement directly contradicted what Private Smith had just told the court – namely his denial of bearing arms (let alone firing them) and of Arzie Martin's involvement. It was left unprobed. Once more the prosecution had put another building block in its own case and simultaneously outmanoeuvred the opponents.

Next, Eresch redirected the examination to get Private Smith to identify the culprits. Despite describing nearly everyone as turning out to strike revenge in Launceston the previous month, there were eight on trial that day whom Private Smith could neither recognise nor place. After naming Privates Clifford Barrett, Henry Tilly, Willis Gibbs, Charlie Geddies, Carl Tennyson and Sergeant Austin, his identification parade went as follows:

> 'I did not see him … I did not see that boy right there, I didn't see him and I didn't see him … I don't remember seeing him … And that boy sitting there, I don't remember seeing him there … I saw him and that other soldier sitting right there, I didn't see him, neither the one sitting next to him …'

Not even being able to place half of those standing trial at the scene said little for Private Smith's reliability as a witness. From what happened next, however, it was hard to believe that anyone – identified or not by Private Smith – understood the gravity of their plight.

For when court took its first break of the day, as if by magic, the seriousness of the situation dissipated into thin air as cigarette smoke rose, whispers became outright chatter and even laughter echoed around the court's four walls. Some soldiers turned around to the press pack to borrow morning newspapers to see what had been written so far. Pointing out headlines and comparing notes, newspapers changed hands repeatedly and Defense Counsel Captain John A. Philbin strode up and down, all the while smoking and laughing with his clients.

But the prosecution team looked set to continue its winning streak as soon as court resumed ten minutes on with an even more senior and credible witness: Staff Sergeant Kenneth Blanchett, of the 581st Ordnance Ammunition Company. He told the familiar story of elusive night passes being tantalisingly within reach of his company, and then withdrawn at the last minute because they lacked the correct dress uniform. Sergeant Blanchett described how even the first pub they visited was packed full of white GIs who prickled visibly and volubly at their presence:

'We walks inside there and all the gang of white soldiers sitting at a table and they said "That way out" and we didn't pay no attention to them and went on to the bar, and the barman told us it was crowded there and said "Go round the other wise. You get served just the same." So we all goes round the other side, and starts drinking this beer.'

But they didn't stop long, leaving a few minutes later for another pub in pursuit of gin drops. It was here, at this second pub, after 'the ladies starts giving us out some gin, and we all starts drinking beer and this gin stuff' that a fight broke out between two white soldiers at the side. During the fisticuffs, 'somebody says "It is not any of your soldiers" so we goes outside and Clifford Barrett brought us all together and starts asking us to stick together', to which they all agreed. Sergeant Blanchett reckoned up to eighteen soldiers stuck together with Clifford Barrett that night on the return armed trip into town.

Sergeant Blanchett was able to name eleven men, including himself. He denied the men were forced to join in – or that he had heard the shots fired at all since he was running away at the time. For the third time that morning, the president weighed in, this time to ask specifically whether Private Barrett had directed soldiers back to camp. Interestingly during his affirmation of this, Sergeant Blanchett said 'it was spoken that "If you are scared you can get out"', which somewhat scuppered the defence's argument of coercion. More devastation came moments later when Sergeant Blanchett denied being fired up that evening by anything other than an age-old ingredient:

Q: 'You were excited at the time?'
A: 'No sir, we wasn't excited. Just drinking, that's all.'
Q: 'And you did it just because Private Barrett asked you to?'
A: 'Because the gang agreed to, sir.'

Nobody pointed out this detracted from the mutiny argument. Sergeant Blanchett was excused, completing the impressive quartet of witnesses who were actively involved in rioting, but having turned army's evidence, were now immune from prosecution themselves. Sergeant Blanchett departed, making way for the company's most senior 581st Ordnance Ammunition Company man to return to court: Captain James Bosson, the commanding officer.

A stalwart of the company for thirteen months, Captain Bosson was temporarily detached elsewhere on 26 September for extra duty. He testified that on the night he was away, only one soldier, Private Clifford Barrett, had a valid pass and that the men had been subjected to the strictest rules and regulations since coming to Launceston on 21 September. As early as 3.00pm that first day, barely after claiming their allocated tents, Captain Bosson gathered all his NCOs to tell them the company was restricted to camp because they did not have 'the proper uniform' and had not yet been orientated. Taking a roll call to ensure all men were present, they were then sent out to spread the word to their various squads and platoons. To ensure there was absolutely no confusion, this came after the entire company had been told earlier that day.

Captain Bosson confirmed that this order banning men from leaving the camp was still in place on the night of the shooting. Responding to Eresch's questioning, he went on to describe that members had also been warned specifically about the use and carrying of knives, although not weapons in general: 'It has been a standing order ever since our early days of training for the men not to carry knives, especially knives with a 3 inch blade or longer.'

In fact the men had no access to these knives on the night of 26 September as they had been confiscated at the company's staging area in Yeovil, Somerset, and did not arrive back to the 581st Ordnance Ammunition Company until the day after the shooting.

Just as Eresch was pulling his case together, Philbin leapt up to catapult the issue of their perpetual camp restriction into the mix. During his cross-examination of the witness, he established the company's 176 men had been restricted for 'a total of about eight weeks' by 26 September. None of them had the blouses that bought access to the town – so neither was there any indication of when or if this prolonged restriction might be lifted. Added to all this, there were no alternative recreation facilities at camp as the nights were drawing in. 'The men had some of that [baseball] equipment and could use it when they were off duty, however, we worked in the magazine so long that we never had any off-duty hours with light sufficient to play.'

This effective denial of 'play' was crucial in the narrative of what 581st Ordnance Ammunition Company men did in Launceston when they finally broke out. It was a deciding factor and had eventually been highlighted by Philbin. But before he could put two and two together for the court, his opponent butted in again with a mundane administrative inquiry – a stocktake of the men's rifles. It was a tactical ploy to stop the defence from shooting holes in its case.

Checking serial numbers for the weapons allocated to each man, Eresch established the rifles and carbines were displayed prominently across the top of men's bunks because 'we had no secure place in which to lock them up, and therefore each man retained possession of his own weapon.' Rifles were distributed in Fort Sill, Oklahoma in August and the carbines were issued at the staging area, Camp Patrick Henry, later that month. The last weapon inspection took place just before they disembarked in the United Kingdom and showed each man to have a gun although three 'had guns whose serial numbers did not agree with our list.' The trio of guns were confiscated and given to the ship's purser. No ammunition had been picked up in the last inspection, on 6 September, and none had been issued since, so to all intents and purposes the men of the 581st were ammunition-less. Despite the company's somewhat misleading name, Philbin's questioning revealed that there was 'none whatsoever' ammunition in the unit.

Captain Bosson was dismissed and when court re-opened at 1.35pm, after lunch, Trial Judge Advocate Frank Eresch was nearly ready to bring his case to a close. There was just a little housekeeping to complete. Three officers who had arrested various 581st men as they returned to camp appeared to describe their night's work: First Lieutenant Robert E. Cohn, Lieutenant Ariel W. Glenn and First Lieutenant Francis H. Blondgren, who went on to spectacularly mis-identify Private Geddies for the court; this howler was made all the worse because of the soldier's distinctive freckled face and scarring on his right hand. When asked to point him out, the court record shows:

Q: 'Lieutenant Blondgren, would you step to the rear and observe the accused who are there and state to the court which of those accused, if any is Geddies, the man you saw there that night?'
A: 'The second man over here (indicating Private Manning).'[7]

It seemed an appropriate enough error on which to finalise the prosecution's case and a double blow for the hapless Geddies, whose own statement had not been read to him, despite him being illiterate, early in the investigation. Moments before resting his case, Eresch tidied up a few administrative details such as correcting dates on charge sheets and clarifying that men referred to by various other nicknames were one and the same as read on the charge sheets. He then submitted prosecution exhibits C to K – and it was done.

The free world's press had spectator seats as Trial Judge Advocate Eresch tried to mould an ironclad tale of rogue soldiers set on murdering the men who policed them – with near-fatal consequences. Over the course of a day-and-a-half, he had somehow overridden countless worrying mistakes such as multiple misidentification of culprits; pivotal words inserted wrongly into statements; and illiterate soldiers not knowing what they were alleged to have said. Additionally, too many testimonies were proved to be sworn incorrectly, if at all, and a singularly unorthodox way of name-taking by investigators had been uncovered.

Eresch had taken it all in his stride, instead hinging his case on evidence from four 581st Ordnance Ammunition Company men who 'were part of the gang' that night, but crucially with whom he had cut a deal.

This pact enabled him to paint an 'angry' menacing ringleader, thirteen willing accomplices – all of whom were in direct contravention of orders restricting them to camp – and a consistent sequence of how events escalated that evening into their prime objective of *gitting* their targets. Eresch had kept on the front foot by working the courtroom and shutting down any semblance of defence or counter-argument when his opponent stood to challenge. Investigators' mistakes and the immorality of restriction (and dearth of alternative recreational camp facilities) were muted simply by his impressive gamesmanship and the defence's timid cross-examination. But the defence's hour had come; their time for limbering was over. Now was the moment to put the accuseds' version of events. Would men of the 581st Ordnance Ammunition Company finally get their chance to be heard?

Chapter 13

Act I: Defending the Defenceless

Rumours about what might have happened in a small Cornish town square had been circulating for nearly three weeks now. In Launceston itself, townspeople were baffled as to what had really taken place in the dark that evening, and why. Tales of Launceston police picking up forty-odd rounds of carbine ammunition abounded. People raged at the danger and damage inflicted. 'They were angry about it. You know what Cornish people are like – very protective of their things. Everyone was talking about it. Cornish people are very good at that too,' said Celia Rolling, then a 15-year-old schoolgirl.[1] Peter Brown, 10 years old and tucked up safely in bed while mutiny unravelled around him, remembers his home town jungle drums beating hard. Press speculation at national and local levels was reaching fever pitch too, especially since the prosecution case began in court. The past day-and-a-half had showcased hours of fascinating testimony and moments of high drama too. Now it was time for the defence to disprove the prosecution case and put together its own narrative and explanation for actions of men from the 581st Ordnance Ammunition Company. The stakes could not have been higher.

Gamely, Defense Counsel Captain John A. Philbin stood up. Surely there was something he could do. The question was what? Clearly large numbers of men had defied orders and broken their restriction to camp to venture into Launceston on 26 September 1943. They had armed themselves at some stage – and then used those weapons to damage people and property. However, that was not necessarily mutiny – or murder. If the facts did not fit the crimes, could Philbin prove it? It was obvious he had some ideas about how to attack. Chiefly he needed to expose gaps in the prosecution's argument and widen them further. But would it be enough to deliver the verdict he needed? The devil would be in the detail, his delivery and how well he handled these two variables. And that was before Trial Advocate Eresch had been factored into things.

Philbin started by targeting those most responsible for the inconsistencies: the investigators. Captain James E. Stevenson, Assistant Inspector General was the first witness and Philbin started by reading out the trio of statements he had taken from Sergeant Henry Austin, Sergeant Rupert Hughes and Private James Lindsey immediately after the shooting. The biggest fractures in the prosecution's argument were over precisely who was involved. But they needed to be forced right open.

Captain Philbin started with someone prosecutors felt was key to events on 26 September: Sergeant Henry Austin, 23. Only testimony from fellow company members (now working for the prosecutors) put him at Clifford Barrett's right hand with central responsibility for rallying mutineers and distributing ammunition. His statement, Exhibit 1, however, was singularly robust in rebutting his alleged role and involvement. The court heard the statement begin with Privates Shaw, Ewing and Tennyson denying even seeing Austin at all that night. Only Private Geddies stated the opposite. The words "Austin had said 'We are all together'" was handwritten on the typed statement. Continuing, supposedly in Austin's own words, the statement described how he and Sergeant Blanchett had visited a pub in town and returned to camp, only to be disturbed later by reports of trouble and the planned armed return.

'I went with them. I followed the rest to town. I didn't issue any ammunition. I work in the office. The others work in the depot. Why should I be issuing ammunition to them when they handle it every day? I didn't have any gun. When the shooting started I ran … I started back to camp. I met Tennyson and Shaw and also saw McKnight … talking to a girl … We went back to camp. That is all I know about it.'

Philbin then moved on to Exhibit 2 – the statement of Austin's fellow Sergeant and so-called mutineer Rupert Hughes, 22. In it, Hughes stated he neither saw Private Arzie Martin nor gave him ammunition, ending: 'I did not swear to the statement made to the CID people although I did sign it.' Lastly, Captain Philbin read out Exhibit 3, the statement of Private James H. Lindsey, 22, which began by putting it on the record that Privates Ewing, Blake and Corporal Joseph had not seen him among the mutineers.

'I was talking with some English civilian and other coloured soldiers. I could see the firing from the gunshot. I was not with that crowd. I did not fire the gun … When I came back to camp I met a jeep coming out of the gate and I gave my gun to the lieutenant.'

This trio of very different statements were linked by one fact – they effectively denied their role as leading mutineers. Philbin was very precise with his first witness, Investigator Stevenson, the man responsible for producing all three statements, by asking quite specifically:

Q: 'Were these men properly sworn?'
A: 'Yes'.
Q: 'In accordance with the notation on the statements were they properly sworn?'
A: 'Yes, sir they were.'
Q: 'In what manner?'
A: 'I had them rise, raise their right hand, and I read the oath to them, "Do you swear to tell the truth, the whole truth and nothing but the truth so help you God" and they said "I do"'.
Q: 'Did you tell them about their rights?'
A: 'Yes.'

But it was not how his interviewees remembered it. Defenders were left in a stand-off, a time-honoured case of Investigator Stevenson's word against 581st Ordnance Ammunition Company men. Holes in the prosecution case existed but widening them further was not going to be straightforward. With that simple, conclusive 'yes', Investigator Stevenson was excused. Defense Counsel decided not to delay to wait for the next scheduled criminal investigator witness. Instead he called upon Sergeant Rupert Hughes and Private Carl Tennyson, of the 581st Ordnance Ammunition Company, to testify. The subject of his questioning, however, was the same.

Following up exactly where he had left off with his previous witness, Investigator Stevenson, Philbin wasted no time in getting to the swearing of statements.

Q: 'Now Sergeant Hughes, when you made this original statement, just how were you sworn as to the truth of the statement?'

A: 'Sir, do you mean to the captain that just left, or to Mr Poltraz?'

Q: 'Well, when you made the original statement. You made that to whom?'

A: 'To Sergeant Poltraz.'

Q: 'The next morning?'

A: 'Yes, sir.'

Q: 'And just how did you go about swearing it?'

A: 'Well, the next morning he had the statements on the table, and he called us up, and he said "Is this your signature?" And we said "yes, sir" and he signed his name to it.'

Q: 'Did he ask you to raise your right hand?'

A: 'No, sir.'

Q: 'Was the whole of the group of you there?'

A: 'There was just six of us, sir ... Myself ... Shaw, Geddies, Blake, Ewing and Tennyson, sir.'

Clearly the 581st's defence was trying to exploit a point of legal technicality involving several of the accused. Keen to continue, Captain Philbin next called in Private Carl Tennyson.

Q: 'Who did you make your original statement to?'

A: 'Sergeant – he was a plain-clothes detective sir.'

Q: 'Did he swear you?'

A: 'No, sir.'

Q: 'When were you sworn?'

A: 'I was not sworn.'

Q: 'Were you taken before anyone? Any officer?'

A: 'Yes, sir.'

Q: 'When?'

A: 'The night after I made my statement, the next morning he took me before a captain.'

Q: 'And did the captain have you – did he tell you to raise your right hand?'

A: 'He did not.'

Q: 'What did he say?'
A: 'He asked me was this my signature, and I said "yes, sir", so he
wrote something down on it, so then he called the next man.'
Q: 'Were you the only one of the coloured boys present in the room
at the time?'
A: 'No sir.'
Q: 'Who else was there?'
A: 'There was Shaw, Blake, Rupert Hughes and myself and Tom
Ewing, sir.'
Q: 'May I suggest Geddies?'
A: 'Yes, sir, Charlie Geddies.'

There were now two detailed, plausible accounts from soldiers testifying that numerous witness statements were not sworn correctly. It should have been easy to exploit a simple legal loophole in the defendants' favour. Asked directly, however, the previous investigator had denied there being any procedural mishaps. In this segregated, *Jim Crow* world of an army, was there any point countering his assertions? There were no prizes for guessing who would be believed by a panel expressly made up of white army officers. Perhaps that was why, instead of making a point or explaining this line of thinking directly after hearing first-hand experience contradicting the investigators, Captain Philbin just moved on.

It was worryingly late in the legal process, but for the first time the defence team was about to introduce something original, new and critical to this court martial: an actual motive for mutiny in Cornwall. In marched Sergeant Charles W. Bury, of F Company, 115th Infantry, 29th Division, to provide an entirely novel twist by talking not about the events of Sunday, 26 September, but the preceding evening when he was on military police duty in town. His testimony alone would lay bare the state of US Army relations with each other – and their British hosts.

Sergeant Bury described how on that Saturday night he and his military police colleagues had been busy sending African American soldiers illicitly in town back to camp:

'The colonel issued orders that no coloured fellows was supposed to
be out of camp, they didn't have passes, they were all confined, so

we had our orders to chase any of them back to camp. If they was seen in town they didn't have passes there, so we checked all the boys, every one we seen, and told them the best thing they could do was hop back to camp before they got themselves into trouble.'

Even so, trouble was coming. Sergeant Bury went on to describe that later on, at the town hall dance they were policing:

'Five coloured fellows came into the dance; the officer of the military police asked them for their passes and they did not have any, so he told them they had to leave, and they did not like it, so he went and got the money back for them and gave the money to them, and they took a good old time going out, and they got outside and this one fellow kept hollering. He said: "If you touch me I will give you what I got in my pocket." So I told them they had better get on up the road before we had to lock them up, so – he was one that was in front – he said "We will get even with you, you wait and see." That was Saturday sir.'

It was a detail without parallel – and obviously what Defense Counsel Philbin had been angling for when he had repeatedly pushed Captain Richard Scott during his cross-examination in court the previous day. For the first time a powerful precedent for trouble had been established between men of the 581st Ordnance Ammunition Company and white 115th Infantry military policemen some twenty-four hours before the shooting. Sergeant Bury just happened to witness both this and the final catalyst the next day, Sunday, 26 September. Because that following evening he happened to be in Launceston again, off duty, and drinking with his girlfriend in the West Gate pub, Philbin asked:

Q: 'Anything unusual occur on that particular evening? Did anything occur?'
A: 'Yes sir. There was a mob of eighteen coloured fellows and five English soldiers came in the West Gate, sir, about 9 o'clock, and the man refused to sell them drinks, and when they walked in a couple of American soldiers got up and walked out, and about four of five of them stood up and stayed standing until they left.'

Quite clearly, British soldiers were very much part of the action that night. Witness statements and oral testimony were littered with reports of 'English' soldiers talking, socialising and drinking with African American troops throughout the evening in Launceston. But this testimony put them solidly side by side as the black soldiers were refused drinks, asked to move or ordered back to camp. And it was displays of solidarity against American racism like this that illustrated fault lines in Anglo–American relations so perfectly and precisely why this case had everyone on the run.

Philbin continued:

Q: 'What else happened?'
A: 'The men came out there behind the counter and refused to sell them something to drink, and they all started mumbling to themselves and drifted out and after they left, one more round of drinks and the man closed the place down and wouldn't sell no more beer.'

The African American soldiers had been told they would be served only if they crossed over to the non-white bar – as indicated ominously by the 115th Infantry soldiers standing up to make sure of it that night. The threat of racial violence was extreme enough to close one pub. Less than an hour later it would paralyse the whole town. But this was not what Trial Judge Advocate Frank Eresch wanted to come to light as he rose to cross-examine Sergeant Bury. His real intent was to rewind to Saturday's dance and turn up the heat on the accused. Digging for dirt, he was set on introducing murderous mutineers. However, the rule of unintended consequences was about to kick in. Eresch was to reveal something else – the type of bully-boy tactics so casually used to police black Americans – and more besides.

Sergeant Bury told the court:

'We was hurrying them all up the road – there were five of them, and the four military policemen and the lieutenant and two regular military policemen [from the 29th Division] – and we was hurrying them up the road, telling them they had better get back up the road before they got into trouble, and one of them said: "White boys, if you touch me I will give you what I got in my pocket." He got his hand in his pocket, and two English Royal Engineers started butting in and said we was picking on them, and we told them they had better keep out of it or we would get the police for them.'

Bury had opened a Pandora's box. Significantly, he had shown it wasn't merely the restriction of troops to camp that was unfair; its method of enforcement was too, exemplified by the chivvying of five weaponless servicemen by seven armed military police. It was precisely the kind of performance that so enraged British bystanders and prompted them to get stuck in on the African Americans' behalf. But it was the wider implications of Sergeant Bury's testimony that were truly revelatory. This was the first open reference to the parlous state of race relations between 'coloured' and 'white' Americans in Launceston – and on which side the Brits were. Here they were again at the heart of things, not just with 581st men, but verbally fighting for them. 'English soldiers' had demonstrably backed the obvious underdog on two successive nights in the town now.

Suddenly, the protracted questions in court the day before were explained: they had been geared at establishing British intervention in the whole affair. Everyone on the crowded press benches already knew it was happening throughout the UK. This so-called mutiny in Launceston was a microcosm of the macro-aggression being played out all over the country; this was the real special relationship in action. It was why they were all here.

The next appearance, after Sergeant Bury finished his testimony, was from Private James L. Gains, of the 581st Ordnance Ammunition Company, whose testimony was short – and none too sweet. He described how his company had been restricted 'for a month' in the United Kingdom and before that 'fifty some odd days' in the United States. If that prolonged restriction wasn't enough, the prospect of it being lifted seemed even longer. Simply no-one in the 581st Ordnance Ammunition Company had the dress shirts needed to unlock cherished passes into town. 'Didn't no-one … have a blouse unless he borrowed one from a soldier in another outfit,' he said. Instead they were kept in the camp.

Q: 'Now when you men had some time off and were restricted to camp area, what did you do?'

A: 'We didn't have no time off.'

Q: 'Well, if you had some time off in the evening, did you have anything special you could do around the area?'

A: 'No, sir.'

It was an appalling indictment of out-of-hours life for African Americans in an army organised and run according to *Jim Crow* rules. But on 16 October 1943 it didn't even merit a comment from the team defending those so drastically affected by it.

Instead, the defence was going to have yet another crack at undermining the validity of statements taken by the investigators now at Paignton police station. Cue Sergeant Marvin F. Richardson, of the Investigation Division, Provost Marshal General Detachment, who had caused a 'sensation' the day before when he couldn't identify the witness he had interviewed for the court. He had also faced a barrage of questions concerning the veracity of his statement-taking and swearing of statements. Still, after finally arriving in court, he now only made it to the stand again after the defence won a brief stand-off with Trial Judge Advocate Frank Eresch who withdrew his objection to his two statements being read aloud to the court: firstly, Exhibit 4, the signed PMG Form 16 for Private Henry W. Tilly and then Exhibit 5 from Private Henry McKnight.

Both former farmhands from Texas denied even leaving camp on 26 September 1943. Private Tilly's statement said:

> 'I shot 'craps' from about 7.30pm until about 8.30pm … and stayed around the tent until about 9.30pm. I then left and went to the mess hall and went to sleep. I awoke about 4.00am and made the fires. I did not know anything about any trouble or shooting down town.'

Similarly, Private McKnight denied leaving the camp at all, claiming 'I was awoke sometime around 6.00am the next morning by my platoon sergeant. I went to reveille. At the mess that morning was the first time I knew anything about any shooting downtown.'

Having read the two statements aloud, Defense Counsellor Philbin asked Sergeant Richardson one more time whether he had warned the men of their rights after making the statements. Answering 'yes', Richardson was excused. That was the level of interrogation facing

Sergeant Richardson. For the second US Army investigator, appearing in Paignton police court had been as easy as pie.

Next came colleague Sergeant C. Poltraz, also from the Provost Marshal's Investigation Division, who was asked to identify statements he took from Privates James Manning and Willis Gibbs before they were read out in court. Private Manning was adamant he had:

> 'performed my usual duties at the rail head during the day and after returning to camp at about 5.30pm I stayed on the post the rest of the evening. I went to bed … About 6.00am the next day, I was placed in custody by Major Partin. I don't know why.'[2]

Private Gibbs admitted going into town, albeit on an official pass, where he was refused a drink at the White Horse. At a second pub he said he met Clifford Barrett and a few others but left Launceston before any shooting started.

Less than twenty-four hours earlier, Investigator Poltraz had been accused of using unfamiliar words and replicating phrases in identikit soldier statements. It had also been revealed he failed to read final statements to an illiterate witness, leaving him unsure of what he was supposed to have said. This was in addition to a whole raft of other complaints centring on inadequate or non-existent swearing of statements. But when the defence team had him where they wanted, Sergeant Poltraz was asked only to identify the two statements before being excused and withdrawing. It was as underwhelming as that. All the investigators had to do was deny everything – there was no follow-up or plan B in place to tackle lying or the misremembering of facts.

The defence team's fortunes were mixed at this stage. Captain Philbin had established the true and underlying cause of the shooting and in so doing revealed the rawness of race relations in the US Army. He had flagged the injustice of restriction and policing for African American soldiers fighting under *Jim Crow* and the natural alliance they had with British civilians and soldiers. But despite all efforts to shed doubt on the efficacy and legality of statements, the investigators' repeated denials were not making it easy. It was time to make a quantum leap and the next witness, Private Carl M. Tennyson, of 581st Ordnance Ammunition Company, was quite possibly the man to start the run up for it.

Chapter 14

Act II: Unfinished Business

Private Tennyson braced himself for his court appearance. He might not know it yet, but he was about to take the place by storm merely by describing his role in events. According to his sworn statement narrated by Trial Judge Advocate Eresch the previous day, Tennyson was central to everything on 26 September and very much part of Private Barrett's gang of mutineers from the get-go. But what was penned in Investigator Richardson's neat cursive hand and read out unchallenged less than twenty-four hours earlier would nowhere resemble the contents of what he was about to disclose in his live court performance. In Tennyson's second appearance for the defence in as many days, he begged to differ from the official version. It might just be the game-changer.

Elaborating on his previous appearance, Private Tennyson told how he was in Launceston that night 'mostly hunting for my girl' but definitely not with Private Clifford Barrett; so much so that he hot-footed it to the fish stand after he happened to 'peeps' him in a second pub. Tennyson went on:

> 'Me and a couple of British soldiers we go back … through the heart of the town, and I gets almost to the heart of the town I could hear bullets scooting along and hitting buildings, so I lies down. Me and the soldiers we laid down, so I curls up by a big rock. During the time I curled up there I hear somebody says "Give me your gun." It was a military policeman told Private Shaw to give him his gun, and the shooting was still going on, so when I come up there I ask him, I say "What's the matter, is it a fight?" The military policeman says "Yes" and said to lay down. I saw Shaw, he was already lying down, and I said "What's the matter, Shaw, are you hurt?" And he said "No."

The military policeman had two guns in his hand, and I said, "Let
me have one of them and I will help you shoot back" and he said,
"No, lay down. You will be protected." So I laid down and the firing
began to ring out again.'

When it finished the military police departed and Privates Shaw and
Tennyson started to walk back to camp. At the town hall they bumped
into Sergeant Austin and Private Henry McKnight who 'was talking to
a couple of girls'. Austin told him, 'We had better hurry up and go back
there, there has been some shooting going on, the military police are
picking up everyone.'[1] The next day he was arrested.

The impact of Private Tennyson's court appearance was electrifying
because it diametrically opposed what was written in Sergeant
Richardson's statement – namely that he had followed Private Barrett
as trouble began on 26 September. That statement was beginning to
sound suspiciously like many of those recorded by the same sergeant.
The court had heard both versions so the difference between the two
accounts could not be more acute. Press observers were quick to pick
up on the discrepancies noting that 'several of the men gave evidence
that statements which they had signed and which had been submitted
by the prosecution were not as related by them.'[2] The court could not
afford to ignore the implications. Having taken the stand, under oath, to
be questioned by his own counsel, Private Tennyson was now about to
be grilled not only by the trial judge advocate, but the president himself,
in what would be the longest appearance that any defence witness would
make. Once more, it would reveal more pertinent defence material, this
time by exposing, in gloriously colourful detail, just how interrogation
worked to elicit witness statements.

Trial Judge Advocate Eresch's starter questions promptly established
that Private Tennyson lacked clear vision – 'it was a blackout, sir, and
you can't see, unless you are close up on a man – I'd say at least 2ft', had
heard twenty or so shots and saw a military policeman disarm Private
Shaw. Asked directly to clarify, he said he saw just Private Shaw by the
war memorial and Sergeant Austin and Private McKnight on the way
back to camp.

Q: 'Did you ever talk to anyone about this incident before?'
A: 'No, sir, no-one except the plain clothes man who was there.'
Q: 'Who was that?'
A: 'This agent I think, agent, some kind of Federal Agent I believe.'

Having successfully identified the agent as in fact the recently excused Sergeant Marvin F. Richardson, of the Provost Marshal General's Detachment, Private Tennyson went on to give an extraordinary account of his interview in the shooting's aftermath:

Q: 'What did you tell him when you had a conversation with him about this?'
A: 'Well I told him the next morning, he asked me where was I last night, before the fighting was going on. I told him I was in bed. He says "No you was not." He said. "Now come on, I have seven or eight papers on my desk and each one has the same tale." He says "Who was the rank leaders of the fight?" I say "I don't know." He says "Was Austin and Barrett the rank leaders?" So he wrote something down. I don't know what it was, and then he started calling names. He had some more papers. He said "Did you see—" – I think it was Manning and Martin and Blake – I think he said – "did I see them in town?" I said "No" so he writes down, and that is all I know about it.'
Q: 'But you signed something, didn't you?'
A: 'Yes, I signed it.'
Q: 'Did you read what you signed?'
A: 'No sir, I didn't read it. I didn't pay any attention. I had nothing to be afraid of.'
Q: 'You didn't read what you signed?'
A: 'No, sir.'

The trial judge advocate handed Private Tennyson the signed statement and checked it was his signature, which it was. Eresch could not process the monumental difference in what he had just been told under oath, and the contents of his signed statement.

Q: 'Do you now desire to tell the court that you did not read this statement, it was not read to you, you did not tell Richardson any of these statements that are on it, is that right?'

A: 'No, sir. I didn't tell Richardson.'

Q: 'You didn't tell him anything?'

A: 'No, sir.'

Q: 'But you just signed it?'

A: 'I just signed it.'

Trial Judge Eresch swiftly moved to identify that Private Tennyson had seen Privates Edwards, Manning, Barrett and Martin before the shooting. Private Tennyson only 'thought' he had seen Privates Martin and Blake but denied outright seeing Private Lindsey. He said once again he had eaten fish at the stand and not stayed in the first or second pub because 'There wasn't none of my friends … in there.' But the trial judge advocate was like a dog with a bone. He could not leave the assertion that Tennyson was not part of the gang asked by Private Barrett to stick together, return to camp and exact armed retaliation.

Q: 'Then if you signed a statement in which you said, or which was on that statement which you signed, "We all went outside. Out there Barrett asked us to all stick together. We all agreed. We went from this back to camp. Sergeant Austin and Private Barrett told us all to get our guns. I did not get mine." You don't recall telling Richardson that?'

A: 'No, sir, I did not tell him that. He asked me and I said I didn't know, so he writes something down, I couldn't see what it was.'

Eresch's downright disbelief is still almost palpable in the decades-old court manuscript. The trial judge advocate manically went through Private Tennyson's spoken testimony with a fine toothcomb, establishing that he had dropped to his knees and crawled to the war memorial at the first sounds of gunfire and ended up listening to bullets 'hitting the buildings' with Private Shaw and a military policeman. Private Tennyson also remembered seeing Privates Barrett and Gibbs' passes that evening 'as I was getting my rations.'

It was also too much for Court President Raymond Zickel to comprehend. At this point he chipped in to double-check that Private Tennyson knew the prosecution's witness, Private Smith. He did. President Zickel followed up by asking whether Private Tennyson had seen the prosecution witness that night in town. Private Tennyson maintained he had not seen him. Pushed on whether he had seen Private Barrett, the witness agreed, but stuck to his guns and said they had not spoken. With that, Private Tennyson was excused and resumed his seat with his fellow accused. The soldier had provided an entirely new account of his role in what had happened that night and shed further fresh light on the interrogation and statement-gathering process. Moreover, Private Tennyson had maintained his line throughout, regardless of what questions had been flung at him. Surely this was what Eresch had feared might happen from the beginning. The prosecution team was clearly vulnerable.

Another soldier identified by the same 581st Ordnance Ammunition Company prosecution witness, Private Smith, was called next. Private Henry Tilly, a father-of-one from DeWitt County, Texas, had joined up at 16 and held good records in both civilian and army life. In the statement he made to Sergeant Richardson, he swore he had slept in the mess hall that night – as he was responsible for keeping the place warm – and had not been into town. Private Tilly was intransigent on the point. He told his own counsel under oath in front of the court: 'I was fireman … and rather than get up and leave the tent early in the morning for the mess hall, and there wasn't any locks on the doors and we stayed there, one of us firemen, in the mess hall.' The mess was 150 yards from the camp's entrance, he said, and he woke at 4.00am to make the fires, unaware of the night's commotion.

Immediately, Eresch sprang. He was anxious to outsmart this witness from the very outset and prove him a liar. This was a crucial ploy to maintain the reputation of his own witness, Private Smith, who had said both Privates Tennyson and Tilly were there – something they both resolutely denied.

Q: 'Will you describe to the court, Launceston, England?'
A: 'I have never been to Launceston. I don't know how Launceston look.'

Q: 'You have never been there?'
A: 'No, sir.'
Q: 'Have you ever been away from Camp Pennygillam?'
A: 'No sir, I have not.'

Hopes dashed, Eresch asked directly about Private Tilly's relationship with the prosecution witness, Private Smith. Private Tilly confirmed he knew the prosecution witness, Private Smith, but doggedly denied seeing him in Launceston that night.

Q: 'You heard Private Smith testify that he saw you in the company street, do you not?'
A: 'Yes, sir, I heard him.'
Q: 'He was mistaken about that, was he?'
A: 'Yes, sir, he was.'

The fourteen accused men's defence team had made nearly all the arguments it could. Almost as an afterthought, their lawyer, Defence Counsel Captain John A. Philbin, said another accused, Private Willis Gibbs, wished to be sworn in. His purpose in doing so was soon evident: almost immediately he produced an official pass into town 'signed by Lieutenant Songy, sir.' Trial Judge Advocate Eresch leapt to his feet, objecting on pretty much any grounds he could find, including the facts 'it is not dated and it does not show that it has anything, is not pertaining to the incident now being considered before the court, as pertaining to that day or any other day for which that pass was good.' However, the president inspected it and overruled Eresch's objection.

Private Gibbs testified how he went into town on his official pass, was refused service at The White Horse, but met up with Private Harry Wall and Clifford Barrett in the second pub for 'a glass of beer.' The private alleged he returned to camp and changed into fatigues for work the next day before shooting started but was woken up at 4.00am. The ever-vigilant trial judge advocate asked whether Private Gibbs had heard the prosecution witness Private Smith name him as one of the gang – and whether he heard his own statement read to the court.

Q: 'You say you heard it on that statement?'

A: 'Yes sir.'

Q: 'But you are now telling the court that you were not in this crowd?'

A: 'I wasn't sir.'[3]

The defence's job was nearly done. It had shown that much of the critical prosecution evidence rested on a bizarre identity parade disputed by every defendant appearing in court that afternoon. Those who admitted being in town had not seen the prosecution witness, Private Smith, who said they were there and given descriptions of their roles. Nor had those who denied leaving camp in the first place seen him.

Captain Philbin's chance to dismantle the prosecution case was over and it was time to finalise his own version of events for closing arguments. Recess was called. Late in the closing light of that autumn afternoon, the court martial was at a critical juncture. The case was moments from being handed over to the watching army panel, party to the entire dramatic legal procedure so far. These ten men alone would decide upon the innocence or guilt of the fourteen accused – and their eventual fate.

Philbin was about to bring this crux-point closer still. Just five of the men he represented had raised their voices during the past two days. Was their evidence – among everything else he had established in the past three-and-a-half hours – enough to persuade the army panel's mind? About to face Trial Judge Advocate Frank P. Eresch for their final exchange, there was still time and opportunity enough to besmirch the prosecution, or at least implant enough uncertainty to ensure the burden of proof could not be met. Philbin needed his closing argument to seek out and expose the prosecution's Achilles' heel for the watching public. This required wit, pith and determination. The only problem was his counterpart Trial Judge Advocate Eresch was aiming for the exact same.

Chapter 15

Closing Arguments

As this extraordinary psychodrama was playing out within Paignton police court's four walls, one stand-out feature towered above everything else for the British audience: its glamorous Americana. This inimitable quality, spelling red-carpet movie allure for rapt readers, was rapidly becoming a national talking point. Reporters writing for communities from Land's End to John o'Groats were hooked, comparing the legal action they were following to that of a suspenseful Hollywood movie. Struck by the number of theatrical 'objections', lawyers thrillingly 'spinning' around on witnesses and armed personnel bestriding the courtroom, it was as if they were spectators at something fantastically make-believe. The gritty reality was in fact more dramatic than anything film directors could dream up: in real life, court action over the past forty-eight hours had been loaded heavily to favour the prosecution and members of the British press had been completely hoodwinked if they believed anything else.

In the final analysis, this was never destined to be a match between equals. For a start, the prosecution was headed by more senior ranking army officers – two majors – compared to the defence team's captains. This additional experience and rank showed. Eresch's legal presentation outlining the prosecution case read persuasively, its arguments well thought out and reflected in a super-smooth flowing court manuscript. His experience allowed him to stay the course and not be distracted by his opponent's challenges. Prosecutors also had the lion's share of court time to make that case – dominating roughly 10 out of 14 court hours. Trial Judge Advocate Frank P. Eresch had twenty witnesses, more than double the defence's tally, to make his point. Most of them came from the 115th Infantry or 29th Division, but there were also two British civilians and four 581st Ordnance Ammunition Company members who were themselves part of the action on 26 September and proved pivotal once aligned to the prosecution's side. In addition to these live appearances in Paignton, the prosecution team used ten full statements which they read out to further persuade the court of its argument.

In contrast, the odds seemed stacked against the defence team. Defense Counsel Captain John Philbin and assistant Captain Alvin E. Ottum were ready for their day in court, but it turned out to be only an afternoon. Within just four hours they were preparing to make closing arguments. In the intervening time they had read seven statements and called nine witnesses – not even half the number used by their opponents. Interestingly, they had invoked witness-stand appearances from all three inspectors involved in statement-gathering, one 115th Infantry military policeman and just over a third of the accused – five 581st Ordnance Ammunition Company men – who stood and spoke up for themselves. Much of what the defence team's line-up was saying was good and made significant wider points – such as the true cause of mutiny in Cornwall and the raw reality of black and white relationships in America's army, complete with its surprising British reaction. But they were handicapped by many factors, not least inspired by their junior experience and status. Clearly not all performances from American players in Paignton police court were as Oscar-worthy as others.

Newsmen didn't report that defenders were often hamstrung by a stuttering delivery. The team seemed thrown by objections and were sometimes unable to regain momentum after certain lines of interruptions. The court transcript clearly indicates an incohesive argument, neither spelling out the implications of certain facts nor joining the dots between cause and effect. The lawyers sometimes failed to follow up a thread of questioning or respond to what people said in court, falling back instead on questions which had clearly been pre-planned – a classic indication of their greenness. Just a hint of the biggest inhibitor of all, however, was contained in a single line of *The Herald*'s report that second day. Reporter Murray Edwards wrote that at one intense point, despite all the theatrical shenanigans on both sides, 'the trial went on with tempers unruffled.'[1] Perhaps it was a simple case of the defence just not caring enough about the outcome for those they were legally meant to protect. They certainly seemed unconcerned by their frequently lacklustre performance. Even in the dying moments of time allotted to argue their case, they acted with extreme and unnecessary haste.

Mindful that this was a critical and late stage, immediately before matters were removed from the hands of both legal teams forever, Court President Zickel interjected. Intricately spelling out their rights, the court president reminded them it was their very last chance to give their own account of what happened that night.

> 'Now before your Defense Counsel closes I am going to call upon him to speak with you to determine what your course shall be,' President Zickel continued. 'I want it understood that once the case is closed by the Defense that will be the last opportunity you have to testify or to make a statement in those proceedings.'
>
> (To Defense Counsel) 'Now Captain, will you confer with them all. Captain, do you want the court to recess while you confer with them?'

But the accuseds' defence did not think it necessary to give them that last opportunity to think in private. When time was there to be bought, Captain Philbin just passed it up.

> Defense Counsel: 'Not necessarily, no sir.'
>
> Defense Counsel (after conferring with each accused). 'I am satisfied, sir.'[2]

With that, the defence rested. It was time for both sides to formulate closing arguments to bring their cases to an official end; to make their final pitches. This was the opportunity for each to have the last word about what really happened on 26 September 1943. Both parties knew what came next could change everything. They wanted army panel members to remember solely their version of events, to have their arguments alone ringing longest and loudest before retiring to decide on a verdict. Army court martial protocol dictated the defence's closing statement would be sandwiched between the prosecution's opening and closing arguments.

Sadly, the prosecution's written arguments are not included in the archived court martial paperwork although Trial Judge Advocate Frank P. Eresch's words are widely preserved in the press reports. He had to prove the men guilty of six counts, namely rioting (violating the 89th article of war); attempted murder (contravening the 93rd article of war); mutiny (breaching the 66th article of war); and unlawfully seizing firearms and ammunition to discharge them while making inflammatory statements. Had his twenty witnesses said enough to prove all fourteen men guilty on every count? Like any self-respecting prosecutor, he curated the evidence carefully to build an ultimately bullet-proof hypothesis.

Trial Judge Advocate Eresch started at the beginning, with soldiers' testimony depicting numerous servicemen being out of camp illegally with illicit weapons and ammunition – and dead set on murderous mutiny. After finding and surrounding military policemen in the town square, they specifically shouted 'hands up', he argued, before firing, indicating their murderous intent. Prosecution witnesses had said this intense shooting resulted in life-changing injuries for one soldier – and bullet-riddled shops, hotels and an army jeep in the town of Launceston. The general thrust of Eresch's arguments, described in *The Sunday Post*, centred on proving attempted murder via this precise sequence of events: 'The prosecution contended … the military police were ordered to put their hands up, and when that was done the accused opened fire. It was only by chance that the two sergeants were shot in the legs instead of in more vital parts of the body.'[3]

Eresch reminded the court that the captain in charge had testified to graphic violence but denied racial tension; several sergeants reported hearing one mutineer's crucial line that night, questioning why 581st Ordnance Ammunition Company men were banned from town. Several medics confirmed wounds sustained by the two military policemen. Identities of soldiers packing Paignton police court benches were confirmed by the company commanding officer. Statements taken by Investigators Poltraz and Richardson were read out loud. But the knock-out blows came from four 581st Ordnance Ammunition Company men who appeared for the prosecution. They alone were able to name Private First Class Clifford Barrett as ringleader, and portray him as an ammunition-hoarding villain, ably assisted by Sergeant Henry Austin. Together they were portrayed as rushing into action after a pub skirmish with white soldiers from the 115th Infantry Regiment. Imploring fellow soldiers to 'stick together,' the pair were then described as inspiring 'the whole company' to break for town, drilled and armed as a small private army, to *'git'* even with the 'motherfucker military police.'

Trial Judge Advocate Eresch pulled together all these elements, no doubt delivering both opening and closing statements with a flourish. Admittedly, he had made a compelling case in forty-eight hours, but by no stretch of the imagination was it conclusive. The biggest glaring omission was that not one of his sixteen white witnesses could identify any of the accused African American soldiers. Close behind was the quirk that no 581st Ordnance Ammunition Company defendant remembered seeing fellow unit members who had identified them as being there for the prosecution. In other words, none of the defence witnesses for 581st saw the members who placed them at the scene and assigned their roles. Is it just possible that some saw the trial as a chance to settle old scores and get even?

Now was the time for Eresch's sparring partner to step up. It is worth remembering what the defence managed to uncover not only in their own all-too-brief afternoon in court, but also during their cross-examination of prosecution witnesses. Throughout the first day-and-a-half they had established, by probing an injured military policeman, that there had been a pub incident earlier on – although it took much cajoling to get there. Then there was the whole shadow cast by army investigators' statements being incorrectly sworn, if at all. This wasn't the worst thing. Many documents produced by Investigator Poltraz were suspiciously similar; words not even known by those supposed to have said them were included in others and one illiterate soldier was left in the dark about what he was supposed to have uttered. Another soldier appearing for the prosecution even described how names were given to him during his interview, while those he offered up in return were ignored. Investigator Richardson, on the other hand, could not identify a soldier he interviewed and had to be stopped from trying with others, so poor was his recollection.

During the prosecution's hour in court, the defence had also probed British involvement, teasing out portrayals of 'English soldiers' drinking happily with African American soldiers; buying drinks – or having drinks bought for them by British servicemen; being directed by each other to the next pub; walking together to various pubs as part of the same group; or talking to each other on street corners around the town. They tried to establish a line of defence that Private Clifford Barrett had bullied people into joining him and that many were scared not to do as he said.

Meanwhile, testimony from the four crucial 581st Ordnance Ammunition Company men who appeared for the prosecution had posed as many questions as they answered. One revealed shooting was deliberately low, thereby challenging in the strongest possible terms that murder was intended that evening. Another said they were out to get even with the white GI drinkers, who had forced them to move from one bar to another, rather than military policemen – which called into question whether usurpation of military power was on the cards. Someone else had said that nothing more sinister than 'drinking' was doing the talking that night and that there had been no coercion of the rioters as people were told they could 'get out' if scared. There were strange contradictions between what one witness said in court and his previous statement. More than anything, however, despite sharing months of training and living with these same men sharing the courtroom that day, these four prosecution witnesses could name only a handful of the fourteen. Other than Private Clifford Barrett, they couldn't even agree on which few were there. It was by no means clear how the fourteen sitting in the dock had earned their places there in lieu of others. This was before the defence had even tried to tell its side of the story.

Tragically, although these gaps and inconsistencies in the prosecution case leap out to even a casual contemporary reader of the court martial transcript, it obviously was not the case in October 1943. Not all these flaws were necessarily noticed or even pointed up by the defence. More was left unsaid than was stated. But what argument of their own had the defence presented when given the chance to nail it?

Although Defense Counsellor Captain John A. Philbin had far fewer witnesses, he organised a solid enough line-up comprising three investigators, one 115th Infantry military policeman and five accused soldiers. Putting Inspectors Stevenson, Richardson and Poltraz on the stand was brave, but did not result in them admitting any mistakes in the procedural swearing of statements. Nor did Philbin further pursue any of the more sensational claims that had emerged previously about these witnesses: such as their responsibility for inserting unknown syntax, not reading statements back to illiterate soldiers and an inability to even recognise some of those who had been interviewed. But in using the testimony of the five 581st Ordnance Ammunition Company men, he was able to try exploiting a legal technicality by getting admissions under oath that at least twelve statements were not sworn correctly. Although it came down to these five's word against the army investigators, it was a staggering claim about the evidence upon which most of the soldiers would be judged. It also set the stage for one witness's scandalous claim that his statement, produced by an investigator, bore absolutely no relation whatsoever to their discussion after arrests were made. So different was it that he was subjected to a lengthy cross-examination by both the prosecution and president.

The defence also built on British friendships with African American soldiers by establishing it was 'English soldiers' who 'butted in' on their behalf when the going got tough with military policemen on Saturday, 25 September 1943. They uniquely established a precedent for racial tension a good twenty-four hours before shooting started, revealing longer-term factors too such as never-ending *Jim Crow* restrictions and heavy-handed harrying by military policemen.

On paper, the defence team had a good chance of giving the prosecution a run for its money. This was the moment to do it – the once-in-a-lifetime chance to bring together every loose end, flag all prosecution anomalies and fine-tune the alternative narrative they had worked so quickly to present.

In reality, when Defense Counsellor Philbin summarised his points for the very last time, his ultimate courtroom statement took less than a couple of minutes to read out. Admittedly, the speech was sandwiched precariously between his opponent's opening and closing arguments, but to call it an over-simplification of what happened would be too generous. Clearly not a lot of time had been spent preparing this. It was scrawled in large, loopy writing with multiple crossings out, added bracketed words and vertical additions penned in the margins climbing the page. In total, it comprises a single, hastily produced scrap of paper. Summing up the entire discovery and legal process after two days, he read out:

> 'The 581st Ord Ammo Co to which these men belong was closely restricted before coming over here and have been, according to the evidence, restricted while here. On the night of the incident the men were highly excited having had trouble with the whites. They were warned by one of their numbers that they had better go along

with all the rest as they would get in trouble later on. These men apparently followed a few (disgruntled) leaders.

The evidence does not prove the charges or specifications (especially as it relates to so many of the individuals accused). The testimony showed that from five to fifty soldiers participated in the disorder – no clear evidence on this point. Most of the accused present are (blameless) innocent of any participation in the events indicated on the evening of 26 September 1943.'[4]

The argument, submitted as defence Exhibit 9, does not even take up a side of A4 paper. Its vague content does not include a fraction of what had been discovered through the cross-examination of prosecution witnesses and direct examination of those for the defence. Defense Counsel Philbin's own brief arguments were not substantiated by one single piece of pithy evidence – an inexcusable omission given so much was readily available. This is perhaps where the movie comparisons fell flattest of all. It was nowhere near the silver-screen production standards described by its press pack audience and was closer to a shabby amateur dramatic production where few knew their lines and even fewer had practised them. Blindsided by American accents, journalists were simply lavishing and attributing praise evenly where it was not deserved – when instead they should have been probing the defence's timid, toothless performance.

The best part of a century later, the question still remains: why was the defence so shoddy? Was there more to it than a lack of experience and confidence on the part of the defenders – or was something more sinister afoot? The defence had potential, but anything they started that second day in court they simply could not finish. Although it can never be known for sure, there must be some weight in the argument that it was the result of a deliberate attempt to secure the result required by the US Army. Although these questions went unasked in 1943 and now no-one can ever answer for sure, suspicion screams out from between the lines of the court martial transcript.

Seconds later, Trial Judge Advocate Eresch stood for the last time to make his closing argument. By 5.20pm it was all over. Time was up. Both sides had exhausted all their chances to persuade the court. It was over to a ten-strong army panel – the fourteen's fate was now in its hands.

Part V

Day Three 17 October 1943

Chapter 16

Hiding in Plain Sight

Cogs in each of the Second World War's geopolitical theatres had continued to grind throughout Paignton's fifteen minutes of fame. While court resumed in Devon for the third day on 17 October, barely alive allied prisoner-of-war work gangs, slaving under excruciating conditions in Thailand and Burma, were inching ever closer towards a macabre milestone. Opposing track-building teams comprising British, Australian and Dutch servicemen would that day collide with each other in Konkuita, just south of Three Pagodas Pass, to complete the 258th and final mile of Burma's brutal, death-riddled railway to Thailand.

Six thousand miles closer to home, in the European sphere of action, another landmark – once again for allied prisoners - was also about to be reached. This historical footnote was being written in a sleepy Victorian seaside resort hosting the third and final day of a public trial involving Americans in Britain. The central drama occurred on British soil, but its real weight lay in the fact this episode shouted volumes about the nation's spirit and feelings toward African American soldiers. Effectively, what would later be termed as the 'special relationship', was itself on trial. And today a verdict would be reached, the guilt or innocence of fourteen US servicemen judged and, if necessary, sentenced.

Classic British seaside weather including torrential rain, driving wind and a miserable sub-average temperature of 11°C set an ominous tone that morning.[1] But when court opened at 9.30am it proved to be a mere formality as the ten-strong army panel, comprising majors and captains from hospitals, quartermaster departments and headquarters in Britain's south-west corner, promptly retired outside to a private room. For most of that final day, they would be locked solidly in top secret debate headed by Court President Lieutenant Colonel Raymond E. Zickel, Law Member, from the 307th Quartermaster Battalion. Three-quarters of the army panel, acting in private as jury, needed to find against each of the accused to secure a guilty verdict via secret ballot.

Although 17 October 1943 was a significant wartime yardstick for allied prisoners in Burma and Devon, it did not seem that way for the court-based soldiers that day once the army panel upped and left. Their fate was being decided behind closed doors, but the prisoners seemed to relish the waiting game they were playing in a court now largely officer – but not prison-guard – free. The longer deliberations continued, the more they kicked back, able, it seemed, finally to enjoy the freedom so long denied them by their perpetual restriction to US and British camps. Appearing neither to understand nor care that their lives might be altered irrevocably, they relaxed unashamedly. Amid the smoke and chatter, incomprehensible scenes including that of a prisoner circulating photos of his girlfriend were reported. All the while, 'everyone sat back and lit cigarettes in the courtroom, and the prisoners cheerfully borrowed newspapers from journalists sitting behind them. A hum of conversation broke out and wagers were made on what the verdicts would be,' was how *The Mirror* reported it.[2] Everyone was considering their fortunes it seemed, including Torquay's star blonde, the 21-year-old Joyce Packe, who by now had filled five notebooks. The court darling divulged her sole 'grouse' to another national newspaper – that the trial's unexpected longevity had forced her to miss a typing exam that would have entitled her to a weekly pay rise of 4 shillings. Meanwhile, other reporters delighted in 'odd incidents' such as an armed guard falling asleep and being awoken only by the clatter of his automatic gun hitting the floor.

What onlookers couldn't have known as they observed the accused so casually contemplating their fate, was that the prosecution witnesses chosen to appear had been ruthlessly whittled down from a much wider – and more significant-starting base. Far more men from the 115th Infantry and 29th Division (eleven in total) had given statements than taken the stand. The number of court witnesses neither tallied with nor reflected the mighty tome of written exhibits included in the archive. Why? Because only a fraction of the evidence was picked out for mainstream consumption. Evidently, the body of witnesses used to testify against men of the 581st Ordnance Ammunition Company had been manipulated in the same way as statements of the accused. On top of this there was a whole raft of other people interviewed by investigators originally, but then airbrushed from the story by prosecutors. Two reports had been quickly but comprehensively compiled by Captain Richard Thrift and Captain William Sullivan respectively, of 29th Division, within twenty-four hours of the mutiny. They included recommendations about what really happened. Seeing how Trial Judge Eresch removed or included various witnesses from these reports pointed to the same unequivocal conclusion. Quite simply, those selected to speak in public court were chosen to tell a story carefully edited by prosecutors. Scrutinising the content of what these witnesses said indicates precisely why they, over and above the rest, were chosen to testify before the press. Because there was another side of the story to be told – and it was something the highest powers in Washington and London wanted obliterated from public view.

Well before ink on the investigators' initial report was dry, army bosses were scrambling to concoct and spin a story that would envelop and distort the truth of what really happened. They needed the right charges to fit – and stick. The boldest strand to be eliminated from the prosecution's official version of events was that this so-called mutiny was in fact a racial rebellion that had been fermenting for some time. It would have at least given it context, if not some serious mitigation. In statements written in the immediate aftermath, two white military police sergeants from the 115th Infantry and 29th Division described vividly the racial stresses and strains felt on Launceston's streets on 26 September. What they said was compelling. Sergeant Alfred Faria, of F Company, 115th Infantry, described how at 10.00pm that night the whole military police detachment was milling around the town square's monument. At that point there was only one topic of conversation, said Sergeant Faria:

'We talked about what was going on. Everything was so tense that evening that we thought that something might start. We saw forty to fifty soldiers coming up the street. They had overcoats on. They walked up almost in formation, and straight toward us. I realised that they were Negroes, and thought the trouble was about to begin.'[3]

Another military policeman standing alongside Sergeant Faria in the town square that evening was Sergeant Fred Unger, of H Company, 115th Infantry, who remembered the point at which soldiers moved in close:

'I saw the Negroes … They closed in in a semi-circle … there had been trouble brewing all evening. Whenever Negroes walked into a pub, things got a little tense. There had been some trouble between two white boys which we had quelled a bit earlier. You could feel the tenseness in the air.'[4]

Neither sergeants showed a shred of surprise at the turn events took shortly afterwards. They clearly and repeatedly described how they had been expecting trouble all night – in direct contrast to what every other prosecution witness had articulated in court – starting with top brass Captain Richard Scott. It had in fact dominated the very first report created by Captain Richard B. Thrift, Assistant Investigator General, from the 29th Division. Publican G.F. Clark, of the Bell Inn in Launceston, told Captain Thrift that although he never had trouble individually with white or black soldiers the bald truth was 'The coloured and the whites have it in them that they don't agree.' Never was it clearer that night, said hotelier J.L. Ball, of the New Market Hotel, who described how he had closed half-an-hour earlier because 'I knew there was something brewing.' The investigators learned a racially-motivated knife 'incident' had also occurred on 18 September. All this preliminary evidence had landed on Captain Thrift's commanding general's desk as early as 29 September, but significantly, these two publicans' witness statements, which backed up the sergeants excluded from court, were also left out of the prosecution case.[5]

Both Sergeants Faria and Unger also talked candidly about racial discrimination and of the calm in Launceston town square before the storm they were both expecting broke. Pointedly, however, this NCO double-act was blocked from the stand. The sergeants' personal testimony in open court was not required and by not speaking up to testify, their descriptions would remain only in the hefty paper bundle in front of each army panel member, and crucially barred from public scrutiny. Accused Private Arzie Martin, of the 581st Ordnance Ammunition Company, also added to this censored tale of mercury rising in an unread statement to the court. In fact, Private Martin used anticipated racial violence as a reason for arming himself ahead of venturing out into the Cornish evening. In a transcribed interview, recorded as exhibit 15b, Private Martin said:

'I had taken Blake's bayonet along because when I had snuck away
before I had had trouble with a military policeman in town who
had called me bad names and also because the boys in the QM
[quartermaster] had told us that they had had trouble with both
white military policemen and white soldiers.'

The quartermaster company was also African American.[6]

All three 'buried' exhibits of simmering racial tension and violence
contained within the official record flew in the face of what the white
military police sergeant eventually selected as witness for the prosecution
said. It can have been no coincidence that Sergeant William Edward
Neilson Jnr, of G Company, 115th Infantry, was the one military
policeman out of this trio of sergeants who appeared in court. In what
was submitted as Exhibit 23, Sergeant Neilson said that when forty or
fifty 'coloured' soldiers arrived in the square 'the whole affair seemed
planned and intentional … Nothing happened during the evening that
could have made them hostile towards us.'[7] Predictably Sergeant Nielson
said much the same on the first day in court, reinforcing the words of
Captain Richard Scott and his driver Private Fred Racey – and in so
doing, obscuring those of his two silenced colleagues who spoke up about
rising racial tension. Mutiny was a much more convenient explanation
for what went on that night.

A total of fifty-three separate exhibits were included in the court
martial paperwork, representing testimony from thirty-three soldiers.
But a third of these soldiers, such as Sergeants Faria and Unger, were
not called to appear. Most of these excluded witnesses also wrote pacy,
punchy tales with a sting about events on 26 September, but by keeping
them out of open court and therefore, under the radar, these narratives
never came to light. Furthermore, those barred from the stand were
often echoing observations and stories from investigator Captain Thrift's
original interviewees. Prosecutors had overlooked these witnesses, not
bothering to include their statements. The result was overpowering.
By blocking them, and eleven others, from testifying in front of the
court-based press pack, an entire version of events was doctored for the
watching public, leaving only the army panel to see the written exhibit
submission in its entirety.

Another broad brushstroke edited out of the prosecution's version of events was the British involvement heavily suspected by many of the duty military policemen in Launceston. The Brits had form, it seemed, in stirring things up, according to Sergeant Charles W. Bury, of F Company, 115th Infantry, another military policeman gagged by prosecutors from describing the dire state of American race relations. Sergeant Bury did at least get to tell his side of things when he appeared as witness for the defence, but in his written submission he went further. Describing escalating tensions earlier that weekend at the Saturday night dance, he pointed unwaveringly at the pivotal role Brits had played. Describing this, in Exhibit 30, as the truer catalyst to 'mutiny', he said:

'I think quite a bit of the trouble springs from last night when we made five Negroes leave the dance. The Negroes, who were restricted last night, were willing to leave until some Englishmen interceded in their behalf. The Negroes, the Englishmen said, should have the same right to attend as well and if the Negroes were restricted to their camp, the Englishman claimed it was our fault. Then the Negroes didn't want to leave.'

He was also careful to specifically name Royal Engineers as accompanying black soldiers on their illicit pub crawl the following night.

More alarming was what the other white military victim, Sergeant Charles J. Cox, of New Jersey, revealed when stating his initial gut feeling about overall British culpability. In the 28-year-old's own statement describing the final moments before soldiers opened fire, he said:

'We were standing near the jeep in front of the White Hart hotel at approximately 10.45pm when I saw a lot of coloured soldiers, sixty-five or seventy at least, coming down the road. There seemed to be a lot of English soldiers with them and I thought that the whole group was English soldiers.'[8]

He cannot have been alone in his suspicions. Sergeant Cox suffered a compound fracture of his left femur and was left in what doctors called 'fair condition' by the shooting, but when it came to who appeared in court it was his fellow victim Sergeant Ralph Simmons, who significantly had nothing whatsoever to say about British involvement – perceived or otherwise – who limped up to testify.

Prosecutors had effectively stamped on racial tensions and potential British support as factors in the Launceston shooting by choosing not to call on certain witnesses to testify once court opened. Significantly, they vetoed three more who had been interviewed by Captain Thrift and said much the same as Sergeants Cox and Bury, just louder, perhaps. Mrs Winifred Titley, from the Westgate Inn, was one of them and remained under no illusion about the role British soldiers played in siding with African American soldiers. She told the investigators that: 'It is my belief that our British soldiers are beneath all this trouble, for there have been several instances where the British soldiers egged the coloured soldiers against the white soldiers. It is also rumoured that the coloured troops often buy the British soldiers drinks.' Technician Fifth Grade Harry W. Beall, from the 2nd Battalion, 115th Infantry, described to Captain Thrift just how it worked on the night of the shooting. When two 581st Ordnance Ammunition Company men were asked to move away from the 'white' bar to their correct area in the Bell Inn, before they even started to turn 'two Englishmen joined them at the bar and set them up with drinks.'

After Captain Thrift's preliminary investigation, Captain William B. Sullivan, of E Company 115th Infantry, was asked to do the follow-up examination and report. Writing to his commanding officer, he was treading softly when he concluded that things on 26 September 'were not improved by the attitude of the British military personnel, who treated the coloured troops in such a manner as to make them dissatisfied with the consideration they received from the white American troops.'[9] Given this was one of just four conclusions this second investigating officer came to, it is extraordinary it was not included in the prosecution's court case.

On the other hand, it was hardly surprising that he who had deprived 581st Ordnance Ammunition Company men of passes in the first place was himself barred from court. One sniff of his withering regard for black soldiers said it all. The guileless Second Lieutenant Guy S. Songy, of F Company, 115th Infantry had blocked passes into Launceston that night for everyone, it seemed, except himself and his friends. Off-duty and out in town with a couple of girls, he wrote how:

'Lieutenant Pressley and myself were walking west of town on the road facing the main Bodmin road. We passed about twenty Negroes headed toward town. They were all in overcoats. The girl I was with asked what they were up to. I answered that you never knew what they were up to.'

It was a throwaway comment in a statement (submitted as Exhibit 31) but surely a risk to put him on a stand where he might prove himself a racist liability under cross-examination.

Grave doubts had been raised in court the previous day over the veracity of witness identifications by 581st Ordnance Ammunition Company men working for prosecutors. Private First Class Alexander Shaw's repeated request for Private Albert Smith to be called in are preserved in his interview, submitted to the court as Exhibit 5b.

He said: 'I know Smith could not have seen me firing a rifle because I was behind the monument with the military police the whole time.' Again, this question mark was one never written in open court and remains only in the trial's transcript.

If casual racism and identity disputes were enough to bar some witnesses from the stand, others can only have been omitted because their version of events was simply too good to be heard about an incident the army was keen to play down. Private Leonard L. Garrett, of the 29th Division Military Police Platoon, told how suddenly

'I heard a rifle bolt crack. A shot landed at our feet. Someone hollered "Duck". One of the military police sergeants hollered, "I am hit." I reached out and pulled him down. I could have shot wildly down the street, but I didn't think it was wise. I might have hit some of our own boys ... Cox was hollering.'[10]

Analysing the court martial manuscript many decades later, it is impossible to escape the unavoidable truth that was established well before court even opened on 15 October 1943: that key elements of the Launceston shooting had been methodically expunged from the public forum. After the US Army legal team had performed its expert evidence sweep, this slight-of-hand was virtually impossible to detect. Members of the general public, picking up on hints and indications in spoken testimony, might rightly have suspected this was not the full picture, but they could not have known for sure. Only a subsequent reading of the full court martial transcript could show that factors such as racial conflict within visiting American forces and latent British sympathy for African Americans had been cut but not pasted for public consumption elsewhere.

Above all, however, there was one stand-out recommendation from the investigators' preliminary and subsequent reports that was glossed over – with potentially terrible and lasting consequences for the fourteen destined for Paignton police court. The biggest elephant in the room was left, seemingly forgotten, in Captain Sullivan's confidential memo to his commanding officer on 27 September 1943. Army detectives did not believe attempted murder should be on the charge sheet. There was not the evidence to back it up – and this was according to the man in charge of the investigation leading up to Paignton. Captain Sullivan said: 'From the number of casualties inflicted, taking into consideration the close range and the number of shots fired, it would seem that it was not the intention of the mob to hit anyone.'[11] Unbelievably, this was the investigators' second recommendation to the prosecuting team to be unceremoniously dropped. They ignored half of Captain Sullivan's thoughts and suggestions.

Meanwhile as the clock ticked on that day, those currently facing the most severe possible sentences were in fact relaxing, weirdly, as if without a care in the world. From 9.30am till lunchtime was announced in court at 1.05pm, they continued to play cards, pass photos and place bets on predicted verdicts. These men suspended so surreally in court limbo could rely on one thing alone: that the army panel deciding their fate would have unfettered access to the entire, unedited catalogue of exhibits to gain a more faithful reading of what really happened. Men of the 581st Ordnance Ammunition Company needed to count on this ten-man band to consider each wider factor, peculiarity and omission concealed in the fifty-three written exhibits and especially the words of the eleven excluded from court. The question was, could they rely on this white army panel to find them at all and, if so, would and could they put two and two together?

Chapter 17

The Verdict

That a US Army panel was considering a verdict in Britain at all was due to some quick-thinking parliamentary action the previous year. Quite by chance, the germ of this remarkable court martial had been contained within the briefcase of Home Secretary Herbert Morrison as he strode through Parliament Square one summer morning. The sun was certainly shining on the ambitious Home Secretary, who harboured not-so-secret prime ministerial aspirations. The date was 4 August 1942 and he and Labour colleagues in the National Coalition Government were deputising for Churchill and his team, who were now en-route to review the Middle East's military situation, before heading to Moscow for meetings with Soviet leader Joseph Stalin. Mr Morrison had to sharpen his step, as he had sensitive business concerning the Anglo-American alliance which needed immediate attention. 'The corridors of the Home Office are paved with dynamite,'[1] he was fond of saying. Today would prove no exception.

In fact, the contents of the right honourable gentleman's leather briefcase that day would be critical, not just to Paignton but to every single American court martial conducted in Britain during the war. A little-known proviso of American participation in the Second World War – designed specifically to accommodate the nation's colossal troop numbers in Britain before D-Day – was an obscure piece of legislation which came to be known as the United States of America (Visiting Forces) Act. Shortly after Franklin D. Roosevelt signed up to the Grand Alliance against Hitler, the need for American law to maintain order amongst servicemen overseas was highlighted and a draft bill swiftly cobbled together. It was this that was in the firm grip of Herbert Morrison's hands as he headed grimly towards the House of Lords.

What precisely was the content of legislation so particularly required by Britain's American allies? Based on its smooth passage earlier through the House of Lords, even the most diligent parliamentary watcher could reasonably assume it was something straightforward. Six days earlier, the United States of America (Visiting Forces) Bill had galloped through the Upper House without any hesitation. Now, Home Secretary Herbert Morrison MP (grandfather of New Labour's celebrated spin doctor Lord Mandelson) was ready to present the Bill to gathered members of the Commons. He was hoping for the same speedy passage it had enjoyed through the Lords to ensure its swift enactment into law.

Somewhat appropriately therefore, it was the Lords in which Herbert Morrison now readied himself. Bombed out of the House of Commons since 10 May 1941, the lower house now sat in the Lords' chamber while the upper house assembled in the robing room. That Tuesday, the first of Parliament's three-day wartime week, waiting MPs were already settled on the aged, blood-red leather benches grounded amidst gilt-encrusted walls and ceilings. Morrison wasted no time in getting to the point: 'The short and clear-cut purpose of the Bill is to provide that all criminal offences, on the part of members of the Armed Forces of the United States, shall be removed from the jurisdiction of the British.'

There was no doubt as to who was calling the shots. Emphasising the importance to which American allies had attached to the passage of this bill, he continued:

> 'It is the considered opinion of the Government of the United States that it is most expedient, and from their constitutional point of view is right, that any offences on the part of members of the American Armed Forces should be tried by their own military courts and not by the British courts. The American authorities have pressed that point of view upon us with great vigour and earnestness; in short, the American view is that constitutionally it is desirable, and indeed necessary, that where their troops go American legal authority should go with them.'

Invoking the relationship underpinned by its 'interests of good feelings before the two countries' he concluded: 'I know the whole House is glad to see them in our country and will do what it can to give them a cordial, pleasant and happy welcome.'

The immediate significance and ripple-effect ramifications of this proposed legislation should not be underestimated, even today. Effectively it would mean that the 4 million US servicemen who were based on British shores before passing to Europe's theatre of operations in the Second World War would be subject to American military law, rather than the law of the land in which they were resident. At its peak one-and-a-half million US citizens were in Britain at any one time. What would happen if British citizens were swept up in the crimes? The bill was tantamount to sanctioning a state within a state. As Morrison succinctly surmised for MPs: 'What this Bill does is to oust the British courts of justice from jurisdiction in cases of criminal offences.'[2] What is more, there was very little British understanding or knowledge about the nature of American military law.

This velvet-cloaked assault on Britain's unwritten constitution was unprecedented. What made it even more sinister was the warm welcome which greeted it. When the Bill was read in the House of Lords the previous week, strangely, since so many lawyers were included in its ranks, just three sitting peers had anything to say at all. Even then, the trio simply made small technical points which they counter-balanced with heart-felt wishes for the bill's Godspeed.

In contrast, on 4 August 1942, when MPs considered it, they were feeling more punchy about English law being usurped on the home-front. But only a bit. Once again, just three spoke up. First to his feet was Liverpudlian lawyer Sydney Silverman, MP for Nelson and Colne, who said:

> 'I concede that the Americans are entitled to think theirs [law] is better, but that is no reason for seeking to apply it without necessity on foreign soil. Usually it has been held that any country has a right to defend its own institutions against anyone within its own territory, with the reciprocal right for others to do the same with theirs. I say that we have gone a very long way. It is entirely without precedent.'

The Right Honourable member wanted to know who from the American administration had made the request and why, before going on to hope gloomily it wasn't a sign of things to come in Anglo-American relations, asking rhetorically: 'Are all our affairs to be dictated from Washington, or are we to retain some rights of our own, some rights to the sovereignty of our own law in our own land, except in cases where the necessity for a departure from that principle has been proved?'

Pressing for more time to consider the Bill, he implored: 'It would be a grave dereliction of their duty as executive custodians of our institutions and our principles to ask the House to pass a measure such as this hastily, in an ill-considered way, and without time for thought.'[3]

Next it was time for a Conservative to underline the magnitude of what was being asked of Britain. Professor John James Craik-Henderson, who had swept into Parliament with more than 97 per cent of the vote in his constituency's 1940 by-election, said: 'The Bill which we are considering is, as far as our law and constitution are concerned, of a completely revolutionary character. It is very far-reaching indeed.' The member for Leeds, North-East continued:

'There is no need for any Uriah Heep attitude here. We are giving up, out of friendship, rights which have been won over a very long period. It is a serious change in our constitutional and legal practice and principles, and the British Government, in the interests of the British people, should have been very specific in their demands, and should have laid down conditions in the most unambiguous terms. I am not going to oppose the Bill, but I hope that at some time we shall be given a statement showing how all these problems will be dealt with, and that they will be thought out now, and not when friction arises later.'[4]

Former Royal Naval Commander Sir Archibald Southby, member for Epsom, added to the outrage, lamenting the fact that 'Once again, the House is being asked to express its approval of a fait accompli.' While the Surrey MP acknowledged the nation was 'very glad' to welcome American troops he reminded members that:

'We in this House are charged with looking after the interests of the British people, and it seems to me that we are being asked to

> express our approval of this measure without having been told what
> code is to be operated in the American military courts, the code
> to which, to a certain extent, British citizens will, of necessity, be
> subject. We have only been allowed to see a very small portion of
> the correspondence which must have passed between the respective
> Governments. I think that the Home Secretary was a little
> unfortunate in the language he used in moving the Second Reading
> of this Bill. He referred to the demand from the United States.'[5]

Such salient criticism was bang on point, but it was largely brushed aside.
So keen was the British government to press the agenda of its much–
needed and powerful American allies that these final reservations were
allowed to ring hollow around the chamber. With that, the Bill passed.
Just two days later, the 'revolutionary' legislation, ensuring American
crimes committed on British soil were dealt with by a non-British penal
code, was written into the statute book. There was precedent from the
First World War in which the British enjoyed jurisdiction over their
own troops in France, but however much the comparison was made, the
situation earlier that century had been entirely different. The soldiers
in First World War France were already in a war zone – whereas Britain
was a home-front hosting millions of American soldiers. Some divisions,
like the 29th Infantry, were nestled at the heart of British communities
for some considerable time, giving ample opportunity for crimes to be
committed and British citizens to become involved and then dealt with
in this unusual manner.

Despite the Lord Chancellor's and Home Secretary's sincerest
assurances to the odd awkward question raised in Parliament during the
Bill's consideration in 1942, the United States of America (Visiting Forces)
Act was a very big deal with enduring consequences, not least for soldiers
of the 581st Ordnance Ammunition Company. For them specifically, it
meant that they would be facing down accusers in a small Devonshire
police court specially swathed in stars and stripes. It meant the same for
thousands of GIs wherever they were court martialled in Britain during
the Second World War: that every criminal action committed in Britain
would be treated with the full force of an antique military law born in
revolutionary times specifically to ensure the strictest compliance.

Eighteenth-century in style, it had remained largely untouched for 170-odd years and worse still, would be delivered in twentieth-century courts where legal training or knowledge was not a pre-requisite – but a *Jim Crow* mentality largely was.

The final rub was that it would be administered on a titanic scale. At the zenith of mobilisation, some 12.3 million Americans were in the armed services – almost equal to the nation's population in 1830. At this unparalleled summit, the army military system was processing roughly a third of all criminal cases tried in the entire United States of America during the Second World War. In total, more than 19,000 court martials involving 22,214 American servicemen took place in the European Theatre of Operation alone between 18 July 1942 and 15 February 1946 – the equivalent of nearly 500 court martials every month. Looking back, it is a wonder the US military had time for anything else.[6]

For 581st Ordnance Ammunition men however, most worrying of all was the outrageous racial bias inherent within America's court martial system now operating in the UK. This would not have come as a complete bombshell in 1943. In fact, a British establishment member raised these precise fears during the Bill-reading stage. Somewhat presciently, the Earl of Shaftesbury foresaw potential trouble for African American soldiers if the United States of America (Visiting Forces) Act was implemented. The Lord Chancellor had assured him:

> 'I do not suppose that my noble friend suggests for a moment that any distinction should be drawn between white and coloured soldiers. I am certain that neither the British Parliament nor any one of us would contemplate that for a single moment. I agree with him that the administering of this Bill will call for a great deal of discretion and good sense.'[7]

These were strong words indeed – but surely cold comfort for men of the 581st Ordnance Ammunition Company waiting for the verdict to be announced in Paignton police court? Not even they could have suspected how wrong the well-intentioned Lord Chancellor would be. The evidence speaks for itself. Out of the many thousands of US Army court martials during the Second World War, 141 military personnel were executed for capital crimes – one for desertion and the rest for murder, rape or a combination of the two. Just under half of all those executed – seventy – were killed in the European Theatre of Operation, many in Britain's Shepton Mallet prison in Somerset, which had been commandeered by American Army officials for that exclusive purpose. Analysis shows that overall almost 80 per cent of those hanged in Europe were black (in Somerset's Shepton Mallet prison it was eleven of the eighteen) despite just 1 in 10 armed forces personnel being African American. The race ratios governing the US Army's make-up were virtually diametrically reversed when it came to who was found criminally guilty at trial – and then killed.[8]

The Act inauspiciously passed in August 1942 would affect forever men of the 581st Ordnance Ammunition Company. That it was passed so effortlessly said more about the changing balance of power in Anglo–American relations than anything else. But because of it they were subjected to one of the most stringent codes of old military law which just happened to be loaded against them. By chance a clause, inserted at the last minute by Foreign Secretary Anthony Eden, stipulating that cases involving members of the public should be heard in open court, worked in their favour. It enabled Paignton's court martial to be thrown open to general scrutiny, illuminating the inequities of The United States of America's army, its Visiting Forces Act – and most especially its tendency to punish skin colour.

Outside Parliament, distant rumblings of discord about all these factors had been heard from the beginning. Much as British and American authorities tried, the cover-up of this Bill's enormity was by no means flawless. The British government first tried turning a blind eye to the difficulties of having a racially prejudiced army for an ally. Just a couple of weeks after the Bill was passed, a letter was sent from the Ministry of Information asking the Home Office to keep a lid about this 'negro business' and that 'in general we feel that the least said the soonest mended.'[9] But that policy was destined to be short-lived and later that year the British government came up with its own way of allowing the Americans to practise a colour bar without endorsing it.

As for members of the public, evidence suggests there was a fair appreciation of the enormity of what had been given away so lightly. The month before Launceston's shooting, buried in the *Special Comments* section of the top-secret Ministry of Information Weekly report, was a distressing concern. According to report No. 148, written on 5 August 1943:

> 'In the London Region, it is reported that 'many people are worried because our police have no power or authority over United States soldiers. It is stated that "it is not unusual to hear of the rape of young girls of 13 and upwards in the parks in and around London."'

Keen to pass the buck away from Americans and mask the fact that British courts could not touch them, the report writer fell back on a bit of good, old-fashioned misogyny to explain events. Concluding its description of rapes of women and girls as young as 13, it went on 'It is recognised, however, that the conduct of the US troops depends very largely on the behaviour of our girls and women.'[10]

The inimitable George Orwell was at pains to point out the great conspiracy whenever he could. Writing his weekly *As I Please* column for *Tribune,* he described how the government's policy of not criticising allies – or engaging with their criticisms of Britain – had backfired. Dire consequences for one included the fact that 'American troops in this country are not liable to British courts for offences against British subjects – practically "extra-territorial rights". Not one English person in ten knows of the existence of this agreement; the newspapers barely reported it and refrained from commenting on it,' was how he concluded his column in December 1943.[11]

There was, however, one stand-out incident which became the apogee of disaffection with the United States of America (Visiting Forces) Act – as well as a national debate. For once, the Act's inequities could be neither veiled or left unsaid, when in May 1944 African American soldier Leroy Henry was sentenced to execution by court martial after his alleged rape of a local woman in Bath, Somerset. There was only one problem – the woman in question was not the victim here. The married housewife had spun a ludicrous story in which she had been roused from her bed by a lost American soldier throwing stones at her window to wake her in the middle of the night. Once awakened, she put on her knickers and agreed to accompany this 'stranger' out into the evening (wearing only her nightgown in addition) so as to put him on the right road. The story seemed somewhat far-fetched and proper investigation after the court martial proved she had in fact slept with the unfortunate Henry twice in the weeks before, each time receiving a pound for her troubles. This time, however, she had demanded double and when he refused, she cried rape. Despite describing how he had pulled a knife before attacking her, neither the doctor could find any marks of a struggle – nor could the prosecution adequately explain why a woman abandoned her husband and bed for the wiles of the outdoor evening, simply to direct a random misplaced soldier to Bristol. In many ways Leroy Henry's court martial foretold the drama contained within Pulitzer-prize winning 1964 novel *To Kill a Mockingbird*. It made no difference that Leroy electrified court proceedings when he testified he had been tortured by army investigators into signing a confession which agreed with the woman's version of events. The 30-year-old technician fifth grade was sentenced unanimously to be hanged by the neck till dead. On hearing the verdict, the 6ft 2in soldier burst into tears and shook his head.

United States Army chiefs had not counted on the reaction of the British public to Henry's plight. They railed against the sentence which highlighted the stark difficulties of having different penalties for the same crime; unlike the United States, rape was not a capital offence in wartime Britain. It also revealed that readers took a dim view of the wildly disproportionate number of African American soldiers being found guilty over their white brethren, which in turn unleashed widespread allegations of racism. Ultimately, the storm launched a battery of parliamentary questions, letters to newspapers, petitions (including one from Bath alone with 33,000 signatures) and editorials. Missives from London to Cornwall poured into the Foreign Office, begging for clemency. Writing from his home in the High Road, Chiswick, an infuriated Ernest A. Gladwell wrote: 'I think it is wicked that such a sentence could happen on British soil'[12] while the Rev C. Phillips Cape, of Gunnislake's Methodist Church in Cornwall, wrote: 'Should it get abroad in this country that an American coloured soldier may suffer and suffer terribly because of his colour, a deadly blow may be struck at the vital cause of Anglo-American amity.'[13]

Such was the general outrage that no less a person than General Eisenhower himself became involved. Bombarded by cables from the

NAACP and League of Coloured Peoples, the general quickly overruled the sentence, releasing the prisoner back to duty. Once again, it had been *The Mirror* leading the charge, reporting significant reader outrage at the capital sentence – and suspicion that racism was really behind the guilty verdict: 'Popular sentiment would be much appeased if justice could, in suitable cases, be tempered with mercy, and not least in cases where coloured men are the offenders. In America, which has a colour problem peculiar to herself, clemency might not be possible,' went one.[14] The central crux was, according to historian Graham Smith, that: 'Many found it totally incongruous in the midst of a multitude of incongruities that a black American could be tried by an American court under American law and sentenced to death for a crime that was not a capital offence in Britain.'[15]

But this had not been the first time such shadowy implications, entrenched within the United States of America (Visiting Forces) Act, wormed their way to the surface. They had emerged a full eight months earlier in Launceston. Admittedly there was a big difference between Leroy Henry's so-called rape and the Cornish mutiny. The former directly involved a British citizen whereas the latter merely had British witnesses – although given the flavour of the 'buried evidence' this might equally have been subjected to a hasty pre-trial cover-up. Overridingly, however, the mutiny was not a crime committed against a British subject and no evidence was offered to suggest British people were involved to any greater degree. Launceston was a purely American affair showcasing a uniquely American problem.

Nevertheless, the Launceston shooting would briefly become a crucible for the inequities of the United States of America (Visiting Forces Act) that third and final day. The abuse of power was less overt than Leroy Henry's treatment but no less egregious. It was in the closing minutes of the Devonshire Riviera court martial – as soldiers were still confined to Paignton police court's uncomfortable wooden benches and the army panel continued to deliberate outside those four walls – that the mood changed, as if anticipating the moment.

Initially, the suspension of live court action had been thrilling, but as hourly ten-minute 'smoking breaks' merged into hours, this third morning began to drag interminably for the men on trial. Consequently, excitement levels lowered and the novelty of chatting freely wore away with each passing hour. Inertia took over. 'They smoked or dozed,' observed *The Herald's* reporter, Murray Edwards. 'One leaned against the dock which had been pushed to one side so that the court could be made to look like an American one. Whenever a door opened they would look up.'[16]

Reporters whiled away the time by working on word puzzles or speaking to court spectators. Defense Counsel Captain John A. Philbin tried to dispel Paignton's damp seaside air and, perhaps his own sense of personal boredom, by walking up and down the courtroom all day. Trying to keep body warm – and mind engaged – his relentless pacing was clocked by watching newsmen. And all the while, defendants were flanked by a dozen white military policemen who zealously guarded the door. Just to be safe, two additional military policemen stood against the prosecuting counsel's table to defend 'against any possible outbreak,' according to *The Herald*. So diligent to duty were they that one of these soldier policemen set a dubious record by standing statue-still in the same spot for more than twenty-one hours, a feat noted by one of the national newspapers.

Just after 3.00pm that afternoon, after six hours of secret deliberations, the oak door to Paignton police court swung open, silencing the court. Dozens of heads turned to watch members of the army panel file back into court. All eyes were locked onto this silent incoming body. Their purpose was quickly communicated. They needed one thing of each defendant before retreating to cast the 140 votes required for a verdict. Did any defendant have previous army convictions?

For most, it was a no. Trial Judge Advocate Frank P. Eresch disclosed that Privates Charlie Geddies, 26, James Lindsey, 22, Alexander Shaw, 32, Freddy Blake, 20, Henry Tilly, 21 and Willis Gibbs, 20, as well as the two sergeants involved, Rupert Hughes, 22 and Henry Austin, 23, had no prior records. Observers discovered that each of the army privates who did have convictions – namely James Manning, 19, Henry McKnight, 21, Private First Class Clifford Barrett, 22, Private Tom Ewing, 32, and Private Arzie Martin, 19 – had served 'hard labour' and incurred severe financial penalties but only for being absent without leave (AWOL). In each case they had been AWOL for brief periods spanning the odd hour to a few days. Just two defendants had anything slightly closer to the charge of mutiny – Private First Class Clifford Barrett had a second prior conviction when he 'wrongfully took a pistol and flourished it, in an attempt to escape arrest' while being AWOL. Meanwhile, Private Carl Tennyson, 21, had a further conviction for 'insubordination & disrespectful language to NCO in execution of office.' Still it was hardly *Mutiny on the Bounty*.

A few things rapidly became clear as Eresch filled in the criminal history background for each defendant. Firstly, this group of men was young. The age span was 19 to 32 but the majority (eleven out of the fourteen) was under the age of 23. Secondly, most of them had wives, children or mothers, who were dependent on their salary. These were young, family men with people to support and added incentive to stay gainfully employed. Just five of them lived totally free of dependants. Finally, and most importantly of all, Eresch showed that only six of the fourteen defendants had any previous convictions – which were mostly for being AWOL. Given the 581st Ordnance Ammunition Company had lived in a semi-permanent state of restriction for most of their army life – was this offence really surprising? It was scarcely tantamount to insurrection.

Just after 3.30pm, court closed once more so the army panel could resume its final spell of deliberation. Three hours later, the ten-strong army panel returned for the last time. At precisely this instant the darkest consequences of the United States of America (Visiting Forces) Act began to emerge – and the biggest outrage of an alien justice being practised publicly in Great Britain was revealed.

'The court was opened, and the president stated that the court had directed that the findings and sentence be not announced,' the court martial transcript reads.[17] A blatant cover-up was happening in front of the public's very eyes. As if to punctuate the outrage, 'Just as he spoke a band which had been heard playing outside struck up the National Anthem,' noted one reporter.[18]

Paignton police court had been packed for three days, its American Army panel had deliberated for nearly ten hours straight and myriad reams of British and American newsprint had been devoted to this story. But no-one would know the result. Not even the defendants.

'They came from all parts of the United States. One hundred and forty slips of paper decided their fate. Only the deputy judge advocate knows what it is. Until he himself confirms the findings, none of the men will know,' said *The Daily Herald*.[19]

Before proceedings started, the president had been thwarted in his attempt to censor the case's racial dimension. But in the dying minutes of the court martial, he achieved the next best thing. The US Army had been forced to hold a public trial yet against all the odds – and dogged efforts of a nearly free press – it had triumphed in its bid for a news blackout. Failing to declare the men's sentences was not the kind of public justice stipulated by Foreign Secretary Anthony Eden as the caveat to Parliament's passing of the Bill. It was a kick in the teeth for fairness and the British public, but most of all the fourteen soldiers who walked out still not knowing their fate. They had been confined at Tidworth Garrison Area Guardhouse since 29 September – and were still none the wiser about what would happen next.

The brazen gagging order stole headlines in the following day's newspapers. But what equally captured imaginations was the unfathomable sense of calmness with which the president's astounding announcement was taken. At the end of three days of rare court drama, they fairly mooched out, seemingly 'relaxed and pleased with the announcement, although they do not know yet whether they were found guilty or not,' noted the *Chicago Defender*, hometown newspaper for three of the men.[20] *The Daily Herald* reported that 'They whispered excitedly amongst themselves as they were ushered back by armed police.'[21]

Uncomprehending, they filed out. As they moved forwards under armed guard towards the waiting US star-emblazoned lorry outside, it was to the sound of the same 'band in the street [which] played a cheerful march.' Despite their decidedly Zen-like spirit, however, no-one foresaw future sunshine and rainbows. Impending doom was somehow written in between the lines of many of the prolific newspaper reports. Somewhat ominously, one report predicted that 'the verdict revealed to the unit's commanding officer may never be made public.'[22] It was spot on. In fact it was never to be officially revealed.

Thinking back to her role in a momentous trial that stood out in a truly remarkable US Army career, Joyce Packe could not quite remember what happened next. One of the British journalists that covered the court martial, George Matthews, who went on to become editor of the *Torbay Herald Express*, told Launceston historian Arthur Venning that his recollection was that at least some of them were eventually executed in America. But Miss Packe was dubious. Speaking many years after the trial, she said the fact she could not remember made her think that death sentences were not imposed:

> 'Cases that ended in hanging I can remember clearly … There is another factor which makes a death sentence memorable: when the court returns for the verdict, every officer of the equivalent of the jury has taken off his side-arms and laid them on the table, pointing towards the accused. This is a spine-chilling sight and not one easily forgotten. All this leads me to wonder whether life sentences were imposed, rather than the death penalty.'[23]

After all the drama, press speculation and subsequent legal spectacle, none of the British public were ever to discover what happened after the wildest Launceston happening since 'the pirates'. Most believed the men hanged for crimes they may have committed but for which they were neither blamed nor condemned, at least by the town. Cornish men and women held their breath, waiting for the truth to out. The few alive who still remember the events of 26 September 1943 are still doing so.

Part VI

The Aftermath

Chapter 18

Lambs to the Slaughter

In the near-dark of approaching sunset, fourteen soldiers trooped out of Paignton police station and into Palace Avenue for the very last time. This precise moment is frozen, captured by a photographer who managed to frame all of them in one lucky snap. They are either looking right of shot at their waiting transport or smiling at a group of children who were gawping-on, awestruck. It is a perfect snapshot of the surreal post-trial calmness and was splashed on *The Daily Herald's* final front page coverage of the story. It remains the only surviving picture of those involved. We know that all that staring and smiling preserved in the image, as well as the puffing on cigarettes and pipes, was in fact set to jaunty military music still being belted out by the out-of-sight street band. What they did not know as they clambered aboard the waiting lorry was that they had been dancing to the US Army's tune – quite literally – all along. Ignorant of the court's findings, they walked into public oblivion by meekly taking their seats in the covered lorry, making it all the easier for the US Army to obfuscate their story. The last thing military bosses wanted revealing was that fourteen of the 581st Ordnance Ammunition Company were now condemned men – not that anyone was telling.

Only the court manuscript preserves the result everyone was waiting for, but no-one got to see – unless, that is, they were part of the tight cabal that was the Judge Advocate General's Office (JAGO). The trial judge advocate himself created the mutiny's postscript for posterity – but not the wartime present – by writing the verdicts beside each of the fourteen names. But the small, neatness of Frank P. Eresch's handwriting, plastered all over the official record here, belies the impending catastrophe it spelled for the fourteen accused. They would have been horrified to know, as the star-spangled lorry began negotiating Paignton's sea-sprayed streets, that they were now army convicts and had been for the last hour: all fourteen men had been found guilty and were to be dishonourably discharged.

A little earlier, the trial judge advocate's painstaking penmanship had recorded the sentences. Eleven of them were to serve fifteen years' hard labour. The remaining trio would suffer a punishment even harsher: Sergeants Henry Austin and Rupert Hughes, along with 'ringleader' Private First Class Clifford Barrett, had twenty years of hard labour stretching ahead. Meticulously, he initialled the fact that three-quarters of the panel had agreed with each verdict and sentence, before signing off with a flourish. It was his final act of grandstanding.

Although not the capital sentences many suspected, the fifteen and twenty-year stretches were still incredibly tough, ensuring this group of young, mostly family men, would be incarcerated at least until middle age. And for what? The austere sentencing rode roughshod over many aspects of a case and investigation that didn't add up, to say nothing of the dubious involvement of some – and the extent others were drawn in, if at all. It mattered not one bit. The one place where African Americans were in fact all equal in the eyes of the US Army was their general and frequent exposure to its iron-fisted penal code.

The judge's ground-breaking decision to keep sentencing secret cannot be allowed to lie unchallenged as it was in 1943 under the all-too-convenient blanket of national security. It demands and deserves an explanation – and so much more. Too many important questions were left unanswered, such as: why was it so important to shut down the story before news of the verdict and sentence broke? How seriously did American and British authorities react to this case? And how effective was the news blackout anyway?

When it comes to explaining why the US Army blocked news of the verdicts and sentences, one thing cannot be forgotten or underplayed – the trial's unique timing. It came slap bang in the middle of a quickening tide of racial discontent that was unleashed by summer rioting in Detroit and had spread across urban America. Mere days before the court martial, this wave peaked in Britain with two home-grown episodes of racial controversy featuring cricketing legend Learie Constantine and would-be Land Army girl Amelia King. Passions were still running high when the case began; secret flash polls show it was the number one issue unifying 75 per cent of Brits against a colour bar.

This story would never have seen the light of day had it not been for Foreign Secretary Anthony Eden's public trial amendment to the United States of America (Visiting Forces) Act 1942 for cases involving ordinary UK citizens. But because it was held in public, many holes revealed by the mutiny cracked wider, throwing race relations under an even brighter spotlight when it got to trial. Authorities could not afford for the acuteness of a problem this sensitive to be exposed by announcing the tough verdicts and sentences for 581st Ordnance Ammunition Company men. Rapidly worsening race relations at this particular moment goes a long way to explaining the presiding judge's decision to block news.

Equally straightforward is understanding how Anglo-American authorities viewed the trial. In one word: fearfully. President Zickel's court bombshell reflected the fact that American and British government departments were running scared. They viewed the mutiny and court martial as a sinister threat to the 'special relationship' and were determined to prevent any dangerous repercussions. Evidence that they did so abounds. What happened directly after – and its velocity – are testimony to this. Put simply, US government departments, both in Washington, and its army-command post (ETOUSA) in London's Grosvenor Square, moved fast. They wasted no time attributing fault and quickly began creating measures to prevent another Paignton-like trial.

US Army censors were keen to lay the blame at anyone's door other, of course, than its own *Jim Crow* army. Well before the trial commenced, US military censors set its sights on 'unhelpful' publications, such as the *Chicago Defender*. One of the most successful and powerful African American publications, this particular newspaper had been under strict government surveillance since July when a censorship report concluded it was 'tending to incite racial feeling and to lower morale of troops', citing front page headline examples such as 'Stimson told of Prejudice in England' and 'Current army probe of Yank conduct in Britain is whispered as partly due to British criticism of shameful treatment of US Negro soldiers in social matters.' The military censorship examiner noted after this that company commanders of 'colored' units felt these 'newspapers cause a definite feeling of unrest among the colored troops.'[1]

Reacting directly in proportion with the story's smash sensationalism, US Army censors now came down hard. Barely a week after the trial came a memo from the US War Department to the Assistant Secretary of War, lamenting how the Launceston shooting 'has been widely discussed, particularly since it was carried by all the wire services.' African American readers' interest in stories featuring inter-racial American conflict was, the author noted, 'very keen' so the department took the strongest action possible. It cancelled the press pass of American journalist David Orro, writer of the *Chicago Defender's* front page story '14 Face Court Martial in British Clash'. Barely two days after filing his copy, according to the War Department memo,

> 'The author of the attached story is being recalled by his paper. His services have not been satisfactory, and he has had considerable trouble apparently growing out of repeated acts of misconduct on his part. Undoubtedly, however, on his return he will spread many fancy tales about the treatment of Negro soldiers in England.'

The War Department memo-writer was locked in denial. It was easy to shoot the messenger – aka David Orro – on the basis that his fanciful writing was popular and resonated with readers:

> 'These stories will find a ready acceptance among large numbers of Negroes and whites. After General Davis' visit to England, most of the liberal white publications and Negro newspapers subjected him to bitter but undeserved criticism for having submitted a whitewash report. Many people will use any unfavourable story to support the common contention that our army takes American race prejudice along with it.'

He attributed Orro's 'scaremongering' for stirring things up instead of acknowledging that real racial prejudice – not newspaper words – was the root cause of uprisings and fights. It underlined the disturbing dearth of official understanding about the type of racial conflict which had spread through America that angry summer and was now presenting in Britain. The memo also highlighted the frankly laughable attempts to find honour and dignity in the African American war contribution to date, admitting 'the situation has not been helped by recent newsreels that have been sent out of the UK. One shows a Negro soldier guarding a chicken coop and the other a platoon of Negro soldiers doing a fancy boogie-woogie march step.'[2]

Hot on censors' heels came a move to 'whitewash' racial incidents by the Bureau of Publicity in Washington. Not two weeks after the court martial, Director A.D. Surles, put in place measures to keep colour out of future news stories by firmly making racial censorship the responsibility of local army commanders. The thinking was that by being selective about what information was released, the magnitude of what was happening in ground-based incidents would be dialled down. 'The release of information about unfortunate racial incidents in the field is a matter entirely within the province of the commanding general,' he wrote on 29 October. 'The general policy is to release essential facts while avoiding the magnifying of such incidents.'[3]

In Britain meanwhile, the mutiny and court martial reverberated almost certainly all the way up the chain to Winston Churchill himself. What else could the prime minister have been referring to when describing how 'reports about the behaviour of US coloured troops stationed in this country … cause me great anxiety', two days after news of the sentencing fiasco emerged? Churchill's 'anxiety' flared from a confidential conversation with his cousin, the Duke of Marlborough, about criminality rates among African American troops in the UK before the newsprint was scarcely dry. What, other than the famous mutiny splashed all over the nation's newspapers, could have inspired this top-secret chat about black American soldiers in Great Britain? A flurry of memos and demands quickly ensued. In a letter to Secretary of State for War Sir Percy James Grigg, Churchill went on to demand numerous details about African American soldiers stationed in the UK. Specifically, he wanted to know how many were here; the names of their stations; whether they were segregated; what recreational facilities had been provided; the number of mutinies; and finally 'what steps have been taken, or are proposed to overcome such difficulties as have arisen' in his personal memo dated and initialled 20 October 1943. Why would he be firing off questions so pertinent to the Launceston mutiny – if not inspired by the same, very public and most recent incident? Despite coming at a time of great stress for the prime minister, still grappling with the Russians (over dates for opening a second front) and the Americans (over terms of the Italian armistice and surrender), Churchill prioritised investigating Paignton, demanding 'a full report giving the facts' within two days.[4]

This interest and concern, by the very personification of Britain's bulldog spirit itself, was hugely significant. Not for one moment was the issue off the official radar – and there was an immediate reaction to the trial in many government sectors ending at the office door of the PM himself. The court martial may no longer be news, but it was not history yet. Churchill's note triggered a frantic to-ing and fro-ing of facts and figures about black American troops in the UK between himself and War Secretary Sir James Grigg. More secretly, Churchill also liaised with the Duke of Marlborough, who since 1942 had been attached to American forces as a liaison officer, and felt best placed to feed the premier's concerns first with some confidential data on 21 October.

Referring to a previous exchange in which he had obviously articulated fears about the dangers facing women going about after dark while African American troops were 'on the prowl', Marlborough produced some statistics to back up his claims. The only trouble was the facts did not speak for themselves. What his enclosed analysis did show was that of the 34,875 black American troops in Great Britain between February and September that year (1943), less than two-tenths of 1 per cent of the serving men had committed a crime at all – let alone against women. A measly number of allegations, just thirty-seven involving sixty-five servicemen, had been reported – setting the soldiers' offending rate at 0.186 per cent. It was a piffling amount. What's more, in direct contrast to the duke's fears, the clear majority of these cases (twenty-five out of the thirty-seven) were for attempted murder – and only two for rape. The duke himself grudgingly conceded he may have over-egged the pudding admitting that 'these figures are liable to belittle the arguments I tried to produce yesterday.' In fact, he had demonstrated an uncomfortably clear aristocratic refutation of statistics over prejudice.

Although Marlborough was forced to admit that black troops were generally well behaved on the most part, he couldn't hold back from talking about the 'subversive' side of their presence in the UK. Reflecting precisely on sparks that flared in Paignton's court martial, such as racial tension and the revelatory British reaction it inspired, he went on to write about how this 'element about them … can do much to bring about a great deal of unpleasantness in the relationship between our two countries.' Perhaps revealing more about himself and his own prejudices than anything else, he concluded his personal memo to the prime minister with the repeated and now statistically unfounded observation that 'it is unwise and dangerous to go out into the roads and country lanes after dark and there is a growing resentment that these conditions should be allowed to exist.'[5]

Churchill's personal minutes record his response to Marlborough's fact-finding mission in the days following the court martial: 'You were quite right to come to me … I consider the matter is serious and wish to have the War Office's view upon it.'[6] Meanwhile, over at the receiving end of this request, War Secretary Sir James Grigg was about to live up to his reputation for enjoying a 'considerable flair for frank speech, aggravated by a hot temper.'[7] Having been jolted into a quick response to the mutiny and court martial, Grigg began with a home truth about Anglo–American relations. Asserting the British weighed into situations like these because they loathed the 'unfair' colour bar, he concluded that 'the problem is mainly that of relation with and attitude of the civilian population, which are matters outside the jurisdiction of either military authority.'[8] It can't have done much to improve relations with Churchill who, since 1942 reportedly was 'very dissatisfied with Grigg at War Office' according to Oliver Harvey, who worked for Foreign Secretary Anthony Eden.[9]

Like the Duke of Marlborough however, after grudgingly accepting the toxic colour bar as chief cause of the problems, the war secretary contrived to divert blame elsewhere – to yet another oppressed strata of society. Sir James Grigg reported to Churchill that the Americans 'are much perturbed by the behaviour of the British civilian population … in particular, of some sections of the female population.' Writing on 21 October, he said: 'Senior officers of the American Army have frequently expressed shocked surprise at the attitude of some of our women, and they point out, with some force, that the blame is not all on one side.'[10]

Both British and American government departments had cringed at the implications of Paignton and cast around wildly for explanations such as 'loose' women and mendacious messengers to shoot. Meanwhile, the

American Army was also hard at work, seeking yet more bogus reasons and cure-alls. Rather than using the debacle as an opportunity for some wholesome soul-searching, they saw it as a matter of discipline. After all, it was much easier to create a new micro-rule governing army behaviour than ask why this ammunition ordnance company had been restricted on account of its race for so long – and then wonder why mutiny had resulted. A memo from American Brigadier General G.M. Alexander said smaller units such as the 581st should be either attached to a regiment or held in staging areas until the commanding officer was satisfied with discipline. The 581st Ordnance Ammunition Company had been stationed in Yeovil 'but without enough supervision or check. The company causing the trouble at Launceston was there for about ten days.'

Brigadier General Alexander concluded that going forwards, no black and white soldiers were to be allowed at the same dance and 'coloured' military policemen needed to team up with white military policemen to prevent claims of unfair treatment. 'This feeling was apparent at Launceston and seemed to be held by certain British,' he surmised. But ultimately, he came to the same conclusions as both the stateside War Department and Bureau of Publicity. This was not an opportunity to investigate what caused the mutiny – which was the army's chronic racist treatment of African American servicemen who were risking their lives for a freedom that did not extend to them. It was this dawning realisation that was behind such fast-rising tension. Instead army chiefs saw it as an excuse to turn a blind eye, crack down harder on the reporting of further incidents and blame poor discipline by prescribing more. 'The solution is a matter of censorship and close supervision on the part of all officers,' concluded the Brigadier General.[11]

While the American Army war and publicity departments stamped on over-mighty journalists and under-disciplined soldiers in the wake of Launceston's mutiny, it was only civil rights activists and writers who turned their guns on the system itself. First to attack was NAACP leader Walter White, who was confident that the attempted murder charges should never have been brought at all. Using his own lawyerly logic and training, he said: 'No English people or other person was shot. No military policemen were shot except in the legs, clearly proving that, despite their rage, the Negro soldiers did not want to cause loss of life.'[12]

Writing in *A Rising Wind*, White despaired about the unfairness of evidence pointing overwhelmingly away from murder and mutiny which he presumed had counted for little in the subsequent court martial. Proving how watertight news of the president's sentencing had been, he wrote how he presumed they were all convicted, with some sentenced to death and others imprisoned for long stretches in American jails.

Even more apparent was the immediate shockwave in Britain, according to American journalist Roi Ottley – rated as 'one of the outstanding Negro writers of America' by none other than Ernest Hemingway. Existing indigenous resistance to the colour bar set the tone for a bumpy trial, he recorded. Although getting the specific incident details wrong, Roi Ottley nevertheless epitomised the trial's inflammatory effect on the British public when he noted in his diary:

'The treatment of the Negro soldier by his fellow American has become a burning issue,' he wrote. 'When eighteen Negro soldiers … [who] were refused service because of their colour put up a fight, their trial was covered by every newspaper. The *London Daily Mail* headlined its story: 'FINDINGS SECRET IN US TRIAL FOR MUTINY'.[13]

Underlying the 'burning' racial issue and the clear-cut wrongs of Launceston's shooting and resulting trial was a genuine fear that the court martial system was out to punish African Americans, who did not take army-imposed subjugation lying down. Walter White condemned the way those who knew their rights were seen as 'troublemakers' and treated as such to crush their resolve. He said it was widely thought by 'many British citizens' (as well as American soldiers of both races) that army justice was used to punish people for being 'bad Negroes' who today would be thought of as activists.[14] So strongly did he feel this that the following year Walter White took this complaint to President Franklin D. Roosevelt himself, decrying the 'excessive tendency to court martial and impose heavy sentences on Negroes.'[15]

Unsurprisingly it was only civil rights activists like Walter White who dug deep, calling for a re-booting of the system itself while authorities remained horrified by the publicity generated by such heat-seeking coverage – and blacked out the verdict and sentences. Flailing around behind the scenes, there was much knee-jerking, with federal departments scrabbling to exert control over journalists by revoking press passes and prescribing yet more censorship while stricter army discipline was ordered. Across the Atlantic, Churchill himself reacted by firing off demands for facts and figures about black soldiers here, while his cousin and war minister were forced to admit the African American soldiers were mostly 'well behaved' and the colour bar 'unfair', all the while seeking alternative scapegoats. Such were the rapid Anglo and American governmental reactions to the court martial, but just how successful was the blanket news ban?

Certainly, up until this point, coverage had been intense. United States newspapers from Gettysburg to Amarillo; Athens, Ohio to Hanover, Pennsylvania; and Paris, Texas to Nebraska had scooped this incredible story from the wires. Some had even pipped British rivals by covering the trial in real time, using the Eastern Seaboard's five-hour difference, to break news on the court day it occurred. Conversely, the 12 million-plus tabloid-reading Britons who had to wait an extra few hours for the latest instalment, were then spoilt for choice as an entirely different army of home-front journalists battled for their attention.

Even when spiked, the story's impact was slow to dissipate. The official British body tasked with monitoring national concerns knew it was still very much in the public's mind, if not in its newspapers. 'The shooting affray in Cornwall has once more drawn attention to the colour problem – NB 12 regions in total,' noted the Home Intelligence Division's weekly report a few days after the trial ended.[16] However much they tried to suppress the Launceston shooting and its show-stopping court martial, neither the British nor American governments could deny its impact on the two nations' newspaper-reading populations – however brief. It had proved impossible to shroud the undeniable racism and prejudice which had driven the shooting in the first place and then governed the kangaroo-like court martial.

Nor could they kid themselves about which side the British public generally backed in this specifically American race war. The mutiny and trial underpinned by an institutional colour bar combined to arouse a support for the underdog as traditionally classic in Britain as warm beer and cricket. It revealed a generosity of spirit, singularly lacking in still-rationed austerity Britain five years later when the *Windrush* steamed up the Thames to Tilbury Dock. And all these factors came together in 1943 to put Anglo-American relations in a wholly unfavourable light at that precise moment.

How then had an international newspaper-reading audience of some millions reacted when the curtain crashed down on the final act in Launceston's mutiny – preventing the most crucial part from being performed? What was the response when news of the sentencing was publicly blocked? A profound and deafening silence was the answer. Despite the wide-reaching hum of activity it had driven on both sides of the Atlantic, to all intents and purposes the story now merely slipped over the edge into an abyss. The decision to keep sentencing secret proved to be a masterstroke, promptly squeezing any remaining life from the subsequent court martial. Denied oxygen, the surrounding brouhaha died. The gagging-order had achieved exactly what army authorities wanted – there was nothing more for people to react to and no more news reports to craft. As President Zickel announced the news blackout on the evening of 17 October 1943, it was as if the earth had opened up and swallowed the mutiny whole. At any other point in history, someone at least might have battled on a bit harder to discover the truth. But as winter closed in on 1943 they were too busy fighting another enemy – and the world merely moved on forever.

Chapter 19

And Beyond

Everything else on the home-front blurred into soft focus that November as covert make-or-break war council decisions were taken by the 'Big Three' – Winston Churchill, Franklin D. Roosevelt and Joseph Stalin. Principal grandees of the Second World War's 'Grand Alliance' were secretly slugging it out in Tehran over how to carve up Europe once Hitler had been crushed – and more pressingly – when, and where, a second front would open to relieve pressure on Russia's eastern flank. Back home in Britain, it was as if a magic wand had been waved banishing American Army racial tension from the newspapers. In Launceston itself, the very opposite of discord and grief was being advertised in the form of a musical performance to be staged at the town hall. Light years away from the most recent showcase of African American drama in town, the sell-out gig was dubbed unmissable by local newspapers, introducing it as 'a terrific coloured revue of melody, dance and mirth' courtesy of 'the American Army.'[1]

This celebrated '*Dixieland*' show was indeed the beating heart of Launceston that last winter before D-Day. According to then 20-something resident Joan Rendell, also witness to the September mutiny:

'Launceston had never seen anything like it before. Some of the men were professional entertainers and they put on a splendid show. For weeks afterwards everybody who saw the show was going around humming a catchy tune 'Chocolate Soldier from the USA' a popular hit song of the day. Proceeds from the sale of tickets for *Dixie* were given to charity and the whole event was one of the highlights of the year in the town, helping people to forget the tragedy of war just for one evening.'[2]

If ever there was a quick-fix to help chip away recent memories of ugly racial tension, *'Dixieland'* was it. But despite the overt celebration of African-Americana, and the improving inter-racial harmony it implied, in real terms nothing had changed, either locally or nationally. People were quick to react to the merest sniff of overt racism – as shown by the furious firestorm surrounding Oswald Mosley's release from internment later that month. Contempt for the British bigot, the cartoon-like leader of the British Union of Fascists, poured into a powerful protest against the decision to free him from prison on the grounds of ill health in November 1943. It created for the Home Secretary 'the biggest storm of [Herbert] Morrison's wartime career', concluded biographers Bernard Donoughue and G.W. Jones.[3]

Significantly, neither had home-grown resentment of imported racial prejudice seemingly diminished. Evidence from the Ministry of Information's Home Intelligence report of 23 December 1943 shows British people still raging against United States troops – with criticism continuing to outweigh favourable comments. Once again 'colour-bar incidents' from all regions underpinned that unfavourable opinion of American soldiers. Why would ordinary British people still be voicing these concerns if the violence had truly dried up?

Clues into what was really happening were picked up one month later. By January 1944, the US Army's policy of not disclosing race in the reporting of incidents had obviously kicked in, but it had not fooled observant opinion-formers such as George Orwell. The policy introduced after the court martial into Launceston's mutiny was masking an important aspect of the news, Orwell noticed.

> 'There is much jealousy between American white and coloured troops. The press shuts down on this subject to such an extent that when a rape or something like that happens, one can only discover by private inquiry whether the American involved is white or coloured. Discussion of the inter-allied relations is still avoided in the press and utterly taboo on the air.'[4]

Dwindling incidents of reported racial violence did not reflect the speedy improvement of relations between black and white GIs. More likely the data showed how slavishly recommendations to edit out racial references were being followed.

Nor had wider national views about the 'American invaders' changed discernibly. In February, the BBC passed its *Listener Report*, specially-commissioned to understand changing British public opinion towards America between 1942 and 1943, to the Ministry of Information. It made for dreary reading – but only between the lines. After analysing the changing opinions of 1,000 listeners over the twelve-month period, the BBC breezily concluded there was 'no basis for alarmist statements to the effect that American troops are universally unpopular.' But four months before D-Day commenced, 'Auntie' was playing hard and fast with the truth.

The biggest headline it glossed over was that 'very nearly' 80 per cent of the 'ordinary' man's opinions was that the Americans were 'still not wholeheartedly in the war, and that, man for man, their war effort is on the average not as great as our own.' In other words, the BBC's own analysis showed most British radio listeners, which was pretty much everyone, did not rate America's spirit or war effort. Neither did they think much more of the impression American servicemen were making in Britain. Damning GIs with the faintest of praise, the report surmised that only those who had not met American servicemen believed that with experience the 'American is as good a fighting man as the British', whereas those who had met them felt they 'will never be equal to the British.'

All the while, the root cause of Britain's (at best) lukewarm opinion of its principal ally was America's *'race problem'*. The refrain was always the same – not treating all men equally undermined basic decency. 'The attitude of white American troops to their coloured compatriots was mentioned only to be condemned and used as evidence against the reality of American democracy' while African Americans were largely preferred because of their better manners.

Expanding on the point, the Listener Research Department's report went on to comment that increasing awareness of the colour bar caused fewer people to believe America to be more democratic than those questioned before. Although it attempted to play down the popularity of this view, claiming it was still 'that of a minority,' the report nevertheless concluded it was more prevalent, especially among those who had met Americans. British people had only seen the colour bar in action in the past couple of years, the report explained, and 'this has made a profound impression in some quarters.'[5]

Even though race had been censored from official versions of what was being fought about on British streets, public opinion had not changed. If anything, it had calcified most probably because everyone knew that tension underlying these 'wild outbursts' had not gone anywhere. The factual evidence is that far from dying down in the wake of Launceston's mutiny, racially driven crimes were on the up. And the biggest sign of this was a secret memo from the American Army's Office of the Inspector General in February 1944.

In the three months since 581st Ordnance Ammunition Company men were imprisoned for mutiny, there had been no less than fifty-six 'inter-racial disorders' according to this cumulative total. Robberies, assaults, fights, stabbings, 'manhandlings', arguments, riots and attacks between black and white individuals and gangs were reported from Swansea to Southampton, Coventry to Carmarthen and Belfast to Basingstoke. Even Launceston witnessed two further incidents post-*Dixieland* according to the record, which was based on logs recorded in military police and base censorship reports from 19 November 1943 to February 1944.[6] By mid-April, US Army morale reports warned that 'incidents of violence between the two races have increased noticeably during this period.' Two weeks later, a follow-up memo noted tersely that 'the whites dislike the Negroes and the Negroes dislike the whites … The predominant note is that if the invasion doesn't occur soon, trouble will.'[7]

The situation that had allowed mutineers to muster in Launceston was not getting any better – quite the contrary. What had changed was that these incidents were not being reported in the newspapers, as now precious little could escape the army censor's net.

Displaying an impeccable sense of timing, NAACP leader Walter White blasted into Britain at this precise moment. Travelling to Launceston as well as other 'hot spots', such as Bamber Bridge, Bristol and Newbury, became his main objective. Originally, his visit was in answer to a desperate missive from an African American Red Cross worker already experiencing life in England. The head of the United States' biggest and

most prominent civil rights group was lured by intriguing tales including
that of a dinner for US soldiers hosted by 'a distinguished British family'.
All was going swimmingly until an African American soldier dared to
dance with an English woman, which promptly started an all-out fist-
fight in which 'the British took the side of the Negroes.' Then there was a
story doing the rounds in the US of a publican who posted a sign over his
entrance which read: 'This place for the exclusive use of Englishmen and
American Negro Soldiers.' According to White's own account, he needed
to see for himself the truth of whispers 'some good, most of them bad'
about what was going on between white and black American troops here –
and he started in Launceston.[8]

Once he got here White wasted little of his sixteen days, travelling
more than 1,700 miles to visit black units based from the North Sea
to Plymouth and Liverpool to Southampton, according to his guide,
Captain Max K. Gilstrap. Seconded especially to arrange, conduct
and accompany White on his trip, Captain Gilstrap, whose day job was
associate editor of US Forces newspaper *The Stars and Stripes,* said no
stone was left unturned. Writing to ETOUSA's Public Relations Office,
Gilstrap described how during his whistle-stop tour, Walter White

'rode in jeeps, flew in a Fortress, slept in a Nissen hut, climbed
aboard a freighter, saw a clubmobile in action, heard the US Army
Negro Chorus, watched a bombing mission go out and return,
and observed ground troops manoeuvring in a combat area. He
tramped miles through mud to talk to Negro airdrome engineers at
work with bulldozers, giant cranes, concrete millers and caterpillar
tractors. He rode more miles along the highways and byways of
Britain to chat with colored troops in hospitals, camp theatres and
kitchens, APOs, weapon and tool rooms, supply depots, libraries, at
docks, in Aero clubs, American Red Cross clubs and in a Detention
Training Centre.'[9]

The one thing Walter White had not packed for his fact-finding
mission to Britain was a pair of rose-tinted glasses. He knew the racist
American contingent was a minority – although admittedly a vocal
one. Nor did he ever forget Britain's own double standards over race,
acknowledging that within its empire, India for one 'remains enslaved,

maligned by British propaganda, and its leaders jailed.'[10] Nevertheless, his devastating conclusion was that lasting damage had been inflicted on Anglo–American relations. The British would remember the violence and prejudice they had seen directed at African Americans long after war ended, White believed. And not only would bad British memories widen the existing chasm between both nations, but it would also soften any justified American criticism of its own colonial policy.

This chasm identified by White clearly featured in Home Intelligence Division reports during the next three months to April. Resentment of white American servicemen's attitudes and actions towards their black peers remained prominent in the department's reports to the Ministry of Information: 'This is not liked – the less so because the coloured troops are usually popular and considered well behaved' read a typical example in April 1944.[11] In fact, from this point onwards, complaints about the segregation, weaved so intricately into the United States of America's army, never departed.

Parliament too kept its role as a vessel for hot-tempered debate about the topic. On 10 May 1944, the righteousness of imposing a death sentence on two black GIs for alleged rape was raised by Hugh Lawson MP. The member for Skipton described the sentence as a 'disgrace' and an 'anomaly' asking Foreign Secretary Anthony Eden 'if he will inform the American government that the carrying out of such a sentence would be interpreted by many people in this country as racial persecution and therefore likely to cause bad feeling between the two countries.'[12]

Little more than two weeks later it was Home Secretary Herbert Morrison's turn to stand in the firing line. Originally fielding a general parliamentary question from Denis Kendall, MP for Grantham, about the danger to women in his constituency posed by the 'ineffectiveness of the American military authorities to deal with the improper behaviour of the American Forces and the complete failure to prevent unconcealed immorality and to give proper protection to women', the issue promptly swung back to race.[13] Once again, the disparity in capital sentences awarded to black and white American servicemen was raised, this time by Morrison's friend Major Richard Stokes, MP for Ipswich, who questioned whether the Home Secretary knew that black GIs were being sentenced to death over white GIs: 'Is my right honourable friend aware

... that ... if they are committed by the coloured troops, are subject to the death penalty, and that the white troops are allowed to do as they like?'[14]

Unsurprisingly, after D-Day, support for America and its servicemen increased markedly, but the inequities of its colour bar never faded totally. There was little appetite for flagrant racism – wherever it originated. It was evident, even amid the lofty peaks of London's High Court, most memorably just a couple of weeks after the Normandy landings. On this occasion, plain common-sense received a fillip when cricketer Learie Constantine had his own day in court – and triumphed. Fulfilling the desire of outraged British members of parliament to 'bowl out' the management of London's Imperial Hotel for refusing to honour his family's booking, Constantine was awarded five guineas' damages for breach of contract.

The sorry story was revealed in all its inglorious detail. Readers learned how the cricket star, also a welfare officer in the Ministry of Labour in Liverpool, had been in London to captain the West Indies in a charity fixture against England at Lord's. Constantine's chief at the Ministry, Arnold Roberts Watson, arrived at the hotel to find the cricketer and his wife looking 'disconsolate and unhappy.' On hearing they had been evicted from the Imperial, 'He told the manageress: "You cannot turn Mr Constantine and his party out of the hotel like this."' Court reporters told how the boorish manageress, Miss Margaret O'Sullivan, a stalwart of the Russell Square hotel for nearly forty years, explained her actions simply saying: 'We won't have *niggers* in this hotel' as it was 'practically full of American and Colonial soldiers.' Constantine later reflected that 'The hotel was then too cowardly to resist this American pressure.'[15]

Giving judgement on 28 June 1944, Mr Justice Birkett described 'the distress and humiliation which [the] plaintiff unjustifiably suffered' and accepted 'without hesitation Mr Constantine's evidence and that of his witnesses.' The judge poured cold water on the hotel management's denial of using such insulting words, instead referring to the poisonous Miss O'Sullivan as 'a lamentable figure ... I am satisfied on the material points she was not speaking the truth. She was grossly insulting in her reference to Mr Constantine.'[16]

At least in court cases British judges could control, there seemed little backing for racial prejudice. Even at this post-D-Day stage, when public support for US troops outweighed criticism, the deciding factor against Americans was nearly always to do with colour. Surveying press cuttings about American troops in Britain from March to July 1944, the British American Liaison Board found there were sixty-two articles in the London papers alone: forty-two good and twenty bad. But of the bad reports most of them (65 per cent) referred 'to the British dislike of the treatment of Negroes by white Americans.' Specifically, almost half of the critical reports (9 out of the 20) dealt 'with the alleged unfair treatment of Negroes by US Court Martial … all criticism arises from the trials of Negro soldiers … which British people have considered to be unfairly conducted owing to racial prejudice.'

Overall, almost one-fifth of all the collated press stories about any single aspect of American servicemen spoke out 'in favour of the Negro soldier, and where there is friction between white and black troops, the British opinion expressed sides invariably with the Negroes.'[17]

What precisely had evolved in US Army race relations in the year after Launceston's mutiny? What had happened to the British reaction it engendered? Wide-ranging changes had swept in governing how 'racial' events were reported, black soldiers were disciplined, and inconvenient reporters recalled. Other more genuine measures too came in after Walter White's trip to Britain, such as joint black and white military police street-patrols to put the kybosh on inflammatory scenes of white soldiers picking on black soldiers. This went further than merely attacking the periphery and somewhere nearer to addressing the root cause. Significantly it was also one of the first recommendations from initial investigators at Launceston – who attributed much of the trouble that night to the lack of mixed patrols.

As a consequence, fewer racial incidents occurred in the public eye. But they did not dry up. Not at all. Long after Launceston's mutiny had been forgotten, American bigotry was still frequent and flagrant enough to merit a British resentment, captured in Home Intelligence reports, BBC listener polls, parliamentary questions and press cutting reviews. The unpopularity of home-grown racial prejudice too was manifested in widespread protests against Oswald Mosley's prison release and celebrations of Learie Constantine's court triumph. Admittedly, outside the UK, other US conciliatory tactics including the creation of 'all-black' fighting units did much to repair the damage by building confidence and acknowledging bravery, skill and general equality, but they were still the rare exceptions.

There may have been signs of more sincere attempts to improve equality in America's army. But the fact remains that the British public still saw raw racial prejudice manifested and they still felt it was wrong – at the Launceston Mutiny, three months afterwards and even after D-Day. It was always there. And despite everything, almost a year to the day that 581st Ordnance Ammunition Company men so dramatically trooped back to their segregated camp, armed themselves and then marched in formation back into Launceston town square, the same emotions and feelings military authorities had tried to quash in the Paignton court martial and beyond, were still bubbling up. Perhaps it was easiest for an outsider to sum up the status quo nearly a year after the court martial that shocked a nation: someone like New Yorker Roi Ottley.

One of America's most famous black writers at the time, Ottley had shot to fame in 1943 with his first book *New World A Coming*, a no-holds-barred depiction of segregated America in the 1920s and 1930s. Now, thanks to an army posting in 1944, he enjoyed an unfiltered view of life in Britain. As a newly commissioned captain, he was European war correspondent for *PM* and *Liberty,* embarking on a two-year odyssey which covered nearly 70,000 miles. His impressions of life in Britain three months after D-Day are invaluable. Biographer Mark A. Huddle said: 'It was extremely rare for an African American journalist to write for a white publication in that period. It is a testament to Ottley's celebrity and political connection, as well as *PM's* antiracist editorial position that he was hired for such a high-profile job.'[18]

It was while living in the UK that Ottley observed the following. Writing in his diary just three weeks short of the Launceston mutiny's first anniversary, Ottley sensed the 'noose of prejudice is slowly tightening around the neck of American Negro soldiers.' And what was the reaction to this in Britain – by this time more of a staging post than training camp for allies edging ever closer to victory in mainland Europe? 'Today the British are aggressively resisting the prejudice which certain white American soldiers are intent upon imposing,' the writer continued in his diary entry of 2 September 1944. Describing what happened when an American soldier tried to boot out two black soldiers from their London bus seats, he recorded: 'You can't do that sort of thing here,' a woman conductor protested. 'We won't have it. Either you stand or off you go.'[19] In this particular brief wartime twinkling at least, little had changed.

Epilogue

Court Martial President and Law Member

Nothing can be found in the file for **Raymond E. Zickel**, president of the court martial.

Prosecutors

Unsurprisingly, the most information available is about the undeniable star of the show himself, Trial Court Advocate **Frank P. Eresch**. He had joined up in his home town of Topeka, Kansas, in October 1940, describing himself as self-employed on the enlistment form. Three years on, he was most definitely employed by the army and wasted little time putting his learnings from Paignton police court to good use for them. On the very day after the court martial ended, there was a five-day 'School of Military Justice' held at the Southern Base to train even more officers from various units for court martial duty. It culminated in a final exam after daily tests and mock trials and resulted in thirty-four more officers being prepared for court martial work. It is interesting to speculate what recent lessons Eresch might have shared with his trainees.

From his performance, there was always an implicit sense that Eresch was playing a long game and that he wanted it to improve his future prospects. Given he ended up as a lieutenant colonel before returning to his hometown of Topeka as city attorney, arguably, it did the trick. By 1951, he was appearing for the state of Kansas at the Kansas Supreme Court. At some later stage he moved to Houston, Texas. Given his decisive role in Paignton's court martial, however, it is no small irony that a landmark case in America's civil rights movement started under Frank P. Eresch's very nose. Seven-year-old Linda Brown, from Topeka, Kansas, inspired a legal watershed when a local school denied her entry on the basis of her race. Linda's family joined a class action filed by the NAACP that would become known as Brown v Board of Education to challenge segregated schools. Its ruling in 1954 that segregating schools 'solely because of their race generates a feeling of inferiority' made segregation in public schools unconstitutional. It was a massive first step in the American Civil Rights movement. Frank P. Eresch died twenty-five years later in 1979 with his rank, lieutenant colonel, engraved on his gravestone.

Defence

We know that Defense Counsel **Captain John A. Philbin** retired from the army on 13 January 1947, but little else.

The Guilty

War was over for the fourteen 581st Ordnance Ammunition Company men as soon as the guilty verdicts came in October 1943. During their very last days of army life, the inequalities they had suffered as African American soldiers had been laid bare. Glimmers of botched statement-gathering techniques, an over-mighty prosecution and under-mighty defence shone through an extraordinary legal process. Tantalising glimpses were snatched of the humiliation, segregation and subjugation they had endured in the US Army. Three days spent determining the fourteen's destiny culminated abruptly with the court's secret findings – itself indicative of the gravity with which military authorities viewed events in Launceston. Some might argue the US Army itself should have been on trial for everything it inflicted on those drafted to fight for a freedom in Europe that was unthinkable, let alone attainable for themselves back home. It could be concluded that 581st Ordnance Ammunition Company men had been backed into a corner and that to come out shooting was their only possible exit.

No time was wasted returning the fourteen to prison, this time on a more permanent basis. None of the men involved in the court martial are alive today and it has proved impossible to trace descendants of the 581st men court-martialled. But enough has been gleaned from a second file, included with the court martial manuscript, to show that life afterwards for most of them spiralled into decline. This subsequent document is at least twice as deep again as the weighty three-day court martial transcript itself and contains findings from subsequent review boards into the court martial, prolific six-monthly bids for clemency from the individuals behind bars, as well as tragic letters from those family members they left behind.

Although the first review board, as early as November 1943, simply concurred with Paignton's findings and sentences, a second in February 1944 found it was 'legally insufficient' to prove any of the men guilty of mutiny at all, so within just three months a major strand of the prosecution had been dismantled altogether. Similarly, there was insufficient evidence against ten of them to prove the intent to murder Sergeant Ralph Curtis Simmons. Four of the accused – McKnight, Gibbs, Manning and Tilly – were found to have not shown intent to riot and were therefore guilty only of making inflammatory sentences (which did not carry a penitentiary confinement). The main errors and irregularities were all the prosecution's, the review board found. Not only had it singularly failed to prove mutiny, but the statements Eresch insisted were read at the trial by each of the accused (to which the defence team objected) in fact proved 'highly prejudicial' to others mentioned, according to the review board. In some of the cases, various NAACP branches took up their cases, as well as senators and congressmen.

Ringleaders et al

Henry Austin had been on parole for armed robbery in 1937 when he joined up in 1941, but fortunately his army record was much better. His military service was deemed good and Austin's conduct in confinement 'excellent'. Not only did army psychologists think he was mentally responsible, but his IQ of 120 afforded him well above average intelligence, making him 'not psychotic ... [but] a leader and is mature, rather dominant type.' His case was taken up by William H. Brooks, President of the NAACP's East Long Street, Columbus, Ohio branch on 14 February 1946 and eventually, on 15 December 1947, his sentence was reduced to six years.

Master mutineer **Clifford Barrett** had a fair military record and showed good conduct in confinement, according to army records. The former gardener and groundkeeper of parks and cemeteries in his native Florida had enjoyed an 11th grade education and was deemed 'mentally responsible, average intelligence.' Perhaps influenced by knowledge of the Launceston shooting, his army psychologist reported he was 'Immature, somewhat aggressively inclined, with scattering of psychopathic tendencies. Prognosis for civilian adjustment is poor because of emotional immaturity.' Most shattering of all in his file however, is the wretched letter written by his mother, Mrs Johnnie Barrett, requesting a copy of the court martial from the Judge Advocate General's Office (JAGO):

> 'I am asking you all to have mercy on me because my health are no good and … Clifford all I can depend on … I really don't believe Clifford meant to do what they say he did. Some time I would hasten to give him a whippen when he was a small boy and we all who wants our children to do right do that. I surpose his father was in 1918 war serve eight months and went and died in 1930 … Ay god ble our country and I know he will.'

The official response was a mealy mouthed letter from Colonel R.E. Kunkel saying a copy had already been issued to Barrett and to get another she must send a cheque for $39.80. On 14 February 1946 Clifford Barrett's sentence was reduced to nine years.

The trail runs cold only for **Sergeant Rupert Hughes**.

The eleven others

Former porter **Freddy Blake** saw his sentence remitted to six-and-a-half years on 25 September 1946. His conduct in confinement at Fort Benjamin Harrison, Indiana, was good and he was deemed 'mentally responsible, high average intelligence. IQ of 109. Essentially normal. Quite stable' by the army psychologist department.

Willis Gibbs, a grammar-school-educated carpenter, originally from Arkansas but now settled in Cook County, Illinois was transferred on 5 July 1944 to United States Disciplinary Barracks Green Haven in New York. It is the one and only entry for him in the JAGO file.

By far the most poignant letter on file for former elevator operator and grammar-school boy **Tom Ewing** comes from his wife, Irene. On 12

September 1944 she wrote asking when he would be released from prison in Atlanta, Georgia, and, most of all, for help. Describing how heart and other health issues were preventing her from working and the difficulties this led to her bringing up their child, she said,

> 'just think if you were in his place and I was your wife and …
> after my husband been in the army and then spent eight months
> in England and then they bring you back here and put you in the
> penitentiary for fifteen years … you know that very hard for me to
> have to live like that long without my husband.'

Irene Ewing was not the only one batting for her husband. On 3 April 1945 Senator Scott W. Lucas, a Democrat and First World War soldier who had been nominated as a potential running mate for Franklin D. Roosevelt in the 1944 presidential election, wrote to JAGO on Ewing's behalf. On 2 August 1945, Illinois Senator C. Wayland Brooks, a former marine wounded in the First World War, also wrote a supportive letter. There is no record of when his sentence was reduced in the file.

The later records from Paignton contain a request from the FBI on 6 December 1949 for a copy of the court martial report in connection with an investigation it was conducting into **James Hedekiah Lindsey**. It is the sole document dealing with him.

No reports exist on file for **James Manning**, probably because he was restored to duty on 31 May 1945.

Father-of-one **Arzie Martin** had the NAACP's New York branch write on his behalf to JAGO to track down exhibits missing from the court martial record. On 28 August 1944 Martin wrote himself for more information about the next clemency hearing, asking for a new trial itself – and saying he wanted the opportunity to put things right. 'My reason for writing you this is that I do not feel as if I have had a chance to prove my innocent, [sic] and if I could get the chance, I am sure I could go back to the army and soldier again.' Martin's tenth-grade education had resulted in good records for civilian, army and prison life. His above average intelligence (an IQ of 120) and good temperament prompted army psychologists to conclude he was 'essentially normal … prognosis for civilian adjustment is good.' Still clemency was denied repeatedly as he was moved from Fort Benjamin Harrison in Indiana to Milwaukee, Wisconsin. A moving plea for help was written by his wife Gwendolyn on 9 August 1946 describing how 'I am 20 of age and I have a baby three of age. My husband is 23 yrs … sir I pray day and night that someone can help us … life is hell.' On 12 December 1946 Martin's sentence was remitted beyond six-and-a-half years.

Although boasting a good civil record, father-of-one **Henry McKnight** had a poor military record which turned worse in confinement, according to his clemency consideration report. He actually escaped on 13 July 1945 and was returned to jail only on 7 September 1945. On 6 February 1946, his sentence was reduced to four-and-a-half years.

On 17 October 1946, the sentence of **Alexander Shaw**, originally a semi-skilled warehouser from Tennessee, was remitted to six-and-a-half years. The father-of-one with a fifth-grade education had a poor civil record according to one of his clemency consideration reports, but good reports from his time both in the military and confinement at Camp Gordon, Georgia. Army psychologists judged him to be mentally responsible with average intelligence and 'essentially normal'.

Carl Tennyson witnessed his honourable discharge at Fort Jay, New York on 8 May 1944. The unexecuted portion was remitted and he was released from confinement and honourably restored to duty on 11 February 1946. Sadly, in 1951, JAGO received a letter from the Westchester County DA in connection with a recent conviction asking whether Tennyson was considered a second offender considering Launceston. If that was the case, his sentence would be increased by five years.

Texan farmhand **Henry Tilly** had his sentence reduced to four years on 4 February 1946.

Nothing could be found on **Charlie Geddies**.

Chief Prosecution Witnesses

Predictably the four crucial prosecution witnesses **Kenneth N. Blanchett, L.V. Edwards, Alfred Joseph Jnr** and **Albert Smith**, who were as much part of events in Launceston as the fourteen they turned on, were granted a 'get out of jail card' in return for their case-making evidence. But they had to wait until just four days before the trial started to get this assurance. As late as 10 October 1943 investigating officer, Captain James E. Stephenson, recommended they be charged and referred to court martial for their involvement. It was only once Trial Judge Advocate Frank P. Eresch got his hands on all the material and realised they were the only ones able to identify the defendants that he recommended granting them immunity from prosecution. There is nothing further in the JAGO follow-up file about any of them except **Private First Class L.V. Edwards** who is recorded as being Dead, Not Battle (DNB) in army registers for the Honor List of Dead and Missing Army and Army Air Forces Personnel from Texas, 1946.

New Yorker **James Bosson** was quietly removed from command of the 581st Ordnance Ammunition Company immediately after the shooting on 1 October 1943 and a good two weeks before the trial even started. He was personally named by 29th Infantry Division Commander **Major General C.H. Gerhardt** as most to blame for the mutiny in the preliminary investigation. It was one of the facts never mentioned during the court martial. He retired fourteen years later as a major on 30 April 1957.

Other Prosecution Witnesses

Surprisingly little is known about what happened individually to those 115th Infantry soldiers at the receiving end of the 581st Ordnance Ammunition Company's firepower on 26 September 1943. In every pre-trial report the 115th Infantry's Second Battalion were absolved of any responsibility for events in Launceston, in all probability with some accuracy. It was the brutal training camps in the US that created the problem and precedent for prejudice, investigators decided. It just happened that the last straws – that final restriction, that final eviction from a dance, that final pub fight, all took place in Launceston. Although all three were rooted in the army's *Jim Crow* attitude, the serious damage had already been done to men of the 581st Ordnance Ammunition Company by the time they reached Great Britain.

Captain Richard P. Scott was included in the battle orders for D-Day. Later on D-Day itself he was credited in the 115th Infantry Regiment's history with delivering a map relieved from a captured German, detailing the enemy's defence batteries, to the regiment's command post at 6.00pm. Three days later he himself became a prisoner of war at La Carrefour – just beyond the beachhead on 9 June 1944. The controversial incident involved a large number of American soldiers being surrounded and then either mown down or taken hostage by Germans. A captured American officer supposedly called on his countrymen to surrender before they were shot dead by machine-gun fire. Captain Scott was one of fifty-eight prisoners taken in this contentious encounter which resulted in the deaths of thirty-one of his comrades and the wounding of seventy-seven more.

As with Captain Richard P. Scott, both La Carrefour and the Launceston shooting were to remain indelible parts of service records for **Staff Sergeant Ralph C. Simmons**. Simmons was again with Captain Scott when he was injured for a second time, at La Carrefour, just as he had been on the Cornish streets eight months earlier.

Ariel W. Glenn had little more luck being on the wrong side of friendly fire when he found himself once more the target of blue-on-blue violence on 25 April 1944. On this occasion an African American soldier, Private Donald McGee, of the 3170th Quartermaster Company, was charged with 'wrongfully' rushing at and grappling with him. McGee was reported to have said: 'No second lieutenant is going to tell me what to do' … and by calling said Lieutenant Glenn "second lieutenant" and "sir" in a very sarcastic and disrespectful manner.' The subsequent court martial, into the soldiers' actions, resulted in McGee, a former parking attendant from Columbus, Ohio, being discharged on 1 April 1944.

John Potocki retains a cherished place in the 115th Infantry Regiment's Roll of Honor. He died of his wounds after fighting on 18 June 1944 and was awarded the Purple Heart. He is buried at: Plot F Row 11 Grave 4 in the Normandy American Cemetery Colleville-sur-Mer, France.

Court Reporter

It is thought that **Joyce Packe** was stenographer at the Nuremberg Trials. When her days in the US Army ended, the fearless Miss Packe was instrumental in setting up the Devon and Cornwall Young Liberal

Federation, becoming vice chairman of the newly formed group. Interestingly, it was in this capacity that she took part in a debate on capital punishment in 1947. The argument to keep it won. In 1948 she moved to London for teacher training and returned to Torquay to set up new courses in hotel management for the local college. By the 1960s she was running typing courses at the local technical college before being recruited a few years later to appoint and train local tourist guides. Here the hardy, no-nonsense reputation of the indomitable Miss Packe became legendary. One of her guides recalls an occasion when Miss Packe was leading a group of Women's Institute members on a walking tour when a storm erupted, bringing with it a sudden onslaught of torrential rain, thunder and lightning. The leader of the WI politely told her tour guide that they wanted to turn around, only to hear an infuriated Miss Packe shout back: 'What are you women, a bunch of WIMPS?' She became a local historian, authoring books and many features for her local newspaper, the *Herald Express*, for thirty-plus years – and remained a respected pillar of the community.

Other Witnesses

Former carpenter, **Sergeant Alfred Faria** from Mattapoisett, Massachusetts, was awarded a Purple Heart after being wounded on Omaha Beach while serving as platoon guide for the 29th Division – a perilous role during the Normandy landings. When he came back from war he joined the Mattapoisett Police Department in 1947 rising all the way to chief of police in 1969, a position he had held for eight years when he retired. He died at the age of 83 on 18 November 1995 and in January 1996 a flag was raised in his honour atop Old Glory Tower, a former fire observation tower in New Bedford's North End.

Joan Rendell went on to become a historian, writer and world-class phillumenist – amassing more than 300,000 matchboxes during her lifetime and in so doing, building one of the largest-ever collections. She wrote thirty books, many about her beloved Cornwall, and was parish clerk for Werrington, her home, a mile away from Launceston, for sixty-five years. In 1958 she was awarded the MBE for her voluntary work for organisations such as the National Savings movement and in 1977 achieved the Queen's Silver Jubilee Medal. She died in 2010.

Observers

George Orwell (1903–1950) is justly regarded as one of the greatest British writers, but the works for which he is perhaps best remembered – *Animal Farm* and *Nineteen Eighty-Four* – were published relatively soon after the Launceston shooting, in 1945 and 1949 respectively. His pithy writing style and insight into social injustice – which characterise his comments on the African Americans in Great Britain – were hallmarks of the genius he displayed throughout his prodigious body of novels, essays, journalism and literary criticism.

Roi Ottley was arguably the leading African American writer in the 1940s having set the publishing world alight with *New World A-Coming* in 1943. He reported the war as correspondent for *PM* and the *Pittsburgh Courier* and continued to freelance for these, and other newspapers, before publishing a study into race relations in Europe and America called *No Green Pastures* in 1951 to a less-than-rapturous reception. Leaving his beloved Harlem for Chicago, he continued to write and publish, but never achieved the lofty heights of his war-time writing career. Roi Ottley's unpublished war diaries covering June to December 1944 were found amongst papers at his alma mater St Bonaventure University and published for the first time in 2011.

Walter White won universal acclaim as godfather of the civil rights movement after twenty-five years at the helm of the NAACP. Perhaps his greatest achievement, particularly in the light of the Launceston mutiny, was helping to bring segregation in the US Armed Services to an end. It started when President Truman passed Executive Order 9981 promising 'equality of treatment and opportunity for all persons in the armed services without regard to race, color, religion or national origin' on 26 July 1948 – in response to NAACP pressure. It ended six years later in 1954 under President Eisenhower when the last of the all-black units were abolished. Walter White's premature death in New York in 1955 ended his role and the mantle passed on to others including Martin Luther King. The participation of African American servicemen in the Second World War is seen as a crucial catalyst in the fight for equality. Having lived with less prejudice and more equality in Europe, many returning servicemen came home to join the fight for freedom for themselves.

Associated

After the war **Learie Constantine** (1901–1971) was awarded an MBE for his work at the Ministry of Labour, where, as welfare officer, he had been responsible for helping settle West Indians who had been recruited to work in factories in the north-west of England. As well as gaining a reputation for his work as a journalist and broadcaster after the war, he qualified as a barrister in 1954 and returned to Trinidad where he entered politics and served as High Commissioner to the United Kingdom during the 1960s. In 1962 he was knighted and seven years later was made a life peer, becoming the first black man to sit in the House of Lords.

Having joined the National Guard at just fourteen, **Robert Henne** had time to return to St Mary's High School, Ohio, after the war, where he completed his studies. He then attended The Ohio State University, where he gained a degree in agricultural engineering, and met his future wife, Josephine Ann Kerr. Immediately after graduation he began work with the Motorists' Mutual Insurance Co, where he became claims vice president. Throughout, he continued as a major in the Army National Guard, only retiring in the late 1960s. In 1970, Robert returned to university, completed a PhD in Horticulture and Food Technology and went on to become a full-time professor, becoming Secretary of the Ohio State University School of Natural Resources in 1976. In retirement, Robert and Josephine spent many happy years splitting their time between Columbus, Ohio and Tempe, Arizona.

581st Ordnance Ammunition Company

As for the rest of the 581st Ordnance Ammunition Company men, five days after D-Day on 6 June 1944, they were attached to the 315th

Ordnance Ammunition Battalion under the command of Lieutenant Colonel Prince to help ship ammunition of all types to the invasion beaches and waterproof the vehicles. The unit was put on standby for travel orders on 4 July 1944 and landed four days later on Omaha. The unit was subsequently awarded a 'campaign credit' for its contribution to the Normandy and Northern France campaign.

Second Battalion, 115th Infantry

Better documented is how the 115th Infantry's Second Battalion lived up to their regimental motto of *'Rally round the Flag'* after landing at Omaha Beach in the face of a determined enemy resistance that had all but wiped out parts of its sister unit, 116th Infantry, earlier on 6 June 1944. They played a crucial role in man's biggest, boldest and most ambitious amphibious assault in modern history and were rewarded with a Presidential Distinguished Unit Citation for courage and valour. But how did they get there? What happened immediately after Paignton and beyond?

In November 1943, a couple of weeks after the court martial, the 115th Infantry Regiment travelled to the north coast of Devon to practise new landing techniques at Woolacombe's assault training centre. On 17 May 1944 they got closer to putting these techniques into practice when they moved to assembly areas around Plymouth. Scattered between HMS Raleigh and Fort Tregantle they waterproofed equipment for the next fortnight while checking and rechecking everything they needed to take into battle. Troops were still largely in the dark about what was going on – many believing they were still preparing for another practice. It wasn't until 28 and 29 May that company and battalion commanders revealed the truth and soldiers began to study in detail models of their designated landing areas: Omaha's Dog Red and Easy Green beaches. Their mission was to sweep up after the 116th Infantry had cleared the beach in the first wave and push on up towards the village of St Laurent-sur-Mer before moving to secure Longueville and defend its position.

On the evening of 29 May 1944 the 115th Infantry Regiment assembled to march the one-and-a-half miles to the Torpoint ferry. Here they were loaded onto their landing crafts, each man weighted down with ammo-loaded cartridge belts, mortars, machine guns, extra bandoliers, a one-day supply of K and D rations; a full canteen of water, gas masks, underwear, socks, toilet articles, a raincoat – and fourteen packets of cigarettes to see them through it all. When they reached Plymouth harbour they transferred to the larger craft that would take them to France.

It was here they stayed, suspended in limbo, waiting for orders as days stretched seemingly without end and boredom took over. Eventually the green light was given for Monday, 5 June 1944. After church services on the Sunday, however, they were told it had been pushed back by 24 hours and 20 minutes. On the morning of the original D-Day, the soldiers were indulged with a breakfast of fresh eggs. Late that afternoon, sun broke through the clouds and gave way to a clear night and memorably rough sea. At 10.00pm they moved to an assembly point near Weymouth to travel to France. They were fast approaching a historical watershed.

Soldiers from the 116th Infantry Regiment landed first on Omaha and suffered calamitous losses in their initial and bloody assault on the Dog Red sector; by the end of D-Day more than 800 of them were killed, wounded or missing. Three hours after the 116th Infantry's early-morning assault started, Navy commanders decided it was still too dangerous for the 115th Infantry Regiment to set down on the same stretch and diverted them a mile or so eastwards. Landing at Fox Green after the eleventh-hour decision to divert meant hundreds of men were separated from comrades at a destination more than a mile from where they were supposed to have unloaded. The beach was crawling with troops trying to regroup as quickly as possible while sprinting over mined sands to bottle-necked exits to reach higher ground – under enemy fire the whole time. By 11.00am, 115th Infantry Regiment members were either landed or in the process of landing at Omaha beach. It had been complicated, but they had made it. They reached the village of St Laurent where the fighting was intense enough to prompt their withdrawal, but not without taking their first German prisoners, some of whom held critical maps of the German batteries along the coast line. By nightfall and against all the odds, the 115th Infantry Regiment had accomplished its mission of encircling St Laurent and cutting out a main road south. It was for this that the regiment was awarded a Distinguished Unit Citation which described their 'outstanding performance of duty, the courage, tenacity, aggressiveness and extraordinary heroism.' By Thursday, 8 June 1944, the 115th Infantry Regiment Second Battalion descended on their target, Longueville, where they were met by the French civilians they had liberated, who were bearing flowers and fresh water. It was their first chance in forty-eight hours to dig in, wash up and relax.

As for the beautiful setting for action that put fourteen men into Paignton police court, **Launceston** is very different to its wartime persona. Seventy-five years later, its weekly market has long gone and so too is the town's rail access to London and the west, thanks to Beeching's massacre of regional branch lines. It registered one of the highest percentage votes for Brexit in the 2016 referendum.

Postscript

When I was growing up in the 1970s and 1980s, the Second World War was still a recent memory. It had dominated the lives of a generation – seemingly most grandfathers fought battles while grandmothers worked on the land or in factories and so forth. Wartime brio abounded. I don't remember batting an eyelid when I heard the thrilling story of how my elderly Polish godfather ended up in Britain. He was piloting his bomber to a German target the moment that Poland surrendered. It was when the plane was ordered back to base and Henryk decided to make for freedom instead that the problems began. What followed was a protracted spat between Henryk and the rest of his crew, who feared their inevitable court martial for not returning, and culminated with the navigator jostling for control of the joystick, a terrifying crash-landing in then-neutral Greece and their tortuous onward journey to England. Didn't everyone have a similar tale to tell? That total generational involvement carried through to infiltrate popular culture with television programmes such as *Tenko*, *Shine on Harvey Moon* (not to mention countless repeats of *Dad's Army*) and our reading of books like Nina Bawden's unputdownable *Carrie's War* or Judith Kerr's *When Hitler Stole Pink Rabbit*. Even the *Eagle Comic*, positively drenched in Second World War derring-do when first published in 1950, was relaunched in 1982.

It was all brought so alive for me and my three siblings by my Dad's legendary stories of growing up in the Blitz. Hearing how a German pilot parachuted into his garden and was given a cup of tea by his mum while waiting for the local bobby to arrive – or American GIs competed to shoot rats with live ammunition in derelict bomb sites – was simply riveting. Shrapnel, sirens and rationing were all passed vividly down as if the most normal thing in the world. This all combusted spectacularly for me in the early 1980s on one of our regular summer trips to Launceston,

Cornwall, the town my father's family left for London for the duration of the war, and to which they returned in 1947. Having met my father's former teacher, the Cornish poet Charles Causley, we walked to the ancient market square where we looked at the White Hart hotel and specifically, a couple of holes hammered into its white front walls from a wartime shooting that still fascinated the town. Nobody knew what had really happened, why – or more importantly – what became of the American men that were arrested and charged. Most presumed they had hanged for their crimes. That summer, as I touched these bullet holes, I wondered what the real story was. Nearly four decades later – and having told it to my own four children – I resolved to find out.

My attempts to discover the truth of events that occurred in a pitch-black Cornish market town one night in 1943 rapidly became something altogether larger – and more profound. Despite being generally hushed up and long-forgotten elsewhere, fortunately enough wartime-era children remembered the mystery to pass it on to the next generation. For years it was their recollection alone that preserved this obscure footnote in history; an alarming shoot-out that subsequently proves to have been even more momentous than their childhood memories allowed. For without a doubt while this story of mutiny flickered and flared, it held the newspaper reading populations of Britain and America in thrall. Bullet holes scorched into a war memorial and on the fascia of a seventeenth-century hotel are a permanent reminder of much more than the five manic minutes when American firepower turned on itself in Launceston. It wasn't just the shock-factor of the event – created by a random rallying of racial-tension, social tides and larger-than-life characters during the dynamic of the Second World War. There was far wider significance to that night's shooting than the flesh wounds of military policemen and damage to Cornish brick and mortar. It is a timely reminder, in our own divided world, of an idiosyncratic point in both American and British twentieth-century history. This brief flash, revived by new research, has allowed new scrutiny of this forgotten mutiny – with remarkable results. Why does this shooting, curiously spontaneous and yet simultaneously inevitable, continue to keep us guessing so many years after?

Above all, this was a compelling drama with an energy that leapt out from the sheets of the many-hundred paged court martial transcript as soon as it was opened. Why? Its written record left the shooting bolder than ever after its punchy dialogue and blow-by-blow action reportage breathed new life into the mutiny. Not only that, the court martial itself was a story within a story – following two opposing legal teams as they shaped the destiny of the fourteen accused men. So, on top of the mutiny itself was stacked an intrinsically related legal story – the narrative of what happened next in the courtroom – which was equally fascinating and more powerful yet. Together, working on these two parallel levels, the tales combine to create an irresistible spectacle; a knock-out story.

Added to this was its unique timing. The mutiny's pinpoint on the calendar of growing transatlantic racial tension – starting with riots in American cities and peaking with one of Britain's best-loved cricketers being thrown out of a London hotel – made it a veritable ticking time bomb. Looking back at the precise sequence of events starting with the context, timing and experiences of the 581st Ordnance Ammunition Company's training, it is no surprise they became central to this saga. Given their experiences, it became a question not of whether the men would break out, but when. The final surprising ingredient was that the story inevitably sucked in giant characters, such as the second-wave heroes of Omaha Beach on D-Day. Who would have thought they had been dodging potshots from their own side a few months before bravely shooting their way back into Nazi Europe? It expanded to include Walter White, Churchill and George Orwell who, if not commenting directly on the mutiny itself, at least reflected and railed against some of its underlying causes. There was no escaping this story at the time – however deeply it was buried afterwards – and this was the first big revelation.

Next was that as well as the big names, big events and big theatrics that the story drew on and reflected, the mutiny shone a powerful light on just what it was to be an African American fighting for a freedom they were denied back home. This tragedy is as much a part of the mutiny as the climatic firing of guns. *Jim Crow* meant segregation and was an intrinsic part of the US Army which joined with Britain in the fight against fascism – and its own separation by race. In theory it meant simply a dividing of the races; in practice it meant, if you were black, the worst jobs, accommodation, transport and general treatment with generous doses of violence and racism thrown in for good measure at every stage.

It literally coloured the beginning of their army experience when the draft earmarked most of them for decidedly unglamorous supply jobs, continued with training and ended in the day-to-day treatment they received once working. At every step, those who had joined up to fight under the United States of America's flag were abused and discriminated against. The journey made by men of the 581st Ordnance Ammunition Company is in many ways a microcosm of America's racial struggle at that moment in history.

The so-called mutiny also indicates how frightened army authorities were in 1943 of acknowledging – let alone tackling – its own racial problem. Even the way the shooting was criminalised and prosecuted shows how scared they were of taking it on. Factually, the event that captivated a generation in Launceston started as a drink-fuelled need to 'get-even' for slights received in town. When a fight happened in a pub on the Sunday, for the second successive night, after months of racism and restriction to every base they had ever known, something snapped. They returned to camp, armed themselves and marched back where they shot up the town – and two white military policemen – who they targeted deliberately low. Somehow these events became dressed up into attempted murder and mutiny when charges were brought against the men in October 1943.

There must have been political machinations to get those charges fixed – and maybe even the eventual conviction. It was a way of hiding one of the greatest myths about the mutiny; it was in fact a race riot and arguably a justifiable one at that. Behind the scenes and before court opened, there had been some serious editing of events and whitewashing of one of the boldest themes – namely racial tension. Undoubtedly the incident was racially inspired and trouble had been brewing for some time. Two sergeants there on the night had described that very groundswell to investigators as well as a couple of the publicans working the same evening and one of the 581st men themselves. A cross range of people with diametrically opposed motives were all saying the same thing. Yet it had no place in the prosecution's case. It was much easier to switch a race riot for mutiny. Even worse was the fact that despite the investigators' conclusion that there were no grounds whatsoever for believing the men had attempted murder – and in fact made that one of its key recommendations in its final report – murder charges were brought. This top-level interference continued from the moment the trial opened with the president's clunky attempt to ban the reporting of race to his ultimate banning of news about the sentencing.

The trial also offers a perfect view of how justice worked in the tough environs of a military courtroom. Given the charges, there shouldn't have been the remotest chance of prosecutors achieving a guilty verdict. They presided over a litany of blunders beginning with the fact that not one of the white victims could identify any of the black soldiers standing trial and ending with questionable prosecution witnesses changing their statements – their recollections of who was involved or flip-flopping over whether they were toting two rifles or none at all.

Yet still the odds remained loaded in favour of the prosecution. Not only was the US Army on its side, but leading the trial was the sharp-thinking, charismatic showman Trial Judge Advocate Frank P. Eresch who was determined to secure a conviction. The same cannot be said for the men's defenders. Although there were promising signs when Defense Counsel Captain John A. Philbin pointed out the more obvious bloomers – it never amounted to much more. We will never know whether it was his deliberate efforts or unintentional ineptitude that made it so, but the defence was incredibly poor. The hard truth is that 80 per cent of American servicemen hanged after court martials in the European Theatre during the Second World War were black – despite making up just 10 per cent of the armed forces. Black servicemen were not only more than proportionately likely to be found guilty of capital offences; they were more likely to be accused and found guilty of anything, and the Launceston shooting and its subsequent court martial underlines this too. Perhaps it was the US Army itself that should have been on trial.

To prevent further outbreaks, army authorities did not stop once they had achieved the guilty verdict they sought in Paignton. They punished American reporters who had filed copy about this case by labelling them 'troublemakers' and removing their press passes; they blamed the African American press corps for stirring things up and set about censoring race from news reports of violence – which did nothing to temper the real racial clashes that were breaking out all over Britain. Shootings and fights cracked on regardless after 581st Ordnance Ammunition

Company prisoners began their fifteen to twenty-year stretches of hard labour. Barely weeks before the Normandy landings, a morale report warned that racial enmity was such that 'the predominant note is that if the invasion doesn't occur soon, trouble will'. The Launceston shooting reflects everything bound up with the African American experience of army life in the Second World War. It was the prejudice shown in training camps, courtrooms and gallows which ultimately sparked the racial violence that spilled out onto Britain's streets in the Second World War – and that authorities were so keen to hide when it threatened to raise its head in Paignton police court. The good that was to come from African American participation in the Second World War stemmed from something the same morale report noted; that 'the only bright spot appears in the fact that colored troops look forward to a brighter future after the arrival of their colored officers.'[1] This widening horizon would do much to drive up numbers of veterans registering to vote in African American communities after the war and continue the civil rights fight.

What is even more extraordinary is that the incident spoke volumes about Britain's schizophrenic relationship with its American ally during the Second World War – offering a new insight into the 'special relationship' close-up. Britain had stood alone long enough by the time the US joined and heartily embraced its mighty, new ally. It needed the relationship to work. Indeed, on many levels, it did just that as the allies prepared for invasion. On the one hand in practical terms there was the euphoria of incoming Yanks who brought with them the untold luxury of plenty – be it food or petrol or money. But the story also uncovered some of the rawness of what it was like to have an 'occupying' army – however friendly its intentions. It was felt in the little-known Visiting Forces Act which allowed 581st Ordnance Ammunition Company men to be tried according to American military law – and crucially allowed the sentencing in this very public trial to be shrouded in secrecy and supposition at the end. It was demonstrated in the secret letters and polls of both Britons and Americans in the UK and this ambivalence revealed darker feelings about the 'special relationship'. Recriminations were mutual. There was American criticism of all things British from the food to the weather and its women. There were British complaints of American 'baloney' from their arrogance and inexplicable medals and their greed. And the one constant thorn in each other's side was 'the colour bar', which got in the way of the relationship ever being 100 per cent 'special'. Many Americans couldn't stand to see black soldiers dating white women in a time when miscegenation laws prevented mixed marriages in thirty of the forty-eight states back home. Many Britons could not stand by silently while black soldiers were reprimanded, or shouted at or hit. They got stuck in, they butted in – soldiers and civilians alike. So the same segregation and prejudice that inspired the shooting in Launceston was behind the suspected British aspect to the case.

In other words, the mutiny highlights how ordinary British people felt about African American servicemen who came over in the build-up to D-Day. One of the strands to disappear from the initial investigators' report was the British involvement in the incident. One eye-witness thought it was an entirely British affair – and another testified to how they were always stirring things up or getting involved. This was further reiterated by another civilian pub-worker and soldier (both barred from court), all of which caused investigators to surmise that things were 'not improved' by the attitude of British military personnel. It was mysteriously side-tracked and removed from the prosecution's case and came up almost by accident with a military policeman's statement for the defence.

The British response to imported American racism thrown up by the Launceston story is intriguing. There is no question that British racism was alive and kicking before the Americans came – as demonstrated in the race riots of 1919. It was still here when African Americans came and terrible public examples of it such as Learie Constantine's infamous hotel eviction and Amelia King's snub from the Land Army are not difficult to find, as well as more insidious examples from ordinary censored letters and cabinet discussions – and decisions too. Most probably it was there in the aristocratic mind more than the workers. But by stripping everything away to that precise time tunnel of autumn 1943, there was a surprising, almost tangible British support for American black troops – the obvious underdogs by any reckoning – not just in Launceston but up and down the nation. And considering Britain's subsequent chequered reception of immigrants which mutated into vicious racial violence, especially in the 1970s and 1980s, it makes this specific wartime reaction both amazing and inspirational. Positive lessons like this from history are few and far between. Without being too virtuous or smug about the British reaction to 'black yanks' as they affectionately called them, there is simply too much evidence of a backlash against the colour bar to ignore. There was a real warmth of feeling and comradeship towards the African American servicemen that came. The British opened their doors and their hearts to them. And in another legal case run in a British courtroom a few months after 581st men were transported back to American prison, Learie Constantine took the hotel that so wrongly evicted him to court – and won. With high praise from the judge.

Ultimately, the lost and now found story of Launceston's dramatic shooting provides a window into America and Britain at a certain point in 1943 – their relationship with themselves, each other and the grey area in between. This fleeting flash in British history – however brief – shows a characteristic and a time of which Britain can be proud. Ironically it was a lifetime away from the ugly racism and violence that besmirched the era in which I first discovered this intriguing shooting – and is perhaps also equally removed from our own fractured and fractious world.

Acknowledgements/Credits

All thanks to the wonderful Westwaters in my life starting with **Sandy** for all his love, encouragement and dedicated reading of the story – as well as challenging my ideas and writing style! I couldn't have done it without him. Equal thanks and love to our four little Westwaters – **Max, Nate, Clemmie** and **Laurie** – who are my inspiration. Talking to them about it and trying to answer their questions gave me the final push to find out what really happened.

Huge thanks also to the following stars who went way beyond the call of duty to allow me to tell and illustrate this forgotten story: Research supremo **Dr John Arnold,** of NICOM, Inc. for retrieving the Thrift Report for me from the National Archives in Washington DC; Historian **Joe Balkoski** for consulting the extensive archives of the 29th Division on my behalf; **Kate Bohdanowicz** for her wonderful guidance, advice and encouragement - long may it continue!: **Kim Cooper,** Library Officer at Kresen Kernow who sourced and reproduced the amazing George Ellis stills for me around packing for the big move to the new archives' home in Redruth, Cornwall; **Simon Flavin,** Mirrorpix for helping me source a timely copy of the only picture of the 581st Ordnance Ammunition men after the trial; **Gaynor Haliday** for her insightful, efficient and consistently cheery editing; the late **First Lieutenant Robert Henne** for sharing his powerful memories of Launceston with me; his wife **Josephine** and sons **Bruce** and **Peter** for filling me in on what happened next and filmmaker **Larry R. Cappetto** for capturing the Omaha hero's spell-binding account of D-Day and allowing me to use it; **Lori Hertzel,** Office of the Clerk of Court, US Army Judiciary for finding and reproducing the court martial for me all those years ago; **Wendy Hillgrove** for her insight into the redoubtable Miss Joyce Packe; **John Lyne** (www.johnlyne.com) for his generosity in sharing his brilliant anecdotes and superb stills of Launceston; **John Neale** for his advice on picture research and guiding me to the fantastic Kresen Kernow; **Judy Nokes**, Copyright and Information Policy Adviser, The National Archives, for all her guidance and advice; **Dr John Maddicott**, for feeding my love of history at university and continuing to encourage it; thanks to everyone at **Pen & Sword History** for bringing this book to fruition, especially Laura Hirst; the late **Joan Rendell** for sparing so much of her time to reminisce about Launceston and Cornwall in the Second World War and especially her thrilling account of watching and hearing events unfold on 26 September 1943; **Graham Smith** for his generous support, help and encouragement all those years ago – and suggesting I try and get a copy of the court martial transcript in the first place; **South West Police Heritage Trust's** Brian Edmunds and Peter Hinchliffe for answering all my policing questions; **Philippa & John Stout** for generously entrusting me with their secondary materials on all things Launceston; **Zoe Uglow**, of the *Cornish & Devon Post* for helping me find residents who still remember the shooting; from the **US Army Artillery Museum, Fort Sill, Oklahoma – Gordon A. Blaker**, Director/Curator for digging up the wonderful stills of life at Fort Sill in the Second World War; **Rod Roadruck**, graphics artist and photographer and **Staff Sergeant Jaycob Turner USMC** for getting them over to me; **Lisa Williams**, of the Mariners' Museum and Park, Newport News, Virginia USA for helping me find and use pictures of Camp Patrick Henry; **David Watts**, Chairman of Paignton Heritage Society, for all his help uncovering the history of Paignton's Palace Avenue police station and putting me in touch with so many who shared their memories of the place and era; **Stephen J. Wilch** for generously sharing his father's memories of Launceston during the Second World War and D-Day; **Celia Werran** for remembering life as a teenager in wartime Launceston for me; **David & Sylvia Werran** for everything, but especially for giving us such memorable summer holidays in Cornwall when we were children – and to **Vicky, Jon** and **Nic** for making them golden and funny; and finally **Arthur Wills** for sharing his encyclopaedic knowledge of Launceston and personal anecdotes about the shooting.

Notes

Prologue
1. larrycappetto.com, Lest They Be Forgotten/Voices of History Project, *Transcript of First Lieutenant Robert Henne*, courtesy of Larry R. Cappetto
2. Office of the Clerk of Court, US Army Judiciary, Washington National Records Centre, *U.S v PV1 Clifford Barrett, et al CM 257070*

Chapter 1: Court Opens
1. National Meteorological Library and Archive – Met Office, UK *Monthly Weather Report ©Crown Copyright* 1943.
2. Reproduced with permission of Curtis Brown, London on behalf of The Estate of Winston S. Churchill © The Estate of Winston S. Churchill
3. *The Daily Herald*, 16 October 1943
4. *Herald Express*, 22 February 1991
5. *The Daily Herald*, 16 October 1943
6. Office of the Clerk of Court, US Army Judiciary, Washington National Records Centre, *U.S v PV1 Clifford Barrett, et al CM 257070*

Chapter 2: Making the Case
1. Office of the Clerk of Court, US Army Judiciary, Washington National Records Centre, *U.S v PV1 Clifford Barrett, et al CM 257070*
2. *Western Morning News*, 23 October 1943
3. *The Daily Herald*, 16 October 1943
4. Office of the Clerk of Court, *CM 257070*
5. Ibid.
6. *The Daily Herald*, 16 October 1943
7. Office of the Clerk of Court, *CM 257070*

Chapter 3: Nailing the Ringleader
1. *The Western Morning News*, 23 October 1943
2. *The Daily Mirror*, 16 October 1943
3. *The Daily Herald*, 16 October 1943
4. *Derby Daily Telegraph*, 6 October 1943
5. Office of the Clerk of Court, US Army Judiciary, Washington National Records Centre, *U.S v PV1 Clifford Barrett, et al CM 257070*
6. Ibid.
7. Ibid.

8. *The Scotsman*, 18 October 1943
9. Office of the Clerk of Court, *CM 257070*

Chapter 4: Turning the Tables
1. Office of the Clerk of Court, US Army Judiciary, Washington National Records Centre, *U.S v PV1 Clifford Barrett, et al CM 257070*
2. *Western Morning News*, 23 October 1943
3. *Daily Mirror*, 5 October 1943
4. Office of the Clerk of Court, *CM 257070*

Chapter 5: The Relationship Gets Special
1. Shirer, William L., *The Rise and Fall of the Third Reich*, (Arrow Books, London, 1991), p 830
2. Rhodes James, Robert ed., *'Chips': The Diaries of Sir Henry Channon*, (Phoenix, London, 2003)
3. Records of the US Army's European Theater of Operations (ETO), 1942–1946, from the National Archives and Records Administration's (NARA) Record Group (RG) 498, *History of 100th Ordnance Battalion* [Online version file 604e, Roll MP63-9_0136 from www.fold3.com]
4. McGuire, Phillip ed., *Taps for a Jim Crow Army: Letters from Black Soldiers in World War II*, (University Press of Kentucky, 1983), p 21
5. Ibid.
6. © Imperial War Museum (IWM), (17754), *Oral history of Benny Gordon*
7. McGuire ed., *Taps for a Jim Crow Army*, p 21
8. Ibid. pp 19–20
9. © IWM (17754), *Oral history of Benny Gordon*
10. McGuire ed., *Taps for a Jim Crow Army*, pp 19–20
11. Ibid. pp 104–5
12. Moore, Christopher Paul, *Fighting for America: Black Soldiers – The Unsung Heroes of World War II*, (One World, 2005), p153

Chapter 6: Heading South – the 581st Ordnance Ammunition Company Assembles
1. Records of the US Army's European Theater of Operations (ETO), 1942–1946, from NARA RG 498, *History of 100th Ordnance Battalion* [Online version file 604e, Roll MP63-9_0136 from www.fold3.com]
2. White, Walter, *A Man Called White, The Autobiography of Walter White* (The Viking Press, New York, 1948)
3. Excerpt from *A Rising Wind*, by Walter White, copyright © 1945 by Walter White. Used by permission of Doubleday, an imprint of the Knopf Doubleday Publishing Group, a division of Random House LLC. All rights reserved.
4. Ibid.

5. Records of the US Army's European Theater of Operations (ETO), 1942–1946, from NARA RG 498, *History of 100th Ordnance Battalion* [Online version file 604e, Roll MP63-9_0136 from www.fold3.com]

Chapter 7: White Yanks in the UK: Anglo-American Relations

1. Reynolds, David, *Rich Relations: The American Occupation of Britain, 1942 – 45* (Random House, 1995)
2. *The Collected Essays, Journalism and Letters of George Orwell, Volume III: As I Please 1943 - 1945* by George Orwell (Copyright © George Orwell). Reproduced by permission of Bill Hamilton as the Literary Executor of the Estate of the Late Sonia Brownell Orwell.
3. FO 371/34114, The National Archives of the UK (TNA), comments of Home Secretary Herbert Morrison included in the Office of War Information, Bureau of Intelligence *Memo on Anti-British Feeling By US Citizens And British Reactions Hereto*, 16 December 1942
4. FO 371/30655, TNA, letter from *Daily Express's* New York correspondent CVR Thompson to his editor Arthur Christiansen, copied to the Ministry of Information on 30 April 1942
5. FO 371/34114, TNA, comments from *New York Amsterdam Star News* columnist A M Wendell Malliet
6. Ibid., report summary
7. War Department, Washington DC, *Instructions for American Servicemen in Britain*, 1942
8. FO 371/34116, TNA, *What the American Soldier is thinking about in this Country*, sent by the Ministry of Information's American Division to the Foreign Office on 11 March 1943
9. Mass-Observation 1656–7, *Mutual Anglo-American Feelings*, April 1943. Reproduced with permission of Curtis Brown Group Ltd, London on behalf of The Trustees of the Mass Observation Archive © The Trustees of the Mass Observation Archive
10. FO 371/34117, TNA, *American Attitudes towards the British*, Surveys Division Bureau of Special Services, Office of War Information, in collaboration with National Opinion Research Center, University of Denver, 6 May, 1943
11. FO 371/34119, TNA, *Memo to VIII Bomber Command* by its security officer after analysis of servicemen letters, sent by Lt Col B W Rowe on 24 September, 1943
12. FO 371/34126, TNA, *Army Mail Censorship Report* No. 71, 11 – 25 July 1943
13. Nicolson, Nigel ed., *The Harold Nicolson Diaries 1907–1963* (Weidenfeld & Nicolson, 2005)
14. FO 371/38624, TNA, censored letter

15. INF 1/282, TNA, Ministry of Information (MOI) *Weekly Report* by Home Intelligence Division, No. 79, 8 April 1942
16. Mass-Observation 1569, *Feelings about America and the Americans*, 22 January 1943. Reproduced with permission of Curtis Brown Group Ltd, London on behalf of The Trustees of the Mass Observation Archive © The Trustees of the Mass Observation Archive
17. Orwell, *Collected Essays Vol III*
18. Mass-Observation 1669 Q, *Attitude to Foreigners*, April 1943, p8. Reproduced with permission of Curtis Brown Group Ltd, London on behalf of The Trustees of the Mass Observation Archive © The Trustees of the Mass Observation Archive
19. Mitchison, Naomi, *Among You Taking Notes ... The Wartime Diary of Naomi Mitchison 1939–45* (Phoenix, 2000)
20. INF 1/282, TNA, MOI *Weekly Report* by Home Intelligence Division, No. 136, 13 May 1943
21. Ibid. No 144, 8 July 1943
22. FO 371/34119, TNA, *Memo to VIII Bomber Command*
23. WO 163/161, TNA, *Draft Morale Report* May – July 1942
24. Ibid. *Morale in the Army*, War Office Committee, May – July 1943

Chapter 8 – Black Yanks in the UK: First Impressions

1. Wheeler, Major William Reginald, The *Road to Victory: A History of Hampton Roads Port of Embarkation in World War II* (Yale University Press, 1946)
2. Wardlow, Chester, *The Transportation Corps: Responsibilities, Organization, and Operations* (Center of Military History United States Army, Washington DC, 1999)
3. http://www.dailypress.com/news/newport-news/dp-nws-ww2-port-of-embarkation-hampton-roads-20170616-story.html
4. Morehouse, Maggi M, *Fighting in the Jim Crow Army: Black Men and Women Remember World War II* (Rowman & Littlefield Publishers, Inc, 2000)
5. *Roi Ottley's World War II: The Lost Diary of an African American Journalist*, edited by Mark A Huddle (University Press of Canvas, © 2011, www.kansaspress.ku.edu)
6. Constantine, MBE, Learie, *Colour Bar* (Stanley Paul & Co Ltd, 1954)
7. Dilks, David ed., *The Diaries of Sir Alexander Cadogan, OM, 1938–1945* (Faber& Faber, 2010)
8. CAB 66/30/3, TNA, *United States Negro Troops in the United Kingdom*, 17 October 1942
9. PREM 4/26/9, TNA, *Letter from Bert, His Grace the Duke of Marlborough to the Prime Minister*, 21 October 1943
10. *Sunday Pictorial*, 6 September 1942

11. FO 371/38624, TNA, *Army Mail Censorship Report,* no. 91 for 11–25 May 1944.

12. INF 1/282, TNA, MOI *Weekly Report* by Home Intelligence Division, No. 160, 28 October 1943

13. CAB 66/29, WP (424) 21, TNA, *Notes on Relations with Coloured Troops,* Dowlers Notes, 7 August 1942

Chapter 9: The Real Special Relationship

1. Roberts, Andrew, *Churchill: Walking with Destiny* (Allen Lane, an imprint of Penguin Books, 2018)

2. PREM 4 26/9, TNA, *Memo from War Secretary PJ Grigg to Prime Minister,* 21 October 1943

3. Box No. 1, Butcher Papers, Eisenhower Library, Abilene, Kansas, *Harry Butcher, Naval Aide to Eisenhower, to Maj Gen Surles,* Bureau of Public Relations Washington 10.9.42

4. *Roi Ottley's World War II: The Lost Diary of an African American Journalist,* edited by Mark A Huddle (University Press of Canvas, © 2011, www. kansaspress.ku.edu)

5. Hervieux, Linda, *Forgotten: The Untold Story of D-Day's Black Heroes, at Home and at War* (Harper, 2015)

6. © IWM (17754), *Oral history of Benny Gordon*

7. Records of the US Army's European Theater of Operations (ETO), 1942–1946, from NARA RG 498, Adjutant General section 291.2, *Plank, Leadership of Colored Troops,* 15 July 1943

8. HO 45/25604, TNA, *Letter from Chief Constable of Oxford JE St Johnston,* 22 July 1942

9. Ibid. *War Cabinet minutes,* 5.30pm 10 August 1942

10. Ibid. *Bolero minutes,* 12 August 1943

11. *Sunday Express,* 20 September 1942

12. *The Times,* 2 October 1943

13. CAB 66/29/21, TNA, *War Cabinet minutes,* October 1942

14. ASW 291.2. RG 107. NARA, *Special Report 'Colored Troops' 16–31 August 1943,* 1 September 1943

15. FO 371/34126, TNA, *Postal and Telegraph Censorship Report Opinion on American Troops in Britain,* July 1943

16. Ibid.

17. FO 371/34116, TNA, *What the American Soldier is thinking about in this Country,* Ministry of Information's American Division report sent to Foreign Office, 11 March 1943

18. Longmate, Norman, *The G.I.'s: The Americans in Britain 1942–1945* (Hutchinson, London, 1945) p 129

19. CO 876/1, TNA, *Letter from Royal Air Force Sergeant Arthur Waldron,* 26 June 1943

20. Louis, Joe with Edna and Art Rust Jnr, *Joe Louis: My Life* (Berkley Books, New York 1981) p 171
21. INF 1/292, TNA, Ministry of Information *Weekly Report* by Home Intelligence Division No. 175, 10 February 1944
22. Slaughter, R. J., *For God, For Country … For Love: The True Story of One Man's Journey* (R. J. Slaughter, 2012)
23. *The Collected Essays, Journalism and Letters of George Orwell, Volume III: As I Please 1943–1945* by George Orwell (Copyright © George Orwell). Reproduced by permission of Bill Hamilton as the Literary Executor of the Estate of the Late Sonia Brownell Orwell
24. Harvey, John ed., *The War Diaries of Oliver Harvey 1941–1945* (Collins, 1978)
25. HO 45/25604, TNA, *Letter from J A Newsam*, 4 September 1942
26. Hansard vol 383 cc670-1, Tom Driberg MP, *House of Commons Debate*, 29 September 1942
27. FO 371/34114, TNA, *Letter from Foreign Secretary Anthony Eden*, 30 November 1942
28. Ibid. *Anti-American Feeling in Britain*, a preliminary report by Home Intelligence, 14 January 1943
29. Mass-Observation 1656–7, Mutual *Anglo-American Feelings*, April 1943. Reproduced with permission of Curtis Brown Group Ltd, London on behalf of The Trustees of the Mass Observation Archive © The Trustees of the Mass Observation Archive
30. Mass-Observation 1569 p 37, *Report on Feelings about America and the Americans*, 22 January 1943. Reproduced with permission of Curtis Brown Group Ltd, London on behalf of The Trustees of the Mass Observation Archive © The Trustees of the Mass Observation Archive
31. FO 371/34126, TNA, Postal and Telegraph Censorship Report *Opinion on American Troops in Britain*, July 1943
32. Mass-Observation 1569 p 39, *Report on Feelings about America*
33. FO 371/38624, TNA, *Letter to the Foreign Office*, 25 May 1944
34. Ibid. *Opinion on American Troops in Britain*, July 1943
35. FO 371/34126, TNA, *Opinion on American Troops in Britain*, July 1943
36. Ibid.
37. Mass-Observation 1569 p 41, *Report on Feelings about America*
38. FO 371/34126, TNA, *Memo by Sir Harry Haig*, 6 September 1943
39. FO 371/38511, TNA, *Minutes from the British American Liaison Board*, 21 July 1944
40. FO 371/34126, TNA, Postal and Telegraph Censorship Report *Opinion on American Troops in Britain*, July 1943
41. *Birmingham Daily Gazette*, 14 October 1942
42. Excerpt from *A Rising Wind*, by Walter White, copyright © 1945 by Walter White. Used by permission of Doubleday, an imprint of the Knopf

Doubleday Publishing Group, a division of Random House LLC. All rights reserved.

43. Lee, Ulysses, *The Employment of Negro Troops* (Center of Military History United States Army, Washington D.C., 2001)

44. Records of the US. Army's European Theater of Operations (ETO), 1942–1946, from the NARA RG 498, *Special Report Negro Troops* [Online version file 218, Roll MP63-9_0030 from www.fold3.com]

45. Ibid.

46. Ibid.

47. Ibid.

48. Huddle ed., *Roi Ottley's World War II*

49. © IWM (17754), *Oral history of Benny Gordon*

50. Hervieux, *Forgotten* p 51

51. ASW 291.2 *Negro Troops*, Box 124 RG 107, NARA, United States Military Censorship HQ USA, 24 September 1943

52. Ibid.

53. *Baltimore Afro American*, 19 September 1942

54. RG 330, NARA, *A Preliminary Report on attitudes of Negro Soldiers in ETO*, report ETO-B2, 7 February 1944

55. FO 371/34114, TNA, Office Of War Information, Bureau Of Intelligence *Memo on Anti-British Feeling*, December 16 1942. Sent via Ministry of Information.

56. *Atlanta Daily World*, 2 September 1943

Chapter 10: Coming to Cornwall

1. IWM (5552), *Private Papers of N Appleyard*

2. Balkoski, Joseph, *Beyond the Beachhead: The 29ᵗʰ Infantry Division in Normandy* (Stackpole Books, 2005) p 55

3. Correspondence with the author 2006

4. Interview with the author 2017

5. Interview with the author 2006

6. IWM, *N Appleyard*

7. Interview with the author 2006

8. Interview with the author 2017

9. Longmate, Norman, *The G.I.'s: The Americans in Britain 1942–1945* (Hutchinson, London, 1945) p 126

10. Interview with the author 2006

11. Longmate, *The G.I.'s:* p 125

12. Interview with the author 2017

13. *Personal Perspectives: World War II*, edited by Timothy C Dowling (ABC-CLIO, Inc, 2005)

14. Granger, Lester B, *Victory through Unity*, *Opportunity,* 21 October 1943

15. INF 1/282, TNA, Ministry of Information (MOI) *Weekly Report* by Home Intelligence Division, No 153, 9 September 1943

16. INF 1/282, TNA, Ministry of Information (MOI) *Weekly Report* by Home Intelligence Division, No. 154, 16 September 1943
17. Mass-Observation File number 1944, *Fortnightly Bulletin*, October 1943. Reproduced with permission of Curtis Brown Group Ltd, London on behalf of The Trustees of the Mass Observation Archive © The Trustees of the Mass Observation Archive

Chapter 11: 26 September 1943
1. British Pathé Ltd, *International Football, 1943*, Film id 1091.11
2. *Western Daily Press*, 27 September 1943
3. *Sunday Mirror*, 26 September 1943
4. Excerpt from *A Rising Wind*, by Walter White, copyright © 1945 by Walter White. Used by permission of Doubleday, an imprint of the Knopf Doubleday Publishing Group, a division of Random House LLC. All rights reserved.
5. *Roi Ottley's World War II: The Lost Diary of an African American Journalist*, edited by Mark A Huddle (University Press of Canvas, © 2011, www.kansaspress.ku.edu)
6. White, *A Rising Wind*
7. Statement of John Pearce to Arthur Wills
8. Interview with the author 2006
9. John Pearce
10. Interview with the author 2006

Chapter 12: The Body of Evidence
1. *Daily Mirror*, 5 October 1943
2. *The Daily Herald*, 6 October 1943
3. *Daily Mirror*, 5 October 1943
4. *The Daily Herald*, 16 October 1943
5. Ibid.
6. *Western Morning News*, 16 October 1943
7. Office of the Clerk of Court, US Army Judiciary, Washington National Records Centre, *U.S v PV1 Clifford Barrett, et al CM 257070*

Chapter 13: Act 1, Defending the Defenceless
1. Interview with the author 2019
2. Office of the Clerk of Court, US Army Judiciary, Washington National Records Centre, *U.S v PV1 Clifford Barrett, et al CM 257070*

Chapter 14: Defending the Defenceless – the Second Act
1. Office of the Clerk of Court, US Army Judiciary, Washington National Records Centre, *U.S v PV1 Clifford Barrett, et al CM 257070*
2. *The Scotsman*, 18 October 1943
3. Office of the Clerk of Court, *CM 257070*

Chapter 15: Closing Arguments
1. *The Daily Herald*, 16 October 1943
2. Office of the Clerk of Court, US Army Judiciary, Washington National Records Centre, *U.S v PV1 Clifford Barrett, et al CM 257070*
3. *Sunday Post,* 17 October 1943
4. Office of the Clerk of Court, *CM 257070*

Chapter 16: Hiding in Plain Sight
1. National Meteorological Library and Archive – Met Office, UK *Monthly Weather Report ©Crown Copyright* 1943.
2. *Daily Mirror*, 18 October 1943
3. Office of the Clerk of Court, US Army Judiciary, Washington National Records Centre, *U.S v PV1 Clifford Barrett, et al CM 257070*
4. Ibid.
5. Inspector's Sections, Investigation Reports 1942–1947, RG 498, HQ European Theatre of Operations, US Army (World War II) NARA, *Inspector General reports by Captain Thrift* 29 September 1943 *and Lieutenant Colonel Plunkett,* 7 October 1943
6. Office of the Clerk of Court, *CM 257070*
7. Ibid.
8. Ibid.
9. RG 498, NARA, *reports by Thrift and Plunkett*
10. Office of the Clerk of Court, *CM 257070*
11. RG 498, NARA, *reports by Thrift and Plunkett*

Chapter 17: The Verdict
1. Donoughue, Bernard and Jones, G.W., *Herbert Morrison: Portrait of a Politician* (Phoenix Press, London, 2001) p 311
2. Hansard vol. 382 cc860-931, Home Secretary Herbert Morrison, *House of Commons Debate*, 4 August 1942
3. Ibid. Sydney Silverman MP, Nelson & Colne, *House of Commons Debate*, 4 August 1942
4. Ibid. Professor John James Craik-Henderson MP, Leeds North-East, *House of Commons Debate*, 4 August 1942
5. Ibid. Sir Archibald Southby MP, Epsom, *House of Commons Debate*, 4 August 1942
6. Records of the US Army's European Theater of Operations (ETO), 1942–1946, from NARA RG 498, *Statistical Survey General Court Martial* [Online version file 559a, Roll MP63-9_0102 from www.fold3.com]
7. Hansard vol. 124 cc59–74, Lord Earl of Shaftesbury, *House of Lords Debate*, 29 July 1942

8. *NARA RG 498, Statistical Survey General Court Martial*; The Daily Beast, 12 March 2016, https://www.thedailybeast.com/werethese-us-soldiers-executed-because-of-their-race

9. HO 45/25604, TNA, *Letter from the Ministry of Information*, 22 August 1942

10. INF 1/282, TNA, Ministry of Information (MOI) *Weekly Report* by Home Intelligence Division, No 148, 5 August 1943

11. *The Collected Essays, Journalism and Letters of George Orwell, Volume III: As I Please 1943–1945 by George Orwell* (Copyright © George Orwell). Reproduced by permission of Bill Hamilton as the Literary Executor of the Estate of the Late Sonia Brownell Orwell.

12. FO 371/38624, TNA, *Letter from Mr Ernest A Gladwell to the Foreign Office*, 10 May 1944

13. Ibid. *Letter from the Rev C Phillips Cape to the Foreign Office*, 11 May 1944

14. *Daily Mirror*, 2 June 1944

15. Smith, Graham, *When Jim Crow met John Bull: Black American Soldiers in World War II Britain* (I.B. Taurus & Co Ltd, London, 1987)

16. *The Daily Herald*, 18 October 1943

17. Office of the Clerk of Court, US Army Judiciary, Washington National Records Centre, *U.S v PV1 Clifford Barrett, et al CM 257070*

18. *Daily Herald*, 18 October 1943

19. Ibid.

20. *Chicago Defender*, 23 October 1943

21. *The Daily Herald*, 18 October 1943

22. *Chicago Defender*, 23 October 1943

23. Venning, Arthur Bate, *The Book of Launceston: A Portrait of the Town* (Barracuda Books Ltd, 1976)

Chapter 18: Lambs to the Slaughter

1. ASW 291.2, Box 124 RG 107, NARA, *Memo from United States Military Censorship HQ*, 24 September 1943

2. Ibid. *War Department memo sent to the Assistant Secretary of War*, 25 October 1943

3. ASW 291.2 Box 125 RG 107, NARA, *Memo from AD Surles, Major-General USA Director of Bureau of Public Relations to Executive to ASW*, 29 October 1943

4. PREM 4 26/9, M714/3, TNA, *Personal memo from PM to PJG*, 20 October 1943

5. PREM 4 26/9, *Memo from Bert, his Grace the Duke of Marlborough, to the PM*, 21 October 1943

6. Ibid. *Memo from PM to Bert, his Grace the Duke of Marlborough*, 22 October 1943

7. Morrison, Herbert, *Herbert Morrison: An Autobiography*, by Lord Morrison of Lambeth P.C., C.H. (Odhams Press Limited, London, 1960) p 207

8. PREM 4 26/9, TNA, *Memo from PJ Grigg, Secretary of War, to the PM*, 21 October 1943

9. Harvey, John ed., *The War Diaries of Oliver Harvey 1941–1945* (Collins, 1978), 14 September 1942

10. PREM 4 26/9, TNA, *Memo from PJ Grigg, Secretary of War, to the PM*, 21 October 1943

11. Adjutant General section 291.2, RG 498, HQ European Theatre of Operations, US Army (World War II) NARA, *Memo from American Brigadier GM Alexander to CG Services of Supply*, 6 October 1943

12. Excerpt from *A Rising Wind*, by Walter White, copyright © 1945 by Walter White. Used by permission of Doubleday, an imprint of the Knopf Doubleday Publishing Group, a division of Random House LLC. All rights reserved.

13. *Roi Ottley's World War II: The Lost Diary of an African American Journalist*, edited by Mark A Huddle (University Press of Canvas, © 2011, www.kansaspress.ku.edu)

14. White, *A Rising Wind*

15. Walter White correspondence, James Weldon Collection, Yale University Library *Letter from WW to FDR*, 26 December 1944

16. INF 1/282, TNA, Ministry of Information (MOI) *Weekly Report* by Home Intelligence Division, 28 October 1943

Chapter 19: And Beyond

1. *Cornish & Devon Post*, 31 October 1943

2. Interview with the author 2006

3. Donoughue, Bernard and Jones, G.W., *Herbert Morrison: Portrait of a Politician* (Phoenix Press, London, 2001) p 304

4. *The Collected Essays, Journalism and Letters of George Orwell, Volume III: As I Please 1943–1945* by George Orwell (Copyright © George Orwell). Reproduced by permission of Bill Hamilton as the Literary Executor of the Estate of the Late Sonia Brownell Orwell.

5. INF 1/282, TNA, *Appendix on America* – A BBC Listener Research Report included in Home Intelligence weekly report for the Ministry of Information, 10 February 1944.

6. Adjutant General section 291.2, RG 498 HQ European Theatre of Operations, US Army (World War II) NARA, *Investigations of racial relations in the United Kingdom*, 11080/73

7. Records of the US Army's European Theater of Operations (ETO), 1942–1946, from NARA RG 498, *Special Report Negro Troops* [Online version file 218, Roll MP63-9_0030 from www.fold3.com]

8. Excerpt from *A Rising Wind*, by Walter White, copyright © 1945 by Walter White. Used by permission of Doubleday, an imprint of the Knopf Doubleday Publishing Group, a division of Random House LLC. All rights reserved.

9. Adjutant General section 291.2, RG 498, HQ European Theatre of Operations, US. Army (World War II) NARA, *Gilstrap report 'Tour of Mr Walter White in the ETO' to Colonel Lawrence*, PRO ETO, 11 February 1944

10. White, *A Rising Wind*

11. INF 1/282, TNA, Ministry of Information (MOI) *Weekly Report* by Home Intelligence Division, 14 April 1944

12. Hansard vol 399, Hugh Lawson MP, Skipton, *United States Forces, Great Britain (Death Sentences)*, 10 May 1944.

13. Hansard vol 400 cc 913-5, Denis Kendall MP, Grantham, *House of Commons Debate*, 25 May 1944.

14. Ibid. Major Richard Stokes MP, Ipswich, *House of Commons Debate*, 25 May 1944

15. *Daily Mirror*, 20 June 1944

16. *The Courier & Advertiser*, 28 June 1944

17. FO 371/38511, TNA, *Press cutting survey March to July 1944 by British American Liaison Board*.

18. *Roi Ottley's World War II: The Lost Diary of an African American Journalist*, edited by Mark A Huddle (University Press of Canvas, © 2011, www. kansaspress.ku.edu)

19. Ibid.

Postscript

1. Records of the US Army's European Theater of Operations (ETO), 1942–1946, from NARA, RG 498, *Special Report Negro Troops* [Online version file 218, Roll MP63-9_0030 from www.fold3.com]

Secondary Reading

Acton, Viv & Carter, Derek, *Cornish War & Peace: The Road to Victory – and Beyond* (Landfall Publications, 1995)

Balkoski, Joseph, *Beyond the Beachhead: The 29th Infantry Division in Normandy* (Stackpole Books, 2005)

Binkoski, Joseph and Plaut, Arthur, *The 115th Regiment in World War II* (Battery Press, Nashville, originally printed 1948)

Buckton, Henry, *Friendly Invasion, Memories of Operation Bolero: The American Occupation of Britain 1942–1945* (Phillimore & Co Ltd, 2006)

Butcher USNR, Captain Harry C, *My Three Years with Eisenhower* (Simon and Schuster, 1946)

Constantine MBE, Learie N, *Colour Bar* (Stanley Paul & Co Ltd, 1954)

James, Robert Rhodes (ed.), *'Chips': The Diaries of Sir Henry Channon* (Phoenix, London, 2003)

Donoughue, Bernard and, Jones, G.W., *Herbert Morrison: Portrait of a Politician* (Phoenix Press, 2001)

Dowling, Timothy C (ed.), *Personal Perspectives: World War II* (ABC-CLIO, Inc. 2005)

Dunning, Martin, *Launceston: A Photographic History of Your Town* (Black Horse Books, 2001)

Harvey, John (ed.), *The War Diaries of Oliver Harvey 1941 – 45* (Collins, 1978)

Hervieux, Linda, *Forgotten: The Untold Story of D-Day's Black Heroes, at Home and at War* (Harper, 2016)

Green, Laurence, *All Cornwall Thunders at My Door: A Biography of Charles Causley* (The Cornovia Press, 2013)

Huddle, Mark A (ed.), *Roi Ottley's World War II: The Lost Diary of an African American Journalist* (University Press of Kansas, 2011)

Janda, Lance, *"Fort Sill,"* The Encyclopedia of Oklahoma History and Culture, https://www.okhistory.org/publications/enc/entry.php?entry=FO038 © Oklahoma Historical Society.

Lemann, Nicholas, *The Promised Land: The Great Black Migration and How it Changed America* (Vintage Books, 1996)

Longmate, Norman, *The G.I's: Americans in Britain 1942–45* (Hutchinson of London, 1975)

Louis, Joe, with Rust Jr, Edna and Art, *Joe Louis: My Life* (Berkley Books, 1981)

Mitchison, Naomi, *Among You Taking Notes ... The Wartime Diary of Naomi Mitchison 1939 – 1945* (Phoenix Press, 2000)

Moore, Christopher Paul, *Fighting for America: Black Soldiers – the Unsung Heroes of World War II* (One World, 2005)

Morehouse, Maggi M., *Fighting in the Jim Crow Army: Black Men and Women Remember World War II* (Rowman and Littlefield Publishers Inc, 2000)

https://en.m.wikipedia.org/wiki/Burma_Railway

Morrison of Lambeth P.C, C.H, Lord, *Herbert Morrison: An Autobiography* (Odhams Press Ltd, 1960)

Neale, John, *Old Launceston* (Stenlake Publishing, 2001)

Olusoga, David, *Black and British: A Forgotten History* (Pan Books, 2017)

Orwell, George, *The Collected Essays, Journalism and Letters of George Orwell: Volume 3, As I Please 1943–45* (Penguin Books, 1968)

Rendell, Joan, *The Archive Photographs Series: Around Launceston* (The Chalford Publishing Company, 1997)

Rendell, Joan, *Launceston: Some Pages in History* (Landfall Publications, 1993)

Reynolds, David, *Rich Relations: The American Occupation of Britain, 1942 –1945* (Random House, 1995)

Shirer, William L., *The Rise and Fall of the Third Reich* (Arrow Books, 1991)

Slaughter, R. J, *For God, For Country ... For Love: The True Story of One Man's Journey* (R.J. Slaughter)

Smith, Graham, *When Jim Crow met John Bull: Black American Soldiers in World War II Britain* (I.B. Taurus & Co Ltd, 1987)

Venning, Arthur Bate, *The Book of Launceston* (Barracuda Books Limited, 1976)

Venning, Arthur Bate & Wills, Arthur, *Yesterday's Town: Launceston* (Barracuda Books Limited, 1988)

War Department, *Instructions for American Servicemen in Britain* (Washington DC, 1942)

White, Walter, *A Rising Wind* (Doubleday, Doran & Company Inc, 1945)

White, Walter, *A Man Called White: The Autobiography of Walter White* (The Viking Press, 1948)

Wilch, Stephen J. with Wilch, William A., *Don't Just Kill Them, Murder Em: Shoot Pee Wee, Just Shoot – The Burton E Burfeind War Stories*